BROTHERS IN ARMS

CAMILLE TAWIL

BROTHERS IN ARMS

The Story of al-Qa'ida and the Arab Jihadists

Translated from the Arabic by
Robin Bray

SAQI

ISBN 978-0-86356-480-2

First published in Arabic as *Al Qa'ida Wa Akhawatuha* by Dar al Saqi in 2007
This English edition published by Saqi Books, London, in 2010

A full CIP record for this book is available from the British Library.
A full CIP record for this book is available from the Library of Congress.

Printed and bound by CPI Mackays, Chatham, ME5 8TD

SAQI

26 Westbourne Grove, London W2 5RH, UK
2398 Doswell Avenue, Saint Paul, Minnesota, 55108, USA
Verdun, Beirut, Lebanon

www.saqibooks.com

Contents

List of Abbreviations

AIS	Islamic Salvation Army (Armée Islamique du Salut)
AQAP	Al-Qaʿida in the Arabian Peninsula
AQI	Al-Qaʿida in Iraq
AQIM	Al-Qaʿida in the Lands of the Islamic Maghreb
EIJ	Egyptian Islamic Jihad
ETIM	East Turkestan Islamic Movement
GIA	Armed Islamic Group (Groupe Islamique Armé)
GICM	Moroccan Islamic Combatant Group (Groupe Islamique Combattant Marocain)
GSPC	Salafist Group for Preaching and Combat (Groupe Salafiste pour la Prédication et le Combat)
FIS	Islamic Salvation Front (Front Islamique du Salut)
IMU	Islamic Movement of Uzbekistan
LIDD	Islamic League for Preaching and Jihad (La Ligue Islamique pour le Daʾwa et le Djihad)
LIFG	Libyan Islamic Fighting Group
LNA	Libyan National Army
SIT	Islamic Labour Union (Syndicat Islamique du Travail)
MIA	Armed Islamic Movement (Mouvement Islamique Armé)
MEI	Movement for an Islamic State
MSC	Mujahidin Shura Council
NFSL	National Front for the Salvation of Libya
SIAC	Special Immigration Appeals Commission

Introduction

America's War on Terror under the George W. Bush administration brought dramatic changes around the world. The transformation was triggered by al-Qaʻida's double blow to the United States on 11 September 2001, striking at its political heart in Washington and its economic capital, New York. Bush had entered the White House in January 2001, bringing to an end Bill Clinton's years of active engagement in the international arena. With the transition from Democratic to Republican administrations, the United States, the world's sole remaining superpower since the collapse of the Soviet Union in the early 1990s, had begun to close itself off from the outside world. Yet just as America seemed to be drifting into a kind of political slumber, the spectacle of hijacked aircraft crashing into some of its most iconic buildings brought it to its senses with a jolt. Suddenly the US was confronted by what looked like a new menace: al-Qaʻida. Yet in truth this bugbear had not emerged with the suddenness of those planes from the skies. Its origins lay far away, in the Afghan quagmire of the 1980s and America's own support for the mujahidin in their conflict with Russia.

In the immediate aftermath of 9/11, Washington's instinct was to hit back at its assailants twice as hard. And that is precisely what it did, retaliating within days by launching its own assault on Osama bin Laden's stronghold in Afghanistan. The country's cities fell, in quick succession, into the hands of the Americans and their Afghan allies. It was only a matter of days before the collapse of the Taliban government, which, since the mid-1990s, had played host to al-Qaʻida and many other jihadists. The Americans' success was not down to their vast military arsenal alone: the millions of dollars they had paid the various Afghan factions had also played their part. Yet, whatever it cost them, there is no denying the scale of the Americans' achievement: a mere two months into their War on Terror they had installed a pro-US government in Kabul.

Nor was this the Americans' only accomplishment: just as importantly, they had driven bin Laden and his fellow al-Qaʻida leaders from their lair in Afghanistan, at the same time destroying dozens of training camps erected during their long years in the country. Many of the fighters who now shared bin Laden's fate had never supported his war against America, yet now that their Afghan stronghold had crumbled they scattered all over the world, to be hunted down by intelligence services wherever they went. Thousands were killed and many others imprisoned. The rest vanished without trace.

But after almost a decade, and a change of administration in the US, the rebranding of the War on Terror by the Obama administration as the 'Overseas Contingency Operation' has done nothing to stop the escalating conflict. In Afghanistan, the Taliban remain a formidable force, while in Iraq, which the Americans invaded in 2003, ostensibly because of its weapons of mass destruction, no such weapons have ever been found. Nor has any evidence emerged of the purported relationship between Iraq's former regime and al-Qaʻida, which, far from aligning itself with the secular Baʼathists, had condemned them as infidels. Meanwhile, although US troops formally withdrew from Baghdad in June 2009, thousands of American soldiers remain in Iraq, and many of them are set to stay until the end of 2011.

As the Americans get bogged down in Iraq and Afghanistan, the main beneficiary seems to be al-Qaʻida itself, the principal target of the war. It has largely succeeded in absorbing the blows that the Americans and their allies have dealt it. In certain areas, particularly the border region between Afghanistan and Pakistan, it has managed to rally its forces. But it has become a different organisation in the process. On the one hand al-Qaʻida has assumed global dimensions, something it has aspired to ever since it was first created in 1988. And yet at the same time it is no longer a single entity: it would be more accurate today to speak of multiple al-Qaʻidas rather than a monolithic organisation. Bin Laden still leads 'core al-Qaʻida', based in Afghanistan and Pakistan, but its franchises around the world are many and various, comprising autonomous affiliates from Iraq to Morocco.[1]

In 2001 America was at war with a single al-Qaʻida in Afghanistan;

---

1 Statements have also been issued in the name of an organisation calling itself al-Qaʼida in the Levant, and there have been reports of an al-Qaʼida in the Land of the Two Niles.

now it is fighting several permutations of the group all around the globe, without any prospect of containing them. Since 11 September 2001 al-Qa'ida has gone global; it follows that its conflict with the Americans and their allies has assumed the character of a 'global war' too. Perhaps this is what al-Qa'ida wanted all along: to convert its struggle against the US into a holy war, pitting Muslims against 'infidel' Western aggressors. Such a perception is of course false, even if American policy often serves to reinforce it in the minds of some Muslim observers. Under the Bush administration, the US gradually expanded its War on Terror to include ever more Islamist groups which it regarded as tainted by their association with al-Qa'ida. Paradoxically, the very intensity of this campaign has helped breathe new life into bin Laden's organisation, which, by early 2002, had seemed on the brink of collapse. The Americans' attacks on other jihadist groups ultimately forced many of them to unite behind bin Laden, despite their grave reservations about his agenda. Previously their priority had been to fight the rulers of the Islamic world, whom they regarded as apostates; now their main goal was to wage war on the West, the root of all evil. There was a new logic behind this shift in focus. It was the infidel West which enabled Middle Eastern regimes to cling to power: defeat the infidels, and their apostate puppets would fall with them. Or so bin Laden hoped.

This book examines this transformation in the ideology of al-Qa'ida and its brothers in arms. Al-Qa'ida's history is inseparable from that of its associates, most of whom emerged at the end of the Afghan jihad in the late 1980s and early 1990s. Numerous groups share al-Qa'ida's agenda, that much is certain. This book concentrates on three factions that have been intimately bound up with al-Qa'ida and its shifting agenda: Egyptian Islamic Jihad (EIJ), Algeria's Armed Islamic Group (known by its French acronym, GIA) and the Libyan Islamic Fighting Group (LIFG). In all three, a key role was played by 'Afghan Arabs', as veterans of the jihad against the Russians were known. Both EIJ and its larger rival, al-Gama'a al-Islamiyya (or 'Islamic Group') were admittedly first formed in the late 1960s and early 1970s. However, after they forged an alliance and together plotted the assassination of Egypt's President Sadat in 1981, thousands of their members were rounded up and thrown into jail. In the years that followed, disagreements over doctrine drove the two groups apart again. When the Egyptian government began releasing jihadists in the second half of the 1980s, they set about rebuilding their respective organisations, this time on the Afghan-Pakistani border. Bin Laden founded his own organisation, al-Qa'ida, in 1988. In 1991 the 'Algerian Afghans' established the GIA, while their Libyan comrades followed suit with the formation of the LIFG between 1990 and 1992.

During the 1990s, these three factions were the only jihadist groups in the Arab world to take up arms against their countries' regimes. In Egypt, EIJ and al-Gama'a al-Islamiyya embarked on a vicious campaign of bombings and assassinations against the government of Hosni Mubarak. In Algeria, after the elections were annulled in 1992, the GIA took up the banner of jihad against the junta which had seized power. Meanwhile, in 1995 the LIFG declared its own jihad against Colonel Gaddafi's rule, launching a series of intermittent skirmishes with the regime and assassination attempts against its leader. Al-Qa'ida was never far behind the scenes. Bin Laden had close ties to EIJ and its leader, Ayman al-Zawahiri: it was he who provided al-Qa'ida's earliest members and helped indoctrinate them with jihadist ideology. In Algeria, the true founder of the GIA was Qari Saïd, a leading 'Afghan Arab' and early al-Qa'ida member who had been strongly influenced by the group's ideology. In Libya the LIFG also had close links to bin Laden, even welcoming al-Qa'ida members into its ranks.

Yet, while al-Qa'ida was close to its brothers in arms, it was not inevitable that they would all merge into a single organisation. Each faction retained its own independent agenda until the late 1990s, when the jihadists suffered a series of setbacks. In Egypt, the security forces gained the upper hand in their fight against EIJ and al-Gama'a al-Islamiyya, forcing both of them to retreat. Al-Gama'a al-Islamiyya laid down its weapons and admitted the error of its ways. EIJ remained committed to the jihadist cause, but was incapable of carrying out attacks inside Egypt, where the security services had dismantled most of its cells. Faced with shrinking numbers and increasingly difficult conditions, EIJ became ever more dependent on the support of al-Qa'ida, its staunchest ally throughout the 1990s.

These developments were closely mirrored in Algeria, where, from 1996 onwards, the security forces dealt a series of blows to the GIA, leading it to splinter into various sub-groups. One of them condemned the entire Algerian population as infidels and embarked on an orgy of violence. Meanwhile, the other groups combined to form a new organisation called the Salafist Group for Preaching and Combat (GSPC) in an attempt to relaunch the jihad. At the same time, in parallel with al-Gama'a al-Islamiyya in Egypt, some Algerian jihadists abandoned the armed struggle and engaged with the regime by political means. The LIFG suffered a similar reversal in 1997, when the Libyan security forces destroyed its military infrastructure, forcing it to retreat to safety to lick its wounds.

The jihadists regrouped in Afghanistan. It was there that they relaunched their jihadist agenda, this time from the safety of the 'Islamic Emirate' founded by the Taliban. However, the process differed from group to group. In 1998 al-Qa'ida and EIJ formed an alliance called the World Islamic Front for Jihad against Jews and Crusaders. They blamed the US for the jihadists' failures, concluding that the only way to overthrow the Arab regimes was to fight their American paymaster. But the partnership of al-Qa'ida and EIJ failed to attract any other factions at the time. In Algeria, the GSPC was busy rebuilding itself and trying to win the support of the public, who had been alienated by the GIA's violent excesses. Bin Laden himself had got his fingers burnt by the GIA. He had placed his trust in the Afghan veterans who founded the group, only for them to lose control of the movement to a rival clique of Salafists,[1] some of whom were no doubt manipulated by the Algerian security services. Of all the jihadist factions, the LIFG was most outspoken in rejecting bin Laden's anti-American manifesto. Like other jihadists, the LIFG's leaders had emigrated to Afghanistan but remained committed to combating the Libyan regime. They had no desire to be drawn into conflict with other parties, least of all the United States.

With every passing day bin Laden and al-Zawahiri grew more confident in their plan to fight the Americans, despite the reluctance of other jihadists to join them. And their ambitions grew with the scale of their operations, from attacks on US embassies to an assault on a warship, and

---

1   The term Salafist is derived from the Arabic word *salaf*, meaning 'forebears' or 'ancestors'. In an Islamic context it refers to the earliest generations of Muslims, whose lives are regarded as exemplary by Salafists and others alike.

finally their strike at the very heart of America. The attacks of 11 September 2001 changed the jihadists, just as they transformed America. In the new War on Terror, US intelligence lumped all jihadists together, drawing no distinction between those who belonged to al-Qa'ida and those who did not. In the eyes of the Bush administration the world was divided into two camps: those on America's side and those on al-Qa'ida's, regardless of the differences of opinion within jihadist circles over the war against the United States. Such simplistic categorisations lent weight to al-Qa'ida's self-styled spiritual leadership of the jihadist groups. Al-Zawahiri's EIJ was, as already mentioned, absorbed into al-Qa'ida, and the GSPC pledged allegiance to bin Laden and his organisation, becoming his sole representative in what al-Qa'ida called the 'Islamic Maghreb'. Meanwhile, the handful of LIFG leaders to have survived the War on Terror joined al-Qa'ida in Afghanistan and merged with its ranks.

In the first decade of the War on Terror, America achieved for bin Laden what he had failed to bring about in all his time in Afghanistan: the unification of the jihadists under al-Qa'ida's banner.

My first book, *The Armed Islamic Movement in Algeria – From the FIS to the GIA*, was published in 1998. Work on the present text began a few years later, initially with the aim of reviewing developments in the Algerian factions following the failure of their 'jihad'. Then came the attacks of 11 September 2001 and everything changed.

It would have been impossible to list the ways in which the world had altered in the aftermath of 9/11 so soon after the attacks had taken place. The situation we face today, in which al-Qa'ida acts as a rallying cry for jihadists around the world, had not yet emerged. A truly clear picture probably remains some years off, but it is possible today to identify the broad outlines of how al-Qa'ida and its brothers in arms are developing. It is that trajectory which this book seeks to explain.

I would like to thank everyone who has helped to produce this work, especially those who have related their own part in the history of al-Qa'ida and its affiliates. But first and foremost I would like to thank my family, who patiently bore years of neglect as I dedicated myself to writing this.

I

Afghan Arabs

Afghanistan was where today's Salafist jihadist groups originated, the successors to the Arab world's first jihadist factions. During the 1980s, in the thick of battle between the Afghan mujahidin and the Soviets and their communist allies in Kabul, a new generation of Arab fighters emerged – a generation that believed that the only way to establish a true Islamic state was jihad, a holy war that would sweep away the Arab regimes they regarded as at best failing to implement Islamic law correctly, and at worst apostate dictatorships. These were the Afghan Arabs.

The jihad in Afghanistan began immediately after the Soviet invasion in December 1979. At first it was an exclusively Afghan enterprise, its leaders mainly clerics and intellectuals who had been known since the 1970s for their involvement in the Islamist movement: Abdul Rabb al-Rasul Sayyaf, Gulbuddin Hekmatyar, Burhanuddin Rabbani and Ahmad Shah Massoud.[1] These leaders were quick to rally their supporters, starting in the areas along the Pakistani border where millions of Afghans had sought refuge: people who would in due course provide an inexhaustible supply of fighters and an essential support base for the mujahidin factions.

Nonetheless, the Afghan jihad got off to a slow start. In the early 1980s the mujahidin groups had not yet organised their forces, either at their base in Pakistan or inside Afghanistan itself.[2] The Russians had invaded using

---

1 Hekmatyar, Rabbani and Massoud were all involved in Islamist plots against the Afghan regime after Muhammad Daoud Khan overthrew the king, his cousin Zahir Shah, and declared the Republic of Afghanistan in 1973. Having seized power with the help of both Marxists and Islamists, Muhammad Daoud Khan proceeded to clamp down on extremists within their ranks. He was killed along with most of his family in the military coup of April 1978.
2 Gulbuddin Hekmatyar founded the Hezb-e Islami in Pakistan in 1975.

massive forces equipped with the latest hardware, supplemented by the military resources of the communist government in Kabul.[1] However, as the overlap between the interests of the mujahidin and the United States became clear, the jihad began to gather pace. The mujahidin wanted to free their country from the communist yoke, while America was keen to stop Russia gaining access to the Arabian Sea via Pakistan, given the threat this would pose to the oil fields of the Persian Gulf. Accordingly, the Americans supported the Afghan jihad during the early 1980s through both overt and covert means. They supplied the mujahidin with money and arms, usually via the Pakistani Inter-Services Intelligence Directorate (ISI), while at the same time encouraging Arab countries to provide funds for the Afghan effort themselves, or to send volunteers to take part in the jihad alongside them.

Initially the Arabs played only a peripheral role in the Afghan jihad. In the early 1980s a handful of Arabs went to assist the mujahidin from their logistical base in Pakistan; at that point their involvement was mainly limited to helping the millions of refugees living in the camps that had sprung up along the Afghan-Pakistani border. Of these Arabs, an even smaller number went into Afghanistan itself, to join the Afghan factions and take part in actual combat.

The Algerian, Abdullah Anas, was one of the first Arabs to participate in the Afghan jihad. He claims that in 1984 no more than fifteen Arabs had taken part in the conflict in Afghanistan.[2] He himself decided to get

Sibghatullah Mojaddedi established the National Front for the Liberation of Afghanistan in 1979, while Burhanuddin Rabbani had led the Jamiat-e Islami since earlier that decade. Abdul Rabb al-Rasul Sayyaf assumed the leadership of the Ittehad-e Islami in 1980.

1   Nur Mohammad Taraki became the second president of Afghanistan following the coup of 1978. Taraki was head of the 'Parcham' (or 'Banner') wing of the communist People's Democratic Party of Afghanistan (PDPA); the other wing of the party, known as 'Khalq' (meaning 'People' or 'Masses'), was led by Babrak Karmal. Rivalry between the two factions led to Taraki's overthrow by his prime minister, Hafizullah Amin of the Khalq wing, who replaced him as president in 1979. Amin's own period in office lasted a mere 104 days, before he was killed by the invading Russian forces on 27 December 1979. He was succeeded by Babrak Karmal, also from the Khalq wing of the PDPA.

2   Abdullah Anas, also known as Boudjoumaa Bounoua, was born in 1958 in Ben

involved after reading a fatwa which argued that it was the duty of every Muslim to take part in the jihad.[1] The signatories to this fatwa included the Palestinian, Abdullah Azzam, at that time the undisputed leader of the Afghan Arabs. After meeting Abdullah Anas in Saudi Arabia in 1984, Azzam put him in touch with the Afghan warlords.[2] Anas had gone to Saudi Arabia to perform the pilgrimage to Mecca; from there he went to Karachi and then on to Islamabad, where he met Osama bin Laden for the first time in Azzam's house. Bin Laden was one of the first Arabs from the Gulf to join the Afghan jihad. From Islamabad, Anas flew to Peshawar, where Azzam introduced him to Abdul Rabb al-Rasul Sayyaf, the emir or commander of the Ittehad-e Islami, the Islamic Union for the Liberation of Afghanistan. 'To date, twelve Arabs have rallied to the Afghan cause,' Anas quotes Sayyaf as saying. 'Now that you three have come, there are fifteen,' he added, referring to Abdullah Azzam, the latter's son-in-law, and Anas.[3] However, the Arabs' modest role in Afghanistan soon began to grow, especially after Abdullah Azzam, Osama bin Laden and others established the Mujahidin Services Bureau, or *Maktab Khidamat al-Mujahidin*, in late 1984. Its role was to arrange for Arabs who wished to take part in the jihad to join the various Afghan factions.

It was around this time that the number of Arabs involved in the conflict in Afghanistan increased significantly. Nonetheless, they remained a mere drop in the ocean compared to the Afghan mujahidin, who played the most important part in the war of attrition against the Russians. Initially, the Arabs merely performed an auxiliary role, fighting alongside the Afghan

Badis, near Sidi Bel Abbès in western Algeria. He described his role in the Afghan jihad to the author during several conversations in October and November 2001. His account was published in Arabic as *Wiladat al-Afghan al-'Arab* ('The Birth of the Afghan Arabs', London and Beirut, Dar al-Saqi, 2002).

1   The fatwa defined the duty to wage jihad as a *fard 'ayn*, a term of Islamic law for an obligation incumbent upon each and every Muslim. This contrasts with a *fard kifaya*, a duty which ceases to apply to all Muslims provided some of them fulfil it.

2   Abdullah Azzam was born in 1941 in the Palestinian village of Silat al-Harithiya in the district of Jenin on the West Bank. He was killed by a car bomb in Pakistan in 1989, along with two of his sons.

3   Anas would go on to marry Azzam's younger daughter in 1990, a year after Azzam's assasination.

groups but not independently of them. Throughout the jihad the Arabs were greatly outnumbered by their local counterparts, but they soon began to organise themselves into a fighting force of their own. Between 1984 and 1985 they established a guesthouse in Peshawar known as the Abu 'Uthman Hostel. Then Abdullah Azzam founded the Sada camp for Arab fighters, near the border with Afghanistan. The camp started out with a modest twelve men, increasing to twenty-five in 1985. By the following year the number of trainee fighters had shot up to almost 200.[1]

However, it was not until 1986 that the Arab mujahidin made the transition to fighting in their own right, rather than going into battle as a mere contingent of the Afghan factions. That same year Osama bin Laden established a new camp with more than thirty Arab fighters. It was located on a supply route used by the Afghan mujahidin in a mountainous area of Jaji in Paktia Province, close to the Pakistani border. The site consisted of two parts: a meeting place at the foot of a mountain and another, known as *al-Ma'sada*, the 'Lion's Den', at its peak. It is unclear how much support its creation received from other Arabs in Afghanistan, who had hitherto been distributed between the various Afghan groups. However, it does not appear to have met with serious opposition from either the Arab or the Afghan mujahidin leaders, most of whom visited the site.

Soon after the foundation of the Lion's Den, there was a major clash between the Arab fighters and Russian forces. The Arabs were led by bin Laden and two Egyptian EIJ members known as Abu Hafs and Abu 'Ubayda al-Banshiri.[2] In the spring of 1987 the Russians launched a long-

---

1   Anas says the Arab jihadists began to form their own group between 1984 and 1985, when approximately eighty of them established the Abu 'Uthman Hostel in Peshawar. Until then they had stayed at Sayyaf's guesthouse in Babi, east of Peshawar. See *Wiladat al-Afghan al-'Arab*, p. 31. The number of fighters at the Sada camp cited here is from *Da'wat al-Muqawama al-Islamiyya al-'Alamiyya* ('The Call to Global Islamic Resistance') by the Syrian jihadist, Mustafa Sitt Maryam Nasar (also known as Abu Mus'ab al-Suri), published on the internet in Arabic in December 2004.

2   Both Muhammad Atif (also known as Abu Hafs al-Misri and Subhi Abu Sitta) and Ali Amin al-Rashidi (also known as Abu 'Ubayda) would later become military leaders of al-Qa'ida. According to Abdullah Anas, they both attempted to join Ahmad Shah Massoud's forces to fight alongside them against the Russians. Abu Hafs was unsuccessful, but Abu 'Ubayda took part in the

awaited attack on the Jaji front, having surrounded the area for forty-eight days and pounded the mountains incessantly.[1] Al-Banshiri proved himself a brave and audacious military commander in the course of the fighting. Having discovered that the Russians had sent in paratroopers, he quickly led a group of fighters over the mountains and beyond the point where the Russians had landed, trapping them between his men and the rest of the Arab forces. When the Russians attempted to advance, they found themselves surrounded and suffered heavy losses in the fighting which ensued.[2]

The former Egyptian military intelligence officer, Essam Deraz, covered the Battle of Jaji as a journalist and spent months in the area with bin Laden and his comrades. He says that the Russians bombarded the area very heavily before beginning their assault in late May 1987. In contrast to the bombardment, which lasted almost two months, the fighting itself lasted a mere 24 hours.[3] 'It was epic,' he says of the mujahidin's victory against the odds:

> A group of Arabs led by Abu 'Ubayda and Abu Hafs spotted the Russian commandos landing on a mountain opposite the Arabs' position. The Russians thought the Arabs had been wiped out in the aerial bombardment. But a group of Arabs advanced to the mountain around the other side [from where the Russians had landed] and lay in wait. The Russian commandos consisted of a single platoon of

---

conflict and was wounded in the Panjshir Valley, north of Kabul. It was for this reason that he was subsequently known as al-Banshiri, an Arabic corruption of 'Panjshiri'.

1   Former member of the Shura Council of the Libyan Islamic Fighting Group and founder member of the Libya Human and Political Development Forum, Noman Benotman quotes Abdul Rabb al-Rasul Sayyaf as saying the Russians pounded the mountains 'until they were like cotton wool'. He was speaking in an interview with the author in the summer of 2005. Benotman, also known as Abu Tamama, was born in Tripoli in 1967. In 1989 he went to Afghanistan, where he fought alongside Sayyaf's Ittehad-e Islami.

2   Few people know that a gun pictured at Bin Laden's side during interviews he gave in the 1990s had been looted from a Russian officer in the fighting at Jaji. The weapon was a Kalashnikov AKS-74U, commonly known as a Krinkov, an assault rifle both shorter and lighter than the better-known AK-47.

3   Essam Deraz in an interview with the author in London during the summer of 2006.

twenty to thirty men; they began advancing into the forest, unaware that they were surrounded. It was only when a young Saudi called Mukhtar began shooting at them that they realised the situation they were in. In the heat of battle, the Russians even shot at their own men, unable to work out where the enemy fire was coming from. They were annihilated. In light of the Russians' heavy casualties, the surviving soldiers were ordered to withdraw; on the Arab side, only three mujahidin were martyred in the fighting.

Arabs and Afghans

The Battle of Jaji boosted the confidence of the Arabs who took part, encouraging them to seek greater autonomy from the Afghan mujahidin. This had become more urgent, given the power struggles among the latter, which were often more violent than the fighting against the Russians. Until then, the Arabs had been scattered between the seven Afghan groups, of which the most important were Gulbuddin Hekmatyar's Hezb-e Islami, the Jamiat-e Islami, led by Burhanuddin Rabbani, and Abdul Rabb al-Rasul Sayyaf's Ittehad-e Islami. Sayyaf's group was by far the Arabs' preferred option; Sayyaf himself was a charismatic figure with a Salafist background who enjoyed the support of clerics in the Gulf. His group was not the most powerful militarily, however, especially in comparison with the two other main Afghan factions. Hekmatyar had considerable influence, particularly in Afghanistan's eastern provinces, as well as the support of Pakistan's powerful security establishment. All this had helped him attract numerous aspiring Arab jihadists into his ranks. A certain number also fought alongside Rabbani's Jamiat-e Islami, most notably the Algerian, Abdullah Anas, who became the right-hand man of Rabbani's military commander Ahmad Shah Massoud.[1]

Massoud's successes did not count for much with decision-makers in Pakistani intelligence, however. They continued to allocate most of their Afghan aid to Hekmatyar's group. For the Pakistanis, Hekmatyar's appeal did not lie merely in his military strength: as a member of Afghanistan's majority Pashtun community, which straddles the border with Pakistan,

---

1   Ahmad Shah Massoud was known as the 'Lion of Panjshir' because of his victories over the Russians in the Panjshir Valley, northeast of Kabul.

they also saw him as an instrument of Pakistani influence. By contrast, Massoud was a Tajik whose power base lay not on the Pakistani border but in the Panjshir Valley and the provinces of northern Afghanistan – areas which the Pakistanis do not seem to have considered strategically significant.[1]

It remains unclear whether the Pakistanis were involved in turning the Arabs against Massoud and driving them into the arms of his rivals. But his trusted aide, Abdullah Anas, suggests that that is what happened. He has described how in Peshawar in 1988 the Arabs staged a 'trial' of Massoud *in absentia*, on the basis of a report containing lurid allegations against him. Anas says the original Arabic version of the report was translated into several languages and then widely circulated, hinting that Pakistani intelligence may have played a role in the smear campaign. The trial itself remains a source of division between the Afghan Arabs to this day. At the time, it was an indication that Abdullah Azzam's influence was on the wane: his support for Massoud would no longer suffice to persuade Arab fighters to back the Afghan warlord. The first signs of this had already emerged in 1986, when Osama bin Laden established his own group in Peshawar, separate from the *Maktab al-Khidamat*.[2]

Massoud's 'trial' sheds light on the relationship between the Arabs and the Afghan mujahidin factions at this time. Abdullah Anas was on a training course with Massoud in the Panjshir Valley when he heard about the claims the Arabs had made against his comrade.[3] A message came over the radio from Abdullah Azzam asking Anas to make haste to Peshawar. Massoud was surprised, but told Anas he would have to wait until the course had ended in a couple of weeks. Four days later Anas received another message from Azzam. 'Have you set off yet?' it asked insistently. 'If not, get moving immediately.' Sensing that something important must

---

1   The Afghan population comprises various ethnic groups, of which the Pashtuns are the largest (constituting some 42 per cent of the population). The Tajiks are the next largest group, accounting for 27 per cent of Afghanistan's inhabitants. For further details of the county's demographics see: https://www.cia.gov/library/publications/the-world-factbook/geos/af.html.

2   Bin Laden named his guesthouse the *Bayt al-Ansar* or 'House of the Supporters', an allusion to the Prophet Muhammad's early helpers.

3   Abdullah Anas in an interview with the author in London in May 2006.

have happened, Anas again sought Massoud's permission to leave; this time it was granted. When he arrived in Peshawar nine days later, Anas went straight to see Azzam, who was accompanied by a Saudi called Wa'il Julaydan.[1] Azzam explained that Anas's former comrades in northern Afghanistan had made serious allegations against Massoud, and that Pashto and Persian translations of the report containing their claims had been widely circulated. Azzam had told Massoud's accusers that he needed time to question Anas: as the Arabs' emir in northern Afghanistan, he was in a unique position to corroborate the charges.

Several hearings were held to examine the claims. These were attended by Azzam himself, his Palestinian deputy, Tamim al-Adnani, the Yemeni, Abd al-Majid al-Zindani, Osama bin Laden and Wa'il Julaydan. Bin Laden, Azzam and Julaydan sat on a committee to oversee the working of the makeshift 'court'. Meanwhile, Abdullah Anas stood for the defence, although he still did not know what evidence existed to support the charges against Massoud. The latter was accused of opening a hostel for Westerners where the sexes mixed freely and 'sins' were committed; it was said to be equipped with a swimming pool intended specifically for Western women. Massoud was purported to have handed control of the front lines in his part of Afghanistan to Shi'ites (regarded as heretics by orthodox Muslims), to have imprisoned Arabs with donkeys and to possess a generally 'anti-Arab' outlook. Numerous other allegations were also levelled against Massoud in the course of the hearings, although they had not been included in the indictment against him.

Anas noticed that one of the signatories to the indictment was Muhammad Harun. Yet he had never met anyone by this name in all his time as commander of the Arab fighters in the north. When he asked who this individual was, the Algerian, Qari Saïd, raised his hand and said that *he* was Muhammad Harun.

'You dare to swear by Almighty God to the truth of these charges under a false name?' Anas asked him indignantly. 'If these accusations are true, and your purpose in making them is honest, you should hold your head up like a man, accept your responsibility before God and put your name to them. But

---

1   Wa'il Julaydan, also known as Abu al-Hasan al-Madani, was head of the Saudi Red Crescent in Pakistan and a prominent figure in the Afghan jihad.

if the charges are false, why use this name? I know no Muhammad Harun; no one by that name has ever accompanied me and Massoud in Panjshir who could give such testimony. I will have nothing to do with trumped-up charges of this kind against a man's honour and the integrity of his jihad. Please erase the name Muhammad Harun and write Qari Saïd in its place, to take responsibility for the claims that you make'.

Qari Saïd had spent almost three years on the northern front under Massoud's command. He agreed to Anas's demand, but maintained his claims regarding nudism, women's swimming pools and acts of murder. When Anas challenged him to specify where exactly these excesses had taken place, Qari Saïd replied that he had not witnessed them himself, but had heard about them from another Arab in the north called Abdullah Ja'far. The trouble was that this individual had not accompanied Massoud in person, but had instead been stationed with one of Massoud's local rival commaders, Jamal Agha (of the Hezb-e Islami Party).[1] As the lack of eyewitnesses became apparent, the case against Massoud began to collapse. Nonetheless, the court's decision did not represent an outright victory for either side: at the end of the hearings it was merely agreed that the Arab fighters would desist from either praising or condemning Massoud. This injunction was clearly aimed at Azzam, who was in the habit of eulogising Massoud as the 'Lion of Panjshir' in his sermons. But, in return, Azzam extracted a promise from Massoud's detractors that they would cease their campaigns against him. It was also decided that the Arabs would not send any more financial aid to Massoud, and Anas was warned that he was 'the Arabs' envoy to Massoud, and not vice versa'.

The ink was barely dry before the agreement was secretly broken. About three weeks after Massoud's 'trial', Anas returned to Panjshir to tell Massoud what had happened. Under normal circumstances he would have taken donations for Massoud with him, but this was out of the question given the outcome of the hearings. Much to Anas's surprise, Azzam asked him to take Massoud some money and to tell no one about it. Anas did as he was asked and passed Massoud the funds, totalling some half a million dollars:

---

1 Jamal Agha subsequently gained notoriety for the massacre at Farkhar in 1989, in which Hekmatyar's Hezb-e Islami butchered numerous members of Massoud's Jamiat-e Islami. Jamal Agha was later executed.

a vast sum compared with previous donations. He also took along one of the witnesses who had testified for the 'prosecution' against Massoud at the trial. The Afghan leader accepted Azzam's 'gift' and gave the witness a warm welcome, thus showing how forgiving he was, even to those who were, only days before, trying to prove his 'guilt'.

The fact that the trial had absolved Massoud did not deter other Afghan Arabs from slandering the warlord, or Azzam from sending him more money. 'The supervisors of the Arab jihad in Afghanistan sent a delegation of thirty men to look into the matter in the north [the allegations against Massoud],' says the Syrian Islamist, Abu Mus'ab al-Suri. 'When they returned a few months later, all but two or three of them delivered damning indictments of Massoud's conduct. One of them, a friend of mine from the Levant, described Massoud as a "present-day Atatürk".[1] But for sentimental reasons and a desire not to sully the reputation of the jihad, Abdullah Azzam rejected this testimony in favour of his son-in-law, Abdullah Anas's account.'[2]

The Foundation of al-Qa'ida

Less than two years on from the Battle of Jaji it was obvious that the mujahidin were assured of victory over their Soviet foes. The Russians' defeat was officially sealed when they signed the Geneva Accords of September 1988, under which they agreed to withdraw from Afghanistan. They had already fulfilled their pledge by the following February, leaving behind a communist government in control of Kabul and the main provincial cities, but little else.

It was amid this atmosphere of impending triumph that Osama bin Laden established al-Qa'ida. Few then would have dreamed that it would ever be capable of mounting a devastating attack such as that of

---

1   Mustafa Kemal Atatürk, the secularist founder of modern Turkey, is detested by many strict Muslims, above all for overseeing the abolition of the caliphate in 1924.

2   Abu Mus'ab al-Suri, *Afghanistan wa al-Taliban wa Ma'rakat al-Islam al-Yawm* ('Afghanistan, the Taliban and the Battle of Islam Today') (Kabul, Markaz al-Ghuraba' li al-Dirasat al-Islamiyya, 1998) pp. 28–29.

11 September 2001. The question is how and why this group was created in the first place.

Osama bin Laden observed that 'there was increasing movement of Arabs to and from the front lines, and growing numbers of fighters either wounded or martyred. Yet there were no records of any of this, even though record-keeping is one of the basic elements of military organisation.'[1] The lack of such information was a frequent source of embarrassment for bin Laden, particularly when families from the Gulf asked after their sons who had gone to fight in Afghanistan. To bin Laden, the absence of accurate records was 'a disgrace, as well as a basic failure of administration'. It was for this reason that he decided to keep files on the Arab mujahidin; later, these would expand to include full details of everyone who came to Afghanistan with the assistance of bin Laden and his group.[2] The files noted the date of each person's arrival in Pakistan; his registration at Peshawar's *Bayt al-Ansar* guesthouse; the date of his enrolment at the training camps; and his despatch to the front lines. In time, these records became 'like an administration in their own right, which needed a name to identify it. This was when bin Laden and his supporters agreed to call the records office "al-Qa'ida" ["the Base"], on the understanding that this term covered everything from the *Bayt al-Ansar* to the training camps and the fronts themselves'.[3]

Al-Qa'ida has said little publicly about its own origins. Nonetheless, since 2001 the records of numerous meetings that took place around the time it was established have come to light. They include the handwritten minutes of discussions in August 1988 between bin Laden and a Syrian called Muhammad Lu'ay Bayazid,[4] regarding the establishment of a 'new

---

1 See the report on the foundation of al-Qa'ida published in the late 1990s by the Islamic Observation Centre (IOC), a London-based Islamist opposition organisation. The report, a 17-page document in Arabic, was sent to the author in late 1999. It was later published on the IOC website, and the author has a copy in his archive. Time has proven much of the information contained in this report to have been correct.

2 Ibid, p. 2.

3 IOC report, p. 2.

4 The Americans maintain that Muhammad Lu'ay Bayazid (also known as Abu Rida al-Suri) was al-Qa'ida's head of procurement. As a student in Phoenix, Arizona he had heard Abdullah Azzam speak during a tour of the United

military group'; this was to consist of a 'general camp', a 'special camp', and a 'base' or *qa'ida*.[1] The minutes indicate that this initiative followed a disagreement with Abdullah Azzam: alluding to certain differences of opinion, Bayazid asked bin Laden if he agreed that Azzam's 'military gang' was finished. He also urged bin Laden to reflect on why they had come to Afghanistan in the first place and pressed for jihadist fighters, or what Bayazid called 'the army's forces', to be based there. In response, bin Laden spoke about having raised large sums of money in Saudi Arabia and claimed to have given the mujahidin 'political power'. The time was now right, he said, to take action of his own. These discussions concluded on 20 August 1988; three weeks later, with an initial membership of fifteen men, al-Qa'ida began work.

The Syrian Islamist, Abu Mus'ab al-Suri, moved to Afghanistan in the late 1980s, following a bitter experience of jihad in his own country.[2] He claims that bin Laden established al-Qa'ida for 'reasons related to jihad both inside Afghanistan and abroad ... He had his own jihadist agenda in South Yemen, against the communist government there.' Later, says Abu Mus'ab, 'his aspirations extended to the whole of Yemen,' alluding to the war which ended in 1994 with the reunification of the two halves of the country.[3] In the late 1980s, bin Laden arguably used Afghanistan as other Arab jihadists did: as somewhere to train his men while hoping to establish an Islamic state once the puppet government in Kabul had been overthrown. Between 1988 and 1991 Abu Mus'ab himself worked intermittently as a military trainer in al-Qa'ida's camps. He also gave

---

States. Despite their later differences, Bayazid was greatly impressed by Azzam and subsequently went to Afghanistan to take part in the jihad.

1   See the case presented on 6 January 2003 before the Federal Northern District Court of Illinois, outlining the evidence against Mr Enaam Arnaout, the head of the Benevolence International Foundation (BIF), an Islamic charity with alleged ties to al-Qa'ida. http://news.findlaw.com/hdocs/docs/bif/usarnaout10603prof. pdf.

2   In 1982 Abu Mus'ab al-Suri was a paramilitary leader of the Muslim Brotherhood, during fighting between Syrian government forces and Islamist opposition groups in Hama. Thousands are believed to have died in the conflict.

3   Abu Mus'ab al-Suri, *Da'wat al-Muqawama al-Islamiyya al-'Alamiyya*, pp. 710–711. Abu Mus'ab made similar remarks to the author during the 1990s, when the former was living in London.

lectures on doctrine, Islamic law and guerrilla warfare at training camps run by al-Qa'ida and other organisations. 'I had contact with most of the founders of the Arab jihad in Afghanistan,' he says. 'At that time, al-Qa'ida wasn't involved in any operational activity outside Afghanistan. Likewise, although Sheikh Osama used to donate money to jihadist groups in all sorts of places, he had no specific agenda anywhere except Yemen. At least not as far as I know – and I speak as a member of the sheikh's inner circle at the time. In 1991 I left Afghanistan and returned to Spain, where I had been living previously, and lost contact with them. Sheikh Osama and most of his people also left and went to Sudan; there was no sign that they were thinking of getting involved in any other action. It was not until 1996 that we met again, this time as guests of the Taliban.'

Exporting Jihad

Jamal Ahmad al-Fadl was an early member of al-Qa'ida, but left its ranks in the mid-1990s after he was caught embezzling funds from the group. He has told a similar story about the foundation of al-Qa'ida, but maintains that it harboured more ambitious aims right from the start. In 2001 he gave evidence before the Manhattan Federal Court in New York concerning the 1998 bombings of the US embassies in Nairobi and Dar es Salaam. Al-Fadl claimed that bin Laden had set up al-Qa'ida with the ultimate aim of overthrowing the regimes of the Arab world and restoring the caliphate.[1]

Abdullah Azzam had jointly run the *Maktab al-Khidamat* with Osama bin Laden in the late 1980s; their common goal was to assist the jihad against the Russians in Afghanistan. The two men later went their separate ways; when the Russians withdrew from Afghanistan, 'Bin Laden resolved to set up his own group, because [the jihad] in Afghanistan was over,'

---

[1]   The author attended the hearings in which Jamal Ahmad al-Fadl, also known as Abu Bakr al-Sudani, testified. The four defendants were Wadi al-Hajj, a naturalised American born in Lebanon who had been Bin Laden's secretary in Khartoum; a Saudi called Muhammad Rashid Dawud al-'Awhali; a Palestinian-Jordanian called Muhammad al-Sadiq Awda; and a Tanzanian called Khalfan Khamis Muhammad. Although their defence team sought to cast doubt on the credibility of al-Fadl's testimony, the jury found all four of them guilty.

al-Fadl has said. His ambitions were grandiose. 'We want to change the
Arab regimes', bin Laden told his supporters at the time, 'and establish an
Islamic government.' Al-Fadl claimed that he had learned all this from
al-Qa'ida's leaders directly, in particular an Iraqi called Abu Ayyub, who
was the organisation's first commander. Al-Fadl had first met Abu Ayyub
at the front in Jaji; they later came across one another again in the al-Faruq
camp in Khost, where Abu Ayyub (also known as Abu Ayyub al-Iraqi)
brought his brother, Yasin (known as Yasin al-Iraqi). 'We're going to set
up a group to train people,' they said, 'because we don't want to stop once
the Russians have withdrawn from Afghanistan.' Al-Fadl explained to the
court in New York that this took place in 1989. Abu Ayyub asked everyone
at the camp to read some documents, then lectured them on his aims: the
group that was to be established at the camp would be used for operations
outside Afghanistan. This group was al-Qa'ida.

The Libyan Afghan veteran, Noman Benotman, confirms that bin
Laden was not al-Qa'ida's first commander.[1] 'Al-Qa'ida was established in
late 1988 or early 1989,' he says. 'The organisation's first emir was an Iraqi
Kurd called Abu Ayyub; he was assassinated in the tribal region of Pakistan
shortly after assuming the leadership of the group. His brother, Abu Yasin,
was murdered in a separate incident in Afghanistan.'[2]

Al-Fadl maintains that the documents Abu Ayyub gave him explained
that al-Qa'ida's aim was to wage jihad; they also outlined the respective
duties of the group's emir, its *Majlis al-Shura* or Consultative Council,
and the rank and file. If one agreed with the content of the documents,
one had to swear a formal oath of allegiance to the group's emir; this
meant promising to do whatever the emir asked of you, whenever
he asked.After reading through the papers, al-Fadl swore the oath of
allegiance in the presence of three other people: Abu Ayyub himself,
Abu 'Ubayda al-Banshiri and Abu Hafs al-Misri. This took place 'at the

---

1 Noman Benotman in interviews with the author in the spring and summer of
   2005.
2 Although Jamal al-Fadl refers to the brother of al-Qa'ida's first emir as Yasin,
   while Benotman calls him Abu Yasin (meaning 'father of Yasin'), there is little
   doubt that they are speaking about the same man. An early audio recording
   produced by al-Qa'ida called *Qawafil al-Shuhada'* ('Caravans of the Martyrs')
   compares Abu Yasin to Saladin, describing both men as 'Kurdish heroes'.

end of 1989 or the beginning of 1990.' According to al-Fadl, the emir of al-Qa'ida at the time was Abu Ayyub al-Iraqi, but Osama bin Laden was its commander-in-chief.[1]

Al-Qa'ida's founders included at least five Egyptians. One of them was Dr Fadl, Islamic Jihad's first leader after the group was revived in Afghanistan in the late 1980s.[2] Another was Ayman al-Zawahiri, who took over the EIJ leadership after Dr Fadl stepped aside in 1993. The other three were Abu 'Ubayda al-Banshiri, Abu Hafs al-Misri and Abu Faraj al-Yemeni.[3] Some of the Gulf Arabs who fought with bin Laden at Jaji are known to have been unhappy about the Egyptians' increasing influence over him. They began to distance themselves from bin Laden when they found they could only gain access to him through his inner circle of Egyptians. The role played by Egyptian EIJ members in the creation of al-Qa'ida would become clear later on, when the two groups merged in 2001.

It is significant that several people involved in setting up al-Qa'ida subsequently withdrew from the group to pursue their own plans: evidence that they had been a loose association of individuals drawn from several different movements. They included Abu Mus'ab al-Suri, who set out on his own path in 1991. A well known Iraqi Kurd also broke away at a later date to form his own organisation in Kurdistan.[4] Nonetheless, it is notable that their decision to strike out on their own did not sour their relationships with bin Laden, with whom they were to remain on cordial terms.

---

1 Jamal al-Fadl listed al-Qa'ida's founders as Abu Ayyub, Abu 'Ubayda al-Banshiri, Abu Faraj al-Yemeni, Ayman al-Zawahiri, Dr Fadl, Abu Hafs al-Misri, Abu Mus'ab al-Suri and one Izz al-Din. EIJ is known to have assigned several of its most senior leaders, including Abu Hafs al-Misri and Abu 'Ubayda al-Banshiri, to help Bin Laden establish al-Qa'ida.

2 Sayyid Imam al-Sharif, also known as Dr Fadl or 'Abd al-Qadir bin 'Abd al-'Aziz, is a prominent Egyptian Islamist ideologue and the author of various influential works. They include *al-'Umda fi I'dad al-'Adda* ('The Essential Guide for Preparation'), which became a crucial text for aspiring jihadists, and *The Quest for Holy Knowledge*. He has been imprisoned in Egypt since early 2004.

3 The real name of Abu Faraj al-Yemeni was Muhammad Sharaf; he was known as al-Yemeni partly because he had lived in Yemen, and also to distinguish him from another Egyptian called Abu Faraj.

4 This prominent figure shall remain anonymous.

Gathering Momentum

Until al-Qa'ida began operating independently in 1989, the *Maktab al-Khidamat*, run by Abdullah Azzam, was the gateway to Afghanistan for Arabs keen to take part in the jihad there. They would arrive convinced of their duty to help their fellow Muslims and confident that they would be rewarded with either victory or martyrdom. In the beginning, the vast majority of these volunteers did not belong to the Islamist groups that had taken up arms against their governments only to be brutally suppressed. They were simply budding jihadists of no particular allegiance. However, as the Soviet collapse in Afghanistan became clear, the type of mujahidin attracted to that country underwent a rapid and significant change. Militant groups saw an opportunity to train fighters in Afghanistan and then send them home to prepare for a new phase of the jihad.

Many Arab fighters who went to Afghanistan had found that there was no room in their home countries for their notions of jihad. Some had tried to wage what they considered to be holy war there, only to be violently suppressed by the authorities. Egyptians, Libyans, Algerians and Syrians – all had endured the same fate. In Egypt, members of EIJ and al-Gama'a al-Islamiyya had murdered President Sadat in 1981 and declared an armed uprising which almost brought down the regime. However, when the attempted coup failed, thousands of those who had taken part were imprisoned. Many were subjected to torture and kept behind bars for years: it was not until the mid-1980s that the Egyptian authorities began releasing them. During Nasser's rule in the 1950s and '60s much the same fate had befallen the Muslim Brotherhood[1]; now, as then, the jihadists emerged from jail filled with even deeper loathing for the regime which had punished them so harshly. Since there was no place for jihad in the Egypt of the 1980s, they left: their preferred destination was naturally Afghanistan. The heroic feats of the mujahidin were the talk of jihadist circles, and members of the jihadist networks who had escaped arrest following Sadat's murder had already made their way to Afghanistan.

---

1   This Sunni opposition group was established in Egypt in 1928, and officially opposes the use of violence in its efforts to establish the Qur'an and Sunnah as the 'sole reference point for ... ordering the life of the Muslim family, individual, community ... and state.'

They secretly urged their former comrades to join them if they wanted to persevere with the jihadist cause.

According to the EIJ affiliate, Hani al-Siba'i[1], Ayman al-Zawahiri was not the first to leave Egypt: others, such as Dr Fadl, had fled the country even before 1981. Al-Zawahiri's brother, Muhammad, had also escaped, after being named during the prosecution of EIJ members following Sadat's assassination. The re-establishment of EIJ did not begin in earnest, however, until Ayman al-Zawahiri was released from prison and emigrated, first to Saudi Arabia and then on to Pakistan. There he worked as a medic, treating wounded Afghans in hospitals in Peshawar or in field hospitals inside Afghanistan itself.[2]

The concentration of Egyptian jihadists in the same place allowed them to renew contact with one another and make the most of the Afghan jihad. The first thing they did was regroup. Those involved included Ayman al-Zawahiri himself, 'Abd al-'Aziz al-Jamal[3] and Ahmad Salama Mabruk.[4] They

---

1   Hani al-Siba'i was born in al-Qanatir al-Khayriyya, north of Cairo, but in 1994 sought asylum in the UK, where he has lived ever since. The Egyptian government has accused him of belonging to EIJ, an allegation al-Siba'i denies. However, in 1998 the British Home Secretary rejected al-Siba'i's asylum application, partly on the basis of an assessment by MI5 that he was an EIJ member. See Case No. HQ03X03052 between the Home Office and Hani al-Siba'i, which can be found at http://www.hmcourts-service.gov.uk/judgmentsfiles/j2758/youssef-v-home_office.htm. Al-Siba'i's account of the revival of the group is from a series of interviews which the author conducted with him during the summer of 2002.

2   The hospitals which treated Afghan mujahidin in Peshawar included one run by the Kuwait Red Crescent Society, a branch of the International Red Cross and Red Crescent Movement.

3   'Abd al-'Aziz al-Jamal is a former Egyptian military officer who worked as a trainer in EIJ's camps in Afghanistan during the jihad. In the mid-1990s he fell out with Ayman al-Zawahiri and went to live in Yemen. In 1999 he was sentenced to death *in absentia* in an Egyptian military court's mass trial of Islamist extremists, known in the local media as the 'Returnees from Albania'. 'Abd al-'Aziz al-Jamal was extradited from Yemen to Egypt in 2004.

4   Ahmad Salama Mabruk was a leading EIJ member who was close to Ayman al-Zawahiri. In the 1980s he was imprisoned for seven years for his involvement in the assassination of President Sadat. On his release he went to Afghanistan; his subsequent travels took him to Azerbaijan, where he was arrested and handed over to the Egyptian authorities. In 1999 he was tried in the 'Returnees from Albania' case and sentenced to life imprisonment. At the time of his arrest he had been a member of EIJ's *Majlis al-Shura* or Consultative Council.

chose Dr Fadl as their emir, but decided to refer to him by the alias 'Abd al-Qadir bin 'Abd al-'Aziz, perhaps hoping to prevent easy identification.[1] Yet Ayman al-Zawahiri was already more widely known than Dr Fadl: people used to swear allegiance to him as if *he* were EIJ's leader. Some people would send representatives to pledge allegiance for them by proxy. But others would swear the oath directly, taking their leader by the hand in imitation of the followers of the Prophet Muhammad.

EIJ was seeking new members at this time, but chose its recruits with care. It was this caution which gave the group something of an elitist air and which limited its size and thus its geographical reach. It was not enough that potential new members should simply pray regularly. The group would first make an approach to an individual, then give him books to read and discuss at a later date: any candidates found to be too argumentative were instantly ruled out. And those who made it through the ideological screening stage were subjected to a series of physical and military tests.

Both Abu Hafs al-Misri and Abu 'Ubayda al-Banshiri played a part in re-establishing EIJ at this time. Al-Banshiri was known to be related to 'Abd al-Majid 'Abd al-Salam, one of the people involved in the assassination of Sadat. In 1987 old EIJ members concluded that they had more to gain from working together than pursuing their own separate goals. They were encouraged in this direction by certain benefactors who were keen to donate funds to jihadist causes and came from the Gulf expressly for this purpose. In this way EIJ came to be reconstituted abroad. However, contact with the group's members back in Egypt remained essential to recruiting new members and having them sent out to Afghanistan for training.

Syrian, Algerian and Libyan Mujahidin

What the Egyptian jihadists went through prior to their departure to Afghanistan mirrored almost exactly the experiences of other Arab militants.

---

1   In the eighth century CE, the leader of the 'Abbasid revolution which deposed the Umayyad dynasty in Damascus was unknown to his followers: they would pledge allegiance to him knowing only that he was a descendant of the Prophet Muhammad. EIJ's use of an alias for their emir is reminiscent of this strategy.

In Algeria, members of Mustafa Bouyali's Armed Islamic Movement (or Mouvement Islamique Armé, MIA) failed in their crude attempt to overthrow the regime in 1982. By 1987 the MIA was practically finished, with Bouyali himself dead and most of his group's several hundred members incarcerated. It was a lesson to any Algerians thinking of going down a similar route: many duly began emigrating. Most were not specifically MIA members, but simply would-be jihadists; a lot of them had connections to the Algerian branch of the Muslim Brotherhood.[1]

Syrian jihadists, like their Algerian counterparts, had suffered a major setback in the early 1980s. In 1982 the Syrian army had quelled an Islamist uprising in Hama, led by the Muslim Brotherhood and one of its radical offshoots called the Fighting Vanguard. The armed forces crushed the revolt by surrounding the city and then shelling it. Other Syrian jihadists had already trained in camps in Iraq; these had been set up with Saddam Hussein's approval, in the hope of toppling his rival, Hafiz al-Asad. But the fighters failed in their attempts to return to Syria in their comrades' hour of need. In the face of these repeated reversals, a few Syrian jihadists, including Abu Mus'ab al-Suri, moved to Afghanistan in 1988. Others made their way there from the United States, where they had gone to study. Many of these people had been swayed by Abdullah Azzam, who had toured American mosques and universities drumming up support for the Afghan cause.

Libya had its own part to play in the formation of al-Qa'ida. In the 1980s the opposition to Gaddafi's regime was predominantly secular and nationalist, represented by the National Front for the Salvation of Libya. However, the country's jihadists also tried to take action against the regime, most notably in 1986, 1987 and finally in 1989. That year the country's disparate jihadist groups all made disastrous attempts to resume their activity, and all found themselves locked in clashes with the security services, particularly in the cities of eastern Libya. The authorities

---

1   The Algerian branch of the Muslim Brotherhood was led by Mahfoud Nahnah; he personally assisted many young jihadists travelling to Afghanistan. In 1980 Nahnah helped found a charitable association called *El Islah Oual Irchad* ('Reform and Guidance'). Ten years later he established his own political party called Hamas, which was later renamed the Movement for the Society of Peace. He died in 2003.

responded by detaining hundreds of them, even thousands, according to some Islamists. Those who escaped the mass arrests did not wait for further evidence that the time was not yet ripe for their jihad; instead, they packed their bags and followed their Arab brothers to Afghanistan.

2

Brothers and Rivals:
The Foundation of the Jihadist Groups

In 1984 there were a mere fifteen Afghan Arabs; but by the time Russian forces withdrew from Afghanistan in February 1989, they numbered in their hundreds if not thousands, and the sudden end to the conflict forced them to rethink their next course of action.

They had all known that eventually the Afghan jihad would end and that, with the exception of those who had died as martyrs, they would have to go back home. It was less clear what would happen next: whether they would simply return to their former lives as if nothing had changed or continue their armed struggle, and, if so, against whom. These questions were the subject of much in-fighting between Islamist factions, whether based in Peshawar or the camps inside Afghanistan itself. Groups from across the Islamist spectrum, from the Muslim Brotherhood to the most radical jihadists, were all seeking to promote their ideology and attract as many supporters as possible from among the Arab fighters. Many of these had come to Afghanistan motivated not by any allegiance to a particular faction but by a simple desire to take part in jihad. Few if any had been party to the bitter ideological disputes between the Islamist movements, above all the jihadist groups and Egypt's Muslim Brotherhood. Idealistic but not ideological, these fighters were ripe for the picking.

Given the varied backgrounds of those who had taken part in the Afghan jihad, it is little wonder that they differed over what should follow. Those who had belonged to jihadist groups before coming to Afghanistan regarded their time there as a chance to prepare for the future battle with the regimes in their home countries. This outlook was shared mainly by the Egyptian members of EIJ and al-Gama'a al-Islamiyya. Unlike other Arabs in Afghanistan, they had no need to create an agenda from scratch or to establish a new hierarchy. Meanwhile, for inspiration they could draw on the writings of Sayyid Qutb and Muhammad 'Abd al-Salam Faraj.[1] It was not only the groups' structures that were in place: their ranks had also been swelled after the Egyptian authorities released hundreds of their members from prison. The ex-convicts had made their way to Afghanistan in the late 1980s; foremost among them was Ayman al-Zawahiri, who had emerged from jail more determined than ever to overthrow the regime that had incarcerated him.[2]

The Egyptian jihadists' perspective was not shared by other Afghan Arabs, however, particularly those who were not members of established groups in their native lands. This was true of most of the Gulf Arabs: few belonged to clandestine armed factions back home, where their governments already applied Islamic law to many aspects of daily life. The Libyan jihadists were in a similar position, albeit for different reasons. Unlike their counterparts from the Gulf, the Libyans *did* dispute their government's Islamic credentials: they regarded Gaddafi's regime as apostate because of its reluctance to implement Islamic law. But in contrast to their Egyptian comrades, the Libyans had no single, well-known group to represent them; instead, they belonged to a motley collection of factions with similar ideas but no formal ties to one another.

The same was largely true of the Algerians, Moroccans and Tunisians. Most Algerians who joined the Afghan jihad did not belong to Mustafa Bouyali's MIA. The majority were members of assorted smaller groups,

---

1   Sayyid Qutb, an Egyptian intellectual and leading member of the Muslim Brotherhood, was charged with plotting to overthrow the Egyptian government and executed in 1966. He maintained that nominally Muslim societies, through their failure to implement Islamic law, had reverted to a state of pre-Islamic 'ignorance' or godlessness known in Arabic as *jahiliyya*. They were consequently ripe to be reconquered for Islam. These concepts have been pivotal for later jihadist groups.

2   Ayman al-Zawahiri was tortured while in prison in Egypt, as a result of which he revealed the names of EIJ comrades linked to Sadat's assassination in 1981. After his release in 1985 al-Zawahiri made his way to Afghanistan, where other EIJ members (including Dr Fadl and Abu 'Ubayda al-Banshiri) had preceded him earlier in the decade.

such as the Muslim Brotherhood or the Qutbist movement.[1] But one thing they all shared was a conviction in their sacred duty to drive the Russians out of Afghanistan. Similarly, the Moroccans who rallied to the Afghan cause were not part of a movement dedicated to fighting the monarchy in their home country. Like their North African neighbours, they had come to Afghanistan simply because they believed in waging jihad against the Soviet occupiers of Muslim land. Earlier in the 1980s, the Tunisian regime had thwarted a coup attempt by army officers with Islamist sympathies; in the early 1990s, a handful of the conspirators found their way to Afghanistan.[2] They were joined by aspiring jihadists from Syria, Lebanon, Jordan and Palestine, as well as Iraqi and Kurdish enemies of Saddam Hussein's secular regime.

This panoply of jihadist factions came together for the first time in the mountains of Afghanistan. And it was there that they began a battle for support that would define the very concept of jihad that their members would espouse in the years to come.

Jihad Triumphant

It was the notion of jihad championed by EIJ that emerged the winner in this battle of ideas, as even the group's rivals would concede. The first EIJ members to arrive in Afghanistan in the late 1980s brought with them a coherent set of beliefs which 'Abd al-Salam Faraj summarised in his work *The Neglected Duty*.[3] In it, he justified jihad against all governments that

1 Based on the teachings of Sayyid Qutb as imparted by his brother, Muhammad Qutb, a Professor of Islamic Studies who ardently promoted his brother's work. One of his most famous students was Ayman al-Zawahiri.
2 The Tunisian government accused officers involved in the coup attempt of links to the Hizb al-Nahda (or 'Renaissance Party'), which emerged from the Islamic Tendency Movement (also known as the Mouvement de la Tendence Islamique) founded in 1981. The Hizb al-Nahda itself denies any such connection.
3 Muhammad 'Abd al-Salam Faraj's work, *al-Farida al-Gha'iba* ('The Neglected Duty') was considered a summary of the theological justifications of jihadist ideology. It draws in particular on the fatwas or formal legal opinions of the fourteenth-century theologian, Ibn Taymiyya. Faraj used his judgements to argue, like Qutb, that 'Islamic' societies were not truly Muslim because they applied positive (or man-made) law, rather than Islamic Shari'a law alone.

did not apply Islamic law and 'govern in accordance with divine revelation'. However, Faraj's influential text was not enough for EIJ members, who published a vast tome by their leader, Dr Fadl, as soon as they regrouped. This book, entitled *The Essential Guide for Preparation*, soon became a key text in jihadist training camps. Nowhere was this more true than the al-Faruq camp, which the newly-founded al-Qa'ida had set up in Khost and which was run mainly by a team of Egyptian EIJ members.

The group was not interested merely in justifying the overthrow of Arab regimes: it also launched a stinging rebuke against Islamist movements which had refused to join its armed struggle. This inter-Islamist rivalry intensified when Ayman al-Zawahiri issued a book of his own in 1988, shortly after moving to Afghanistan. Entitled *Bitter Harvest: Sixty Years of the Muslim Brotherhood*, the book contained an interminable string of accusations and recriminations against the group.[1] Meanwhile, the Syrian Islamist, Abu Mus'ab al-Suri, used his work, *The Islamic Jihadist Revolution in Syria*, to inveigh against the Muslim Brotherhood's ideas, blaming it for the failure of what he called 'the jihad in Syria' in the early 1980s.[2] While the Muslim Brotherhood was undoubtedly the Arab world's most recognised Islamist organisation, ideas of violent jihad soon began to gain sway among the Afghan Arabs. It may be that the very nature of their environment lent itself more to the promotion of armed struggle than the Muslim Brotherhood's conciliatory approach.[3]

Perhaps the jihadists' most significant achievement in the late 1980s was to influence bin Laden's thinking. It was they who convinced him to break away from the *Maktab al-Khidamat* and its emir, Abdullah Azzam,

---

1   Al-Zawahiri's book contained a savage attack on the Muslim Brotherhood's non-violent approach to the Egyptian regime and criticised the movement for abandoning its slogan 'Our Path is Jihad'.

2   Abu Mus'ab al-Suri's book, *The Islamic Jihadist Revolution in Syria*, was first published in Pakistan in 1989; he gave a copy to the present author in London in 1996.

3   After the suppression of the Muslim Brotherhood under President Nasser in the 1950s and '60s, the organisation sought to avoid any confrontation with the Egyptian regime. It was this conciliatory approach in particular which EIJ despised. A similar process occurred with the Syrian branch of the Brotherhood, which, to the fury of jihadists, forged an alliance with secular opposition groups following the crackdown of the early 1980s.

who had originally belonged to a school of the Muslim Brotherhood.[1] Two years after setting up the *Bayt al-Ansar* alongside the *Maktab al-Khidamat* in Peshawar, the Egyptians helped bin Laden found al-Qa'ida as a jihadist movement independent of Azzam's control, albeit with little to distinguish itself from him ideologically. The personal affection between bin Laden and Azzam endured. However, those close to the Palestinian leader confirm that by the late 1980s his influence over jihadist circles in Peshawar had begun to dwindle. EIJ's ideas were now in the ascendant.

Abdullah Azzam's son, Hudhayfa, describes the hostility EIJ members, led by Dr Fadl and Ayman al-Zawahiri, showed his father during the late 1980s:

> These Egyptian brothers in Peshawar would stand up to my father in the mosque. They issued statements against him while he was still alive, claiming that he and his supporters had been penetrated by American intelligence and accusing him of stealing funds ... They would refuse to let him lead them during prayers in the mosque. They split the Arabs into two camps. Abdullah Azzam used to pray at a mosque called *Sab' al-Layl*, while the Egyptians would perform the Friday prayers at the Kuwait Red Crescent's mosque in Peshawar. My father once addressed a Friday sermon to them lasting an hour and a half. He would go and pray with them, even though they were the same age as his own children. They were nothing compared with him: his knowledge of Islamic law in particular was much greater than theirs. And yet even so, he would sit with them modestly and listen to sermons delivered by people who had no idea about public speaking. His aim was to lead by example, showing them how Muslims ought to behave towards one another.[2]

---

1 Although Abdullah Azzam was a member of the Muslim Brotherhood, he always stressed the principle of violent jihad, from which the organisation's Egyptian leaders distanced themselves. His outlook may have owed something to his Palestinian background and the armed struggle against Israeli occupation. Azzam's ideology is also espoused by the Palestinian militant group, Hamas (founded in the late 1980s), which is itself a jihadist offshoot of the Muslim Brotherhood.

2 From an interview with Abdullah Azzam's son, Hudhayfa, in July 2005 by the Arabic satellite television station, al-Arabiya. See: http://www.alarabiya.net/Articles/2005/07/28/15351.htm for the Arabic text of the interview.

It is important to set EIJ's hostility to Abdullah Azzam in context. Part of this animosity was ideological and stemmed from the Egyptians' hatred of the Muslim Brotherhood, to which Azzam belonged. But there were also tensions relating to practical aspects of the Afghan jihad, such as the distribution of money donated by Muslims around the world. These funds were controlled by Azzam and his closest associates, a fact which EIJ bitterly resented. As bin Laden moved to establish his own organisation, the Egyptian jihadists placed themselves at his disposal and based themselves at his very residence in Peshawar. This close association must have created a certain friction between the al-Qa'ida leader and Azzam, given EIJ's criticism of the latter. But whatever the Egyptians' influence over bin Laden, he was not prepared to abandon Azzam to their mercy.

Abdullah Anas has described how in 1988 a group of Egyptian jihadists, led by Dr Fadl and Ayman al-Zawahiri, sought to prosecute Azzam on charges of corruption.[1] Paradoxically, it was a suggestion Anas himself had made to his future father-in-law which had set this train of events in motion. Earlier that year he had spoken to Azzam about the lack of aid reaching northern Afghanistan compared with the south of the country, which was much more accessible to Arab charities based in Pakistan. Anas proposed increasing the Islamic relief effort in the north, partly to prove to the local population that the Arabs could offer them more effective support than Western aid agencies. Azzam took up the idea and, throwing down the gauntlet to rival charities, named the scheme *al-Tahaddi*, meaning 'the Challenge'.

Azzam subsequently agreed that an Egyptian-born individual called Ahmad Sa'id Khadr, also known as Abu 'Abd al-Rahman al-Kanadi, should manage the project. Al-Kanadi was a competent administrator, but crucially he also had Canadian citizenship, a fact which would make it much easier for him to travel the world raising funds for the new scheme. He spent much of his time in Islamabad, where he had contacts in the Canadian embassy and various charities, and he even wore Western dress, which meant that Azzam and others were waved through Pakistani police checkpoints whenever al-Kanadi accompanied them. Yet despite appearances, al-Kanadi was committed to jihad and had left Canada to take

1   Abdullah Anas in an interview with the author in London on 16 April 2010.

part in the Afghan war effort, bringing his family with him. Nonetheless, he was not affiliated to any particular Islamist faction. This very neutrality made him even better suited to raising money for *al-Tahaddi* from a broad range of sympathisers, and to this end Azzam dispatched him back to Canada with a letter of recommendation.

When al-Kanadi launched *al-Tahaddi*, he did so in coordination with Azzam's *Maktab al-Khidamat* or 'Services Bureau'. Nonetheless, the two entities remained separate, based in adjacent buildings and equipped with their own vehicles. *Al-Tahaddi* paid a group of Muslim clerics to travel to northern Afghanistan and identify local people's medical, educational and welfare needs. Abdullah Anas was the commander of the Arab fighters in the area, but it was al-Kanadi who decided where the clerics went. Likewise, they submitted their reports on conditions in the area to al-Kanadi, not Anas, and the aid projects that followed were badged as the initiatives of *al-Tahaddi*, not the *Maktab al-Khidamat*. Yet months later, Anas returned to Peshawar to find that al-Tahaddi's offices had been closed down. Worse still, al-Kanadi had embarked on a vicious campaign against Abdullah Azzam, accusing him of embezzling funds destined for *al-Tahaddi*.

Abdullah Anas maintains that Azzam was preoccupied with more important matters at the time; he therefore preferred to let al-Kanadi vent his frustration than get involved in discussions of administrative detail. But al-Kanadi's grievances provided just the ammunition that Azzam's opponents had been looking for. EIJ duly went on the offensive, charging him with misappropriating funds intended for relief work in Afghanistan. The fact that they were coordinating this smear campaign from within bin Laden's own home only added to the dismay of Azzam's supporters. Yet the night before the accusations against Azzam were due to be heard in a Shari'a court, bin Laden personally sent word to his old friend urging him not to attend the hearing: to do so could put his very life in jeopardy. In the event, Azzam stayed away; the self-styled judges ruled that al-Kanadi, and not the *Maktab al-Khidamat*, was in charge of *al-Tahaddi*, but Azzam's absence meant that the accusations against him of corruption were dropped. Bin Laden's intervention had won Azzam a stay of execution, but not for long: within months he would be dead, killed along with two of his sons by a car bomb in Peshawar. The culprits have never been conclusively identified.

Yet for all their apparent shortcomings, Azzam's opponents ultimately attracted many aspiring jihadists away from the Muslim Brotherhood. Abu Mus'ab al-Suri describes the battle of ideas raging in Peshawar at this time and how it was the jihadists who won:

> The late 1970s and early 1980s were a period of intense interaction between the various schools of the Islamic revival. The hostels and training camps in Peshawar and Afghanistan became places where they could meet, discuss ideas and often end up arguing. Arab jihadists found themselves confronted by two main schools of thought. On the one hand were those who believed in democracy, such as the Muslim Brotherhood. They would promote their ideas by publishing research and delivering lectures, even calling for democratic practices in the camps where they were active. On the other hand was the school of official Saudi theology; its adherents rejected the idea of hakimiyya, defended the legitimacy of Arab rulers and demanded respect for official clerics, particularly in Saudi Arabia and the other Gulf states ...[1]
>
> At the same time there was a jihadist fervour in the air ... This was the febrile atmosphere in which the ideology of jihad began to gain sway.[2]

The Emergence of the Jihadist Groups

In the early 1990s the jihadists had yet to consolidate their victory over the Muslim Brotherhood: its only practical manifestations were the formation of al-Qa'ida and the reconstitution of EIJ. However, two years on, the seeds sown by the jihadists in the hostels of Peshawar and the training camps had begun to grow into new factions. In Algeria, jihadist

---

1 The Pakistani Islamist thinker, Abu al-'Ala' Mawdudi (1903–1979), argued that sovereignty, or hakimiyya, belonged to God alone: the only just ruler was one who governed in accordance with divine revelation, the Qur'an. To invest sovereignty in any other authority would cause a nominally Muslim society to revert to the godless condition of jahiliyya, akin to the pagan Arabs' state of ignorance before the Prophet Muhammad's mission.

2 Abu Mus'ab al-Suri, Da'wat al-Muqawama, pp. 717–8.

graduates of al-Qa'ida's camps founded the GIA. Similarly, the Libyans established the LIFG , bringing together most of their country's disparate jihadist factions under a single umbrella. These organisations were by far the Afghan jihad's most significant product in the Maghreb.

The establishment of the two North African groups coincided with events in the Middle East which would have major repercussions for the Afghan Arabs. In the Gulf War of 1991 an international coalition led by the United States drove Iraqi forces out of Kuwait. Osama bin Laden had opposed this action, believing that it had led to 'infidel' foreign forces 'defiling' the sacred soil of the Arabian Peninsula. The same year saw an Islamist uprising in Algeria. At that time the country was seething with popular discontent; the campaign of civil disobedience led by the Islamic Salvation Front (FIS) in the spring and summer of 1991 had ended with the Algerian authorities rounding up the leaders of the FIS, headed by Abbasi Madani and Ali Belhadj.

This period saw the Algerian veterans of the Afghan jihad begin to return home and make secret moves to establish a jihadist group there. Initially, they made contact with well-known associates of Mustafa Bouyali, known locally as the 'first jihadists'. These figures had been released during the period of pluralism in Algeria, when the political process was opened up to the Islamists. However, it was not long before the government of Chadli Bendjedid cancelled the elections which the FIS had been poised to win. This fateful decision handed the Islamists the excuse they needed to declare jihad against the Algerian regime.

It was clear from the outset that there were two very different types of jihadist in Algeria, with distinct agendas. On the one hand were the Islamists, who had declared holy war with the aim of reclaiming their rightful victory in the polls. On the other were people with a more radical outlook, who had declared a different type of jihad, aimed at establishing an Islamic state by force – a state where there would be no room for democracy, pluralism or elections, or even for Islamists with different ideas. These divergent approaches found their expression in two jihadist groups: the Armed Islamic Group (GIA) and the Islamic Salvation Army (AIS).

The Armed Islamic Group

Abdullah Anas admits his failure to rally the Algerians based in the hostels of Afghanistan and Pakistan behind the FIS. He concedes that EIJ's ideology played a key role in prompting them to found an extremist group. Here, for the first time, Anas describes his differences with the founders of the GIA and their leader, Qari Saïd:[1]

> The ideological polarisation in Peshawar began early on, especially once people began arriving who had a background in the Islamist organisations of their home countries. EIJ members, the Muslim Brotherhood, the Salafists – they all brought the baggage of their ideological disputes with them to Afghanistan. Abdullah Azzam and his colleagues disapproved of this, but he could not protect the region altogether from their influence. As a result, one Jamil al-Rahman rebelled against Hekmatyar and set himself up as an independent military leader, claiming that he was a true Salafist while the Afghans were all heretics.[2] There was fierce fighting in Kunar [in eastern Afghanistan] between Hekmatyar's men and the followers of these Salafists and Wahhabis, as they were known. Some men were fervent admirers of Hekmatyar: in their eyes, he was the only leader of any distinction in Afghanistan. Obedience to him was essential: anyone who rebelled against him was undermining the jihad. One of his more fanatical supporters took matters into his own hands and went and killed Jamil al-Rahman. But that was not the end of the trouble.

Anas points to the way that EIJ imported the conflict between the Muslim Brotherhood, EIJ itself and the Salafist movement to Afghanistan:

> The first book al-Zawahiri wrote was called *Bitter Harvest: Sixty Years of the Muslim Brotherhood*. This book has nothing whatsoever to do with the Afghans, or with the problems of feeding the Arabs who had come to join the jihad, or reinforcing the camps or fighting the Russians. You have the sense that any link to Afghanistan is

---

1   Abdullah Anas in an interview with the author in London in May 2006.
2   Jamil al-Rahman was a leading member of Hekmatyar's Hezb-e Islami. He was subsequently influenced by Salafist ideas and founded his own group, only to be murdered by one of Hekmatyar's supporters.

forced, and that the book is really about settling old scores between factions in a specifically Egyptian context. But whether one likes it or not, there was an audience for what he had to say. A lot of this had to do with the fact that most of the Arabs were staying in Peshawar at this point, and not inside Afghanistan. There were two categories of young men: those who were members of various organisations, and those who were unaffiliated. The latter were like a blank canvas in ideological terms. These people had only recently been motivated to take part in jihad, perhaps as a way of doing penance for something in their private lives or as a result of some other emotional impulse. Some of them came from Europe, while others were from the Arab world, but none had any history of involvement in Islamist factional rivalry. Yet these people usually fell prey to the ideological polarisation at the time, attracted either by the Muslim Brotherhood or by the messages of EIJ or the Salafists.

Anas admits that Ayman al-Zawahiri's ideas about the Muslim Brotherhood, which he roundly condemned in his book, soon spread among the young jihadists. Al-Zawahiri argued that the Brotherhood's agenda was misguided and that its members were heretics, a judgement Anas says had considerable influence on certain people. They included some young Algerians, who opened a new camp and set up their own hostel. Anas describes these people as 'normal young men who went to the al-Faruq camp to train':

> During their course, they had al-Zawahiri's ideas drummed into them: they were brainwashed into thinking that what the FIS was doing in Algeria was much the same as what the Muslim Brotherhood believed in. Its approach was based on political participation; but [according to the doctrine the men were fed] for Muslims to found a party was an act of heresy, elections were blasphemous and democracy was tantamount to unbelief. As a result, anyone even remotely involved in politics was a heretic who had strayed from the path of the Prophet. The only way to get rid of the tyrants, the infidels and the apostates was jihad.

Anas himself found this view uncontroversial: any Muslim asked to compare Islam with Western democracy could only conclude that Islam was superior. The problem arose when people were polarised on the basis of this simplistic idea. It was then that 'new recruits began to despise the

Muslim Brotherhood and to hate anyone who believed in the possibility of non-violent reform, such as the FIS, Hamas and the Muslim Brotherhood. The lads who went to train [at the al-Faruq camp] were like blank slates. But when you have control over such people 24 hours a day, when you feed them and train them and give them things to read, within a month or two they become like robots you can use to do whatever you want.' Anas realised that a number of young Algerians had fallen under the influence of this ideology. In response, he tried to preserve a sense of solidarity between the Algerians at his hostel, a place called the *Bayt al-Muhajirin* which provided accommodation for some 200 people with funding from the *Maktab al-Khidamat*. Anas feared that otherwise they would move to hostels run by jihadists who were supported by al-Qa'ida and influenced by al-Zawahiri's ideology. But he admits that he was unsuccessful. Some young Algerians broke away from the *Bayt al-Muhajirin* and set up their own hostel in the area of Babi in Pakistan, under the leadership of the Afghan warlord, Abdul Rabb al-Rasul Sayyaf. Their allegiance was entirely to the Reform and Guidance Movement, led by Mahfoud al-Nahnah. Another group, led by Qari Saïd, opened a different guesthouse, which they called the *Bayt al-Mujahidin*; this was essentially an extension of al-Zawahiri's EIJ and al-Qa'ida's al-Faruq camp.

Anas tried to persuade the Algerians who remained at the *Bayt al-Muhajirin* that the best thing would be for them to support the FIS. At that point the movement was still preparing to contest the Algerian elections: it argued that by taking part in the political process it could protest against the regime. 'I was in a race against time,' says Anas:

> trying to prevent the young men who were left from having their minds poisoned by this [violent jihadist] ideology. I was attempting to keep them on the FIS's side; though I believed in jihad, it was not in the misguided sense used at the al-Faruq camp. But we were overtaken by events. We held two or three meetings, attended by hundreds of young men. We talked to them about the slogan that ordinary Algerians gathered in football stadiums used to chant at that time: 'Chebouti is our general, Abbasi our president and Ali our imam.'[1] We tried to convince them of what this meant: that Algerian

---

1 This slogan referred to the militant Islamist leader Abdelkader Chebouti and

public opinion accepted the existing political hierarchy in the country. After Abbasi and Ali Belhadj were arrested [following the campaign of civil disobedience in mid-1991] Abdelkader Chebouti's name came to the fore. Now that the political process had come to an end, the next phase would be dominated by three men: Chebouti, Saïd Makhloufi and Mansour Meliani, all of whom represented the FIS and its ideas. It is true that they all believed in jihad, belonged to the jihadist movement and had themselves taken part in armed action in the days of Mustafa Bouyali; but they were also inextricably bound up with the political process. Their experience would help ensure that the public's aspirations were achieved without paying too heavy a price. Now that the political process had been suspended, of course it had to be replaced by armed struggle. But that struggle had to be a continuation of political action by other means, and not a question of condemning democracy and the electoral process as blasphemy and unbelief.

Anas relates an incident which occurred when the Algerian veterans of the Afghan jihad were establishing their own group, independently of the FIS:

> I remember that Qari Saïd came to see me at that time, having travelled to Algeria in 1991. He told me that he had visited Meliani and suggested that the latter quit his leader, Chebouti. He had gone to see Meliani and told him, 'There's no reason for you to remain loyal to the leadership of Chebouti and Saïd Makhloufi: they're nothing but an extension of the FIS. We can set up our own camp in Afghanistan and we won't need to depend on anyone. We've got the money and the training; you can send us the men and we'll see to it that they get proper jihadist instruction.' Meliani agreed and promptly informed Chebouti that he no longer recognised him as his emir. This was the first split in the Islamist ranks. 'Well done,' I told him, 'you've broken the armed struggle away from the political process and taken the first step down the road to civil

---

the Islamic Salvation Front (FIS) leaders, Abbasi Madani and Ali Belhadj. It signified that the public would welcome the three men as Algeria's military, political and spiritual leaders respectively. Anas's argument is that Algerian popular opinion was opposed not to the structure of the state, but only to those in control of it and to their policies at the time.

war in Algeria.' I asked Qari Saïd what it was about Chebouti and Makhloufi that had led him to encourage Meliani to reject their leadership. 'Chebouti's a weak, sick man,' he replied. 'He hasn't got the strength to lead a band of soldiers. And Saïd Makhloufi's an oaf.' It wasn't the time or the place to argue with Qari Saïd; the situation was still in its early stages and I had no idea that things would work out as they did. One of the first people to collaborate with Meliani after he broke away from Chebouti's group was Moh Leveilley.[1] Together they formed the nucleus around which the GIA was formed: the group which, paradoxically, would in due course become an instrument of the Algerian intelligence services.

Egypt and the Return of the Jihadists

There were similarly violent incidents in Egypt. Having regrouped in Afghanistan, the jihadists who had been released from prison in the mid-1980s were now beginning to return home in dribs and drabs. Many of them were soon discovered by the authorities and prosecuted in the so-called 'Vanguards of Conquest' trials of 1993. However, many others remained at large and soon embarked on a campaign of attacks on foreign tourists and the Egyptian security forces which was to drag on throughout the first half of the 1990s.

Hani al-Siba'i says that EIJ was rebuilding itself in Afghanistan, training new members and then sending them back to Egypt to prepare for future operations.[2] Some of these recruits began talking about the training they had received. In late 1992 and early 1993, about a thousand men who had attended the camps were arrested and prosecuted in the Vanguards of Conquest trials, which lasted several weeks. Dr al-Siba'i believes they were detained because they did not really know what they had been trained for. 'Some of them thought they would be like al-Gama'a al-Islamiyya, whose members received training in Afghanistan and then went back to Egypt to carry out operations. Some EIJ members knew that they had

---

1   Moh Leveilley's real name was Muhammad Allal; his nickname, by which he was more widely known, was derived from the area of Algiers where he was based.

2   From a series of interviews with Dr al-Siba'i, conducted by the author in September 2002.

been trained in preparation for future action, but many of the others didn't understand this.'

The Libyans: Jihad and the LIFG

The Libyan jihadists who returned home from the battlefields of Afghanistan adopted a more cautious approach than their Egyptian and Algerian counterparts. In their view, the time was not yet ripe for a confrontation with their country's security forces. They may also have preferred to wait and see how the situation in neighbouring countries would develop: the overthrow of any regime in the area was bound to influence the course of events inside Libya. Furthermore, Gaddafi's regime itself did not force the Libyan jihadists into a premature conflict, a fact which allowed them to use the early 1990s to organise themselves. They established cells inside Libya, appointed emirs to the various parts of the country and decided on the type of organisation that would best represent them on their return. This was how the Libyan Islamic Fighting Group (LIFG) was born.

The LIFG did not appear out of nowhere: it was the product of the jihadist circles that had been suppressed under Gaddafi's rule. Numerous small factions with jihadist ideas had been active inside Libya before the LIFG coalesced in the early 1990s, and these groups had themselves been linked to Libyans based in Afghanistan.

Abdullah Ahmad is the *nom de guerre* of a Libyan veteran of the Afghan jihad who was involved in a paramilitary group called the Jihad Movement.[1] He maintains that the jihadist groups first began to appear in Libya in the early 1980s, when 'many young people became more devout, going to the mosques regularly and immersing themselves in the study of Islamic law and theology. They included Muhammad al-Muhashhish, the uncle of Muhammad al-Hami [an Islamist leader], who became a practising Muslim

---

1 In 1996 the Jihad Movement changed its name to the Islamic Martyrs' Movement. The source, called 'Abdallah Ahmad' in these pages, described the emergence of the jihadist movement in Libya to the author in a long letter in 1999. In 2004–2005 he went to Iraq, where he was subsequently reported to have been killed.

as a high school student in 1982.' These young, newly pious Muslims set
up a group which Abdullah Ahmad describes as 'the first Libyan jihadist
organisation, led by 'Ali al-'Ashabi:

> [However,] the nine members of the group were all arrested and
> executed. Meanwhile, Dr Hasan Qtait was detained on charges of
> issuing inflammatory fatwas and inciting murder, then imprisoned
> and tortured...before being released in 1988. It was Muhammad
> al-Muhashhish's contact with these young militants which led him
> to embrace Salafist jihadist ideology. This saw jihad as a means of
> removing apostate governments and replacing them with an Islamic
> state. In 1989 Muhammad al-Muhashhish took part in the 'blessed
> jihad', when intermittent clashes with the authorities took place
> in Benghazi and Ajdabiya. Several brothers were killed, including
> Salih Mahfuz from Ajdabiya and various senior leaders of the
> movement, who died in the fighting in Benghazi. When the jihad
> of 1989 failed, the regime carried out mass arrests of young Islamists,
> rounding up between 5,000 and 7,000 of them and imprisoning
> them in various parts of the country. Many young Libyans went
> abroad, especially to Afghanistan, where they took part in the jihad
> and later founded their own organisations, foremost among which
> was the LIFG. Others stayed behind; they included Muhammad
> al-Muhashhish, who was famed for his courage, eloquence and
> leadership ability.[1] The events of 1989 were the first time that he had
> taken part in jihad. Together with others who had been involved, he
> established the Islamic Martyrs' Movement, which they based on
> a cell which had emerged from the fighting unscathed. They then
> began recruiting and training new members, concentrating on the
> Islamist strongholds of West Salmani and al-Majuri, both districts
> of Benghazi. The movement later expanded to include other parts
> of the city and the surrounding area and attracted support from
> community elders and students alike.

'The brothers first called the movement the Islamic Jihad Group in Libya,
to signal their agenda,' adds Abdullah Ahmad:

---

[1] According to Abdullah Ahmad, Muhammad al-Muhashhish was known as 'the
     Libyan Sayyaf', a reference to Abdul Rabb al-Rasul Sayyaf, the Afghan warlord
     and leader of the Ittehad-e Islami who was widely admired by Arab fighters in
     Afghanistan.

This was back in August 1989. A meeting was held at Muhammad al-Muhashhish's house, in which the formation of the movement was formally declared and its charter was read out. There were twenty-five founder members of the group; of those present, twenty-two swore an oath of allegiance to al-Muhashhish as the movement's first emir and five were appointed members of its Consultative Council or *Majlis al-Shura*.

The Official History of the LIFG

The LIFG's account of its own formation has much in common with Abdullah Ahmad's story. However, the LIFG's history also shows that its origins were very different from those of the Martyrs' Movement. This is itself evidence of the fact that many jihadist groups were operating in Libya at the same time, but in isolation from one another. While the Martyrs' Movement had links to the jihadist movement led by 'Ali al-'Ashabi and later Muhammad al-Muhashhish, the LIFG had ties to a completely different group headed by 'Iwad al-Zawawi.

'The annals of the LIFG', according to the group's official history, 'are testament to the various phases of the Islamic renaissance in Libya in general, and the jihadist awakening in particular.' The group maintains that its origins date back to 1985, 'when 'Iwad al-Zawawi, the leader of the jihadist movement, travelled the length and breadth of the country in search of people to defend Islam alongside him and carry aloft the torch of jihad.' In 1988 many of the LIFG's founding members 'went to the battlefields of Afghanistan to take part in jihad and make use of the opportunities there.'[1] Abu al-Mundhir al-Sa'idi was one of the LIFG's founders; he explains that the group's origins were linked to 'a secret jihadist organisation inside Libya led by Brother 'Iwad al-Zawawi.'[2] Al-Zawawi was a student of Islamic law and a graduate of the Faculty of Education at Tripoli University. His group remained active and continued to recruit new members 'until the events

---

1 From the LIFG's account of its own formation published on its website (currently inactive).
2 From an interview with Sami al-Sa'idi, also known as Abu al-Mundhir al-Sa'idi, conducted by the magazine *Bayariq al-Majd* ('Banners of Glory') and published on the LIFG's website.

of 1989, when some of the group's leading members went to eastern Libya to find out what was happening, particularly in Ajdabiya and Benghazi. Then came the raids and the mass arrests in Tripoli, in which the group's leaders were also swept up. This group [led by al-Zawawi] formed the core of the LIFG, many of whose most senior members today started out in that faction's leadership.' The former LIFG member, Noman Benotman, confirms al-Sa'idi's story, while admitting that there is no single account of the LIFG's formation.[1] 'The LIFG emerged gradually, through various phases of activity, rather than all at once,' he says.

According to Benotman, the LIFG as it is known today was founded after 1990 by a core of five individuals. At the time, they belonged to two other groups: 'Iwad al-Zawawi's faction, founded in Tripoli in 1982, and another organisation established in the mid-1980s and comprising several smaller sub-groups all operating in the capital. Benotman explains the little-known reason behind the LIFG's insistence that it emerged from al-Zawawi's group alone:

> In 1986 'Iwad al-Zawawi went to Afghanistan, where he met [Abdul Rabb al-Rasul] Sayyaf. Al-Zawawi spent several weeks there and left Sayyaf a 36-volume edition of the complete fatwas of Ibn Taymiyya.[2] 'Iwad al-Zawawi went to Afghanistan to find out for himself what was going on there and told Sayyaf that 'some of the brothers' might come and join him [to take part in the Afghan jihad]. This is why some people say that al-Zawawi's group was the nucleus around which the LIFG formed. Al-Zawawi went back to Libya, where he told a select few about his trip. Abu al-Mundhir told me this story himself. When Abu al-Mundhir wanted to go to Afghanistan in 1988, 'Iwad al-Zawawi told him he had left the collected fatwas of Ibn Taymiyya with Sayyaf and that Abu al-Mundhir could use them.

---

1   From the author's interviews with Noman Benotman in London in the spring and summer of 2005.
2   Taqi al-Din Ahmad Ibn Taymiyyah (1268–1328 CE) was a conservative, anti-rationalist scholar of Islam educated in Damascus. Writing in the aftermath of the Mongol invasions, Ibn Taymiyya argued the necessity of opposing tyranny by force. These and other views resonate for contemporary Islamists and jihadists, who often cite his works.

There were many obstacles to be overcome before the LIFG could see the light of day, as Benotman explains: 'In 1989 and 1990 there were numerous problems in Pakistan and Afghanistan related to the foundation of the LIFG. They had to do in particular with the appointment of regional emirs [the group's representatives for the various parts of Libya]. People were arguing over who was to represent which area, which goes to show that the group had not acquired its present form prior to 1990.' According to Benotman, when work first started on establishing the group, it comprised many members of other organisations, including the Muslim Brotherhood. However, with time the LIFG membership crystallised around a particular group, who finished defining the LIFG's structure and drew up a jihadist manifesto for the organisation. It was at this point that Islamists from other movements distanced themselves from the LIFG.[1]

According to Benotman, one of the LIFG's founders was Abu Abdullah al-Sadiq, emir of the group from 1995. Other founder members included Abu al-Mundhir al-Sa'idi, the LIFG's one-time head of Islamic law; the group's first emir, 'Abd al-Ghaffar al-Duwadi; Salah Fathi bin Sulayman; and 'Commander' 'Abd al-Wahhab.[2] All these men were university students when they decided to leave for Afghanistan and join the jihad. Abu Idris, who became a leading member of the LIFG's Consultative Council, was a medical student in Benghazi when he set off for Afghanistan in 1988. Abu Abdullah al-Sadiq was in the final year of his engineering course, and al-Sa'idi was likewise studying civil engineering at al-Fatih University when they both decided to leave Libya for Afghanistan in the same year.

Benotman himself moved to Afghanistan in the late 1980s, having studied political science at Tripoli University. He says that the LIFG's founders could not at first agree on a name for the group. The reason, he explains, was that the LIFG was similar to EIJ in being an agglomeration of smaller factions which shared the same jihadist ideas:

1   One man involved in the initial discussions about the foundation of the LIFG is today a leading member of the Muslim Brotherhood.
2   'Abd al-Ghaffar al-Duwadi, also known as 'Abd al-Salam, is from Sabrata, 60 kilometres west of Tripoli. 'Commander' 'Abd al-Wahhab, also known as Abu Idris, was arrested in Libya in 1996; he is currently imprisoned in the Abu Salim Prison in Tripoli. The prison was supposed to have been demolished by the time this book went to print.

It was one of these, the Libyan Jihadist Group, which had been
the driving force behind the establishment of the LIFG. Various
names were bandied about at the meetings held prior to the group's
foundation, but initially it was launched without an official title. By
the time the group's membership had settled down a few months later
and its structure had become more clearly defined, it was named the
Mujahidin Companies. When a document was drawn up defining
the group's position on Islamic law, it was disseminated under the
title 'An Outline of the Mujahidin Companies' Programme'. Two
hundred copies were printed in Peshawar and handed out to people
to read and then give back. I was in Babi [in Pakistan] when one of
the brothers brought me a copy to read. This was how work began on
bringing together the Libyans in Afghanistan. 'Abd al-Rahman al-
Hattab acted temporarily as the group's emir ... because of in-fighting
between some of its members. This was in the early 1990s.[1]

Relations between the LIFG and the GIA

Given that both the LIFG and the Algerian GIA had emerged from the
camps and hostels dotted along the Afghan-Pakistani border, it was a
matter of course that their founders should know one another. It was also
natural that the Libyans should take a keen interest in the jihad on which
their Algerian counterparts would embark in 1992.

Noman Benotman describes the relationship between the LIFG and
the Algerians as 'normal', since they all worked closely together:[2]

We had contact with dozens of them in Afghanistan, including Qari
Saïd, Chouakri Abdelkader and Rachid Ramda.[3] Most of them had

---

1   The author of 'The Outline of the Mujahidin Companies' Programme' is widely
    known to have been Abu al-Mundhir al-Sa'idi.
2   From an interview with the author in London in the spring of 2005.
3   In 1990 Chouakri Abdelkader, also known as Abou Khaled, took charge of
    the branch of the FIS in Es Sénia in the province of Oran in western Algeria.
    In 1992 he moved to Afghanistan, where he trained at the Khaldan camp and
    joined the GIA. He was imprisoned in Algeria in the latter half of the 1990s, but
    was subsequently released during the country's national reconciliation process.
    See Muhammad Muqaddam, al-Afghan al-Jaza'iriyyun: Min al-Jama'ah ila al-
    Qa'ida ('The Algerian Afghans: From the GIA to al-Qa'ida') (Agence Nationale
    d'Édition et de Publicité, Algiers, 2002), pp. 85–87. Rachid Ramda, also known

a reputation for their love of jihad and spirit of self-sacrifice; if they were typical of the mujahidin in Algeria, then our impression of the GIA was a good one. We couldn't ignore what was happening there: Algeria was of vital strategic importance to our own plans. We could have used it as a stepping stone from Afghanistan back to Libya. Military strategists talk about 'leapfrogging': if you had a military force in Afghanistan, you needed it to 'leapfrog' to the Algerian border with Libya. The alternative would mean leaving that force to stand idle in Afghanistan and rust.

Little did the LIFG know when they dispatched their men to Algeria that they were sending them on a deadly escapade that would have a terrible outcome.

---

as Abou Farès and Ilyas, was a prominent London-based supporter of the GIA during the 1990s. His deportation to France from the UK in 2005 is discussed in Chapter Seven.

3

Libya: Jihadists Supplant Nationalists

When the LIFG finally emerged from the shadows on 18 October 1995, it did so reluctantly. The group had wanted more time to build up its cells within Libya, so that when the time came they would be ready to take on the security forces. But time was not a luxury that the regime was about to grant them. Following a series of incidents in 1995, the group's cells were rapidly exposed, one after another. Yet for the security services the surprise was not that opposition groups had been operating inside the country: ever since the 1980s they had been preparing for a showdown with Libyan patriotic movements such as the National Front for the Salvation of Libya (NFSL). The shock was discovering that the real threat to Gaddafi's regime came from an altogether different quarter: the nationalists had been replaced by jihadists.

The NFSL first appeared on 7 October 1981 as an alliance of Libyan former officials opposed to many of Gaddafi's policies.[1] The front's leader was Dr Muhammad al-Magarief, who had held several senior positions, most recently that of Libyan ambassador to India, before announcing his resignation in July 1980. He was followed a year later by the former army officers, Ahmad Hwas, who had been *chargé d'affaires* at the Libyan embassy in Guyana, and Ibrahim ʿAbd al-ʿAziz, who had held the same post at the embassy in Argentina.

The emergence of the NFSL reflected wider opposition to Gaddafi's rule inside Libya, but it was also bound up with political tensions between the Libyan regime and other Arab states, including Egypt, Morocco, Tunisia

---

1 See *Bayanat al-Jabha al-Wataniyya li-Inqadh Libya 1980–1991* ('Statements Issued by the National Front for the Salvation of Libya 1980–1991), (Dar al-Inqadh lil-Nasher wa al-Iʾlam, Chicago, 1991), pp. 65–66.

and later Iraq. All of these countries embraced the NFSL in a tit-for-tat response to the support which Gaddafi had extended to opposition groups on their own soil.

From the outset the NFSL enjoyed the support of Egypt, which was locked in a long-standing dispute with its neighbour to the west; indeed, tensions between the two countries had almost flared up into military conflict on their border. Relations between Tripoli and Rabat were at a similarly low ebb as a result of Libya's support for Polisario and its criticism of the alliance between the United States and Morocco.[1] In response, Rabat agreed to host the NFSL's first National Congress in 1982, during which the Libyan opposition affirmed its determination to bring down Gaddafi's regime.[2] Libya's relations with Tunisia were scarcely any better; there was certainly no love lost between Gaddafi and the Tunisian president, Habib Bourguiba. The NFSL took advantage of this fact to use Tunisia as a staging post from which to get in and out of Libya. The front's representative in Tunis, 'Ali Abu Zayd, played a crucial role at the time in smuggling NFSL fighters into Libya, as they prepared to make good on their promise to overthrow Gaddafi.[3]

In the spring of 1984 NFSL members launched an attack on the Libyan army barracks at Bab al-'Aziziyya in Tripoli in an attempt to bring down the regime. An act of desperation by militants whose leader, Ahmad Hwas, had been killed shortly after crossing the border from Tunisia, the attack was a miserable failure. With the help of 'Ali Abu Zayd, NFSL fighters had been infiltrating Libya for months, taking up positions in preparation

---

1 Polisario is a rebel movement founded in 1973 with the aim of achieving the independence of the Western Sahara from Morocco. Morocco permitted American rapid reaction forces to use military bases on its territory after the fall of the Shah of Iran in 1979.

2 See the closing statement of the NFSL's first National Congress, in *Bayanat al-Jabha al-Wataniyya li-Inqadh Libya 1980–1991*, pp. 74–75.

3 'Ali Muhammad Abu Zayd was murdered in his shop in London in November 1995. The police never identified his killers, although suspicions lingered about the possible involvement of the Libyan security services. Shortly after his murder, the British government expelled Khalifa Bazelya, *Chargé d'Affaires* at the Libyan embassy in London, for activities incompatible with his diplomatic status. However, no official connection was made to Abu Zayd's death, nor is there any evidence to point to a link.

for the coup d'état. With the death of Hwas and the capture of two of his companions, they became convinced that their plans would inevitably be discovered. Rather than waiting for the authorities to come after them, they decided to go on the offensive. 'Ashur al-Shamis, a leading member of the NFSL at the time, describes what happened:[1]

> The Bab al-'Aziziyya operation was led by the former army lieutenant, Ahmad Hwas, who decided to enter Libya in May 1984. Trained NFSL fighters had already gone on ahead of him and begun taking up positions, ready to move when the time came. At that point I was involved in helping people to get from Tunisia into Libya; Ahmad [Hwas] had stayed with me in Britain before he himself moved to Libya. His family was living in Egypt, but he used to come [to the United Kingdom] from time to time. His last visit was on a Thursday, as far as I recall; he spent that night at my house. On the Friday he flew to Tunisia and from there crossed into Libya. However, somehow the Libyan authorities discovered who he was and after a gunfight lasting several hours the security forces killed him and captured his two companions.
>
> Other NFSL members soon learned what had happened to Hwas from people who had been waiting to meet him. The plot had been blown: within days the regime knew everything. The fighters who had gone to Libya ahead of Hwas had rented a flat near the entrance to the Bab al-'Aziziyya barracks. They set up home there, intending to use it either as a surveillance post or as a base for launching an operation of some kind. When they heard that Hwas had been killed, they decided to storm Bab al-'Aziziyya. Some of them tried to smash their way into the compound using a rubbish truck, but were challenged by the guards and shot. Other NFSL members were killed at the entrance to the flat where they were based; in all, only two people involved in the operation survived. There was no public reaction.

The NFSL claims that the operation involved fierce fighting between its fighters and the security forces, but even it admits that they were acting on impulse after learning of Hwas's death.[2] What no one disputes is that with

---

1 'Ashur al-Shamis in an interview with the author in London in the autumn of 2005. Al-Shamis resigned from the NFSL in 1989.

2 See the June 1984 issue of the NFSL's newsletter *al-Inqadh*, which gives the

H was gone and many of its cells broken up, the movement had suffered a serious setback.

Yet the NFSL remained as determined as ever to topple Gaddafi. Within a year it launched a second coup attempt, this time in collaboration with the Americans. As Reagan and Gaddafi traded insults scarcely befitting two heads of state, the relationship between their countries reached a new nadir.[1] But the hostility was to go much further than a mere diplomatic spat. In April 1986 a bomb detonated in a West Berlin discotheque called *La Belle*, leaving two American servicemen and a Turkish woman dead. Within days the US launched air strikes on Tripoli in retaliation, killing dozens of people, including the Libyan leader's adopted daughter.[2]

In 1985 the NFSL had begun work on a new US-backed plot against Gaddafi known as the 'Algeria plan'. 'The Algerians were willing to train a paramilitary group, while the Americans would engineer a coup inside Libya itself,' explains 'Ashur al-Shamis:[3]

> The scheme envisaged NFSL fighters trained in Algeria lending support to the coup when the time came. The NFSL duly began rallying its members overseas and encouraging them to go to Algeria, either to prepare for military action or to help mobilise popular support for the revolution. The call to arms began in the summer of 1985, coinciding with two developments which were to have a decisive influence on the NFSL's operations. The first was the overthrow in 1985 of President Ja'far al-Numayri of Sudan, where the NFSL had been extremely active. The second crucial development was Iraq's decision to open its doors to the NFSL [in response to Libya's support for Iran in its war with Iraq]. As a result, the NFSL's radio station, which used to broadcast to Libya from Sudan, relocated to Baghdad, while the NFSL's military wing moved to Algeria.

front's perspective on the Bab al-'Aziziyya incident.

1 In early 1986 President Reagan described Gaddafi as the 'mad dog of the Middle East'. The Libyan leader in turn dismissed his American counterpart as 'crazy'.
2 Gaddafi's 15-month-old adopted daughter was killed in the Bab al-'Aziziyya complex in Tripoli.
3 From an interview with 'Ashur al-Shamis, conducted by the author in the autumn of 2005.

The plot was soon to suffer a setback, however, to the consternation of the NFSL fighters who had assembled in Algeria in preparation for the advance on their homeland. Unbeknownst to them, the plan was part of a wider American strategy, and Washington's enthusiasm for the scheme had cooled. The abandonment of the Algeria plan was to cost the NFSL dear. There was the sheer expense of moving its fighters to Algeria, and training and housing them. Yet the NFSL's greatest loss was arguably not financial, but rather the damage to the morale of its members, none of whom wanted to see their movement reduced to a mere tool in American hands.[1] Nonetheless, the NFSL continued to receive generous assistance from Saddam Hussein. Baghdad was to sponsor the front between 1985 and 1986, setting up training camps for its fighters, providing new offices for its radio station and hosting its second National Congress in 1985. Iraq had become a refuge for every Libyan opposition member in need of shelter.

Yet for all the Iraqis' support, after the collapse of the Algeria plan there was no prospect of the NFSL taking military action inside Libya. But the autumn of 1987 brought a glimmer of hope when Libyan expatriates passed a letter to the movement from the Chadian president, Hissène Habré. At the time Chadian forces were winning one victory after another in their conflict with Libya over the mineral-rich Aouzou Strip in northern Chad.[2] Habré referred to 1,500 Libyan soldiers whom the Chadians had captured, including one Colonel Khalifa Abu al-Qasim Haftar. The colonel had a distinguished record of service in the highest echelons of the Libyan military establishment. And now he wanted to talk to the NFSL.

The movement could hardly ignore such an important request, even if it had come from someone who until recently had taken his orders from Gaddafi. The NFSL decided to open a channel of communication with Haftar to find out what he wanted. Several meetings followed in late 1987 and early 1988 in the Chadian capital, N'djamena, during which

---

1   From an interview with 'Ashur al-Shamis, conducted by the author in the autumn of 2005.

2   Saddam Hussein provided substantial support to Hissène Habré's regime in its conflict with Libya, which resulted in the Libyans losing control of the disputed Aouzou Strip. In the 1990s Libya accepted Chadian sovereignty over the territory after the International Court of Justice ruled in favour of N'djamena.

Haftar expressed his willingness to help bring down Gaddafi. His offer was accepted and, at a press conference in April 1988, Haftar announced to the world that he and his forces were joining the NFSL.[1]

The Chad Plan

Haftar's offer had been too tempting to resist; and in accepting it, the NFSL became embroiled in its third plot to overthrow Gaddafi's regime in less than three years. Once again it issued a call to arms, this time urging its supporters to head to Chad, where it relocated its radio station from Baghdad. For their part, the Iraqis welcomed the move: the NFSL's departure relieved them of a burden while offering the prospect of a friendly regime in Tripoli, willing to return the favour of Iraq's support during its years in opposition. However, the NFSL's move to Chad did not mean the end of Iraqi assistance; on the contrary, Baghdad began supplying the front with massive quantities of arms, enabling it to form the Libyan National Army (LNA), comprising Haftar and 750 other former prisoners of war. The NFSL now started to consider how to get its forces into Libya. The most plausible idea was to orchestrate some form of action inside Libya, which would provide the cue for the troops based in Chad to move in and provide assistance. Their advance from Chad to Libya would mean marching through the desert, where they would be vulnerable to attack by the Libyan air force. But it was widely believed that the Americans would protect them.

Two years on, the LNA was ready and its training camps were running at full tilt. But the order to advance on Libya never came. Any residual prospect of the 'Chad plan' coming to fruition vanished in 1990, when Hissène Habré was deposed in a military coup.[2] Most NFSL members moved to Zaire (now the Democratic Republic of Congo), their exodus supervised by the Americans; some later went on to the United States

---

1   Haftar and his group joined the NFSL on 16 April 1988. See the statement issued by the NFSL on 24 June 1988, in *Bayanat al-Jabha al-Wataniyya li-Inqadh Libya 1980–1991*, pp. 173–175.

2   Habré was ousted by Idriss Déby, a former high-ranking Chadian military officer and leader of the Chadian Patriotic Salvation Movement.

itself. With the demise of the Chadian option, the NFSL pinned its hopes on a group of serving Libyan army officers seizing power.[1] Yet these officers had never belonged to the NFSL, and had begun scheming even before they made contact with the front. In the event, the Libyan government suppressed the plot, rounding up the conspirators in late 1993 and prosecuting them in the Supreme Military Court on charges of espionage for the United States and planning to overthrow the regime. In early 1997 six senior army officers and two of their civilian associates were executed for their part in the plan. The NFSL's hopes of ever taking power in Libya were to die with them.

The Islamists Step Forward

As the NFSL lurched from one fiasco to another, a different band of opposition members was preparing to take on Gaddafi's regime. But they were biding their time, in no hurry for the conflict to begin before they were ready.

In the late 1980s the men who would go on to found the LIFG were content to remain in Afghanistan, where conditions suited their strategy at the time. To embark on armed conflict back in Libya would require trained combatants; Afghanistan, where the war was continuing against the communist regime led by Mohammad Najibullah, offered the ideal location for preparing fighters for martyrdom and holy war.[2] The LIFG's men already had the necessary ideological motivation, as in their eyes Gaddafi's regime was an apostate abomination. What they needed now was military experience. And that was what Afghanistan could provide.

Noman Benotman, who himself served in Afghanistan, claims that the LIFG fought on various fronts throughout the country, including Kandahar, Jalalabad, Logar, Kama and Khost. But the most important front from the LIFG's point of view was undoubtedly Gardez, for it was there that the group was in sole control of a number of positions.[3]

1 The officers belonged to the powerful Warfala tribe from western Libya, to which Gaddafi's own clan is connected by blood ties and patronage.

2 Mohammad Najibullah was elected president of Afghanistan in November 1986, only months before the Soviets announced their plans to withdraw from the country.

3 From interviews with Noman Benotman in the spring and summer of 2005.

The Return to Libya

As the Afghan mujahidin prepared to seize Kabul in 1992, the several hundred Libyan fighters in Afghanistan were getting ready to take the jihad to their own country.[1] The LIFG began sending members back to Libya to start setting up cells and preparing for the conflict ahead. These small groups were well trained and battle-hardened; they were also fired up with indignation at what they considered the 'infidel' regimes in power throughout the Arab world. It was a zeal which had been fuelled both by the war in Afghanistan and the indoctrination they had undergone in the Arab hostels and camps, where EIJ's ideology now reigned supreme.

No sooner had LIFG representatives returned to Libya than they began amassing weapons and recruiting new members. No one was in the slightest doubt that they were arming in preparation for a showdown with the security forces. 'Nonetheless,' says 'Ashur al-Shamis, who was in contact with LIFG members at the time, 'I don't think they had a clear military strategy or a definite political programme. The men were passionate and eager to fight, convinced of their duty to wage holy war. They started collecting weapons and identifying targets, with the intention of attacking military sites to begin with. They also started finding safe houses and began recruiting policemen and army officers, which was a smart move. All these arrangements took two or three years.'[2]

The Advance on Libya

The initial phase of the organisation's development was not without its problems. To begin with, there was the fate of the group's first emir, a former medical student called 'Abd al-Ghaffar al-Duwadi. He had left Afghanistan and travelled to Egypt with the intention of moving on to Libya to maintain close contact with the LIFG's cells there. Yet almost

---

Benotman was involved in the sieges of both Khost and Gardez, which ended in 1991 and 1992 respectively.

1   In an interview with the author in early 2006 Benotman estimated that there had been between 800 and 1,000 Libyan fighters of various affiliations in Afghanistan in April 1992.

2   From an interview with 'Ashur al-Shamis in London in the autumn of 2005.

as soon as he arrived in Egypt he was arrested and handed over to the Libyan authorities.[1]

The LIFG has always been reluctant to identify al-Duwadi's immediate successor. Whoever he was, he remained head of the group until 1995, when 'Abd al-Hakim Belhaj took over. It was he who would lead the LIFG out of the shadows. The group took many people by surprise when it released its first statement on 17 October 1995, not least the other Libyan opposition factions, which had no idea of the LIFG's true size. Little did they know that for five years it had taken advantage of the security forces' preoccupation with the NFSL to build up its network inside Libya.

Yet, ironically, it was the LIFG's exposure by the security forces four months earlier which had prompted it to make itself known to the Libyan public. In June 1995 a member of the group called Khalid Bakshish was under armed guard in a Benghazi hospital, having been wounded in a fire-fight with the authorities. In what was to be a remarkable feat of brazenness, his comrades decided to get him out. 'The LIFG commander for eastern Libya, Sa'd al-Farajani, decided to spring Bakshish,' explains Noman Benotman:[2]

> The operation was carried out by ten men disguised as Special Forces commandos, who drove up to the hospital in a couple of security service cars they'd stolen. They simply walked in and took Khalid away, without anyone realising what was going on: the whole thing passed off without a drop of blood being shed. Al-Farajani, known to everyone as 'Wahid', was a close friend of Khalid's. They took him straight to al-Fa'akat, an area outside Benghazi, where they hid him on a farm. But within days the security forces had got wind of them and surrounded the place.

After some fierce fighting, the men who had freed Khalid Bakshish were all captured; Wahid and two comrades managed to get away to Umm al-Razam, 300 kilometres east of Benghazi. But their fate was also sealed: it

---

1 'Abd al-Ghaffar al-Duwadi was extradited to Libya in 1992, where he remained in prison until early 2009.

2 Noman Benotman in interviews with the author in the spring and summer of 2005.

was only a matter of time before the security services tracked them down too and killed them.[1]

The documents recovered from al-Fa'akat and Umm al-Razam and the security services' subsequent investigations made one thing clear: that the cell they had found hiding out on the farm was by no means an isolated example. Other LIFG cells – indeed, whole organisations with similar ideas of jihad – had already spread throughout Libya.

Up to this point, Benotman argues, the Libyan regime had assumed the LIFG's powerbase lay outside the country: this was why it had not seen the group as a serious threat. What the authorities did not realise was that hundreds of LIFG members were already operating *inside* the country. 'The regime had no idea what was going on,' says Benotman:

> We'd been establishing our cells for years, but we weren't intending to make any public announcement just yet. The regime had a zero-tolerance approach to fighters returning from Afghanistan: any that it got its hands on, it locked up. But the regime was unaware of the size and the strength of the LIFG. The incident at the farm took place in June 1995; four months on we announced the formation of the group. But we did so only when we knew that the authorities had found us out, and that unless we acted they'd smash the organisation in an instant.

---

1 The man in charge of the farm at al-Fa'akat was a Libyan army deserter called Salih al-Shuhaybi; he blew himself up with a hand grenade. The two men who accompanied Wahid to Umm al-Razam were Rajab 'Urfa and a founder member of the LIFG called Salih 'Abd al-Sayyid al-Maghribi.

4

Algeria: The Descent into the Abyss

The situation in Algeria erupted soon after the Libyans established the LIFG in Afghanistan. In January 1992 the Algerian authorities cancelled the country's parliamentary elections, which the Islamists had been poised to win: it was a decision which was to trigger a catastrophic sequence of events. The Libyans could hardly ignore what was happening, nor stand idly by as mere spectators. On the one hand they felt a religious duty to support their Islamist brothers, who had been denied the power that was legitimately theirs. While on the other hand the Libyan fighters in Afghanistan observed a steady stream of their Algerian comrades heading home to take part in the new jihad there. It was natural that the Libyans should want to get a clearer picture of what was happening in the state bordering their own country. Yet, as this chapter will show, the Libyans' quest would have terrible consequences, with some of their leading men butchered by the GIA, the very group they had gone to help.

The Armed Islamic Group

The resignation of the Algerian president, Chadli Bendjedid, the cancellation of the elections, the dissolution of the FIS and the imprisonment of thousands of its members in 1992 led the already precarious situation in Algeria to explode.[1] Yet when the GIA suddenly embarked on a murderous

---

1 After the heads of the FIS were detained in 1991, the front swiftly appointed new leaders and went on to contest the general elections later in the year. The FIS won an overwhelming majority of seats in the first round of voting in December 1991, prompting the authorities to annul the elections the following month. Some 40,000 people were subsequently arrested and transported to

campaign targeting journalists, civil servants and policemen, few people
had even heard of it. The whole world knew about the FIS and its party's
rightful electoral victory being snatched away at the last minute; it was
a legitimate organisation whose leaders, members and supporters were
all a matter of public knowledge.[1] Yet within months of its closure a
new generation of Islamists had emerged, focused on waging a jihad to
overthrow the regime and replace it with an Islamic state.

These neo-Islamists had little to unite them beyond this single, simplistic
goal. Some of them were extreme Salafists, some passionate jihadists, while
others were more sympathetic to the FIS's agenda. Certain groups had
undoubtedly been penetrated by the security services. But the leading role
was played by the Algerian veterans of the Afghan jihad.[2]

It was the Afghan veterans who began moves to establish the GIA,
fired up by the ideas of jihad they had brought with them on their return
to Algeria in 1991. They had immediately set about contacting well-known
leaders of the Armed Islamic Movement (MIA), founded in the 1980s by
Mustafa Bouyali.[3] Qari Saïd, a leading Afghan veteran, was the lynchpin
of these efforts, which focused on trying to persuade two of Bouyali's
senior associates to assume the leadership of the new group. One of them,
Abdelkader Chebouti, declined the offer, setting up his own Movement for
an Islamic State (MEI) instead. Meanwhile the other, Mansour Meliani,
accepted the offer, becoming the GIA's first emir.

The group's core membership did not consist solely of Afghan veterans.
True, the latter were experienced fighters and had certainly played their
part in the conflict in Afghanistan, but urban guerrilla warfare required a
different type of training. It called for an intimate knowledge of the narrow

   detention centres deep inside the Algerian desert. See Camille Tawil, *al-Haraka
   al-Islamiyya al-Musallaha fi al-Jaza'ir: Min al-Inqadh ila al-Jama'a* ('The Armed
   Islamic Movement in Algeria: From the FIS to the GIA') (Dar al-Nahar, Beirut,
   1998), p. 94.
1 The FIS received official recognition in September 1989.
2 For more on the foundation of the GIA see Camille Tawil, *al-Haraka al-Islamiyya
   al-Musallaha fi al-Jaza'ir*, pp. 53–90.
3 The jihad declared by Mustafa Bouyali's group ended in early 1987 near Médéa,
   south of Algiers, when Bouyali himself was shot dead by the Algerian security
   forces.

alleyways of Algeria's towns, where fighters could vanish after carrying out their operations – and it needed those fighters to be familiar with every building in every neighbourhood, as well as their inhabitants and their allegiances. The Afghan veterans, who had spent years overseas, were not equipped for this kind of conflict; moreover, the sudden appearance of outsiders in a given area would be sure to attract the attention of the security services. But what the Afghans could not do, the new generation of urban Islamists could. Some of them had served time in prison for minor offences, only to emerge as neo-Islamists, occasionally with extreme Salafist ideas. And it was these groups that were the most active on the ground, because they knew the territory like the backs of their hands.

It was not long before these two Islamist movements, one of local origin and the other imported from Afghanistan, came into contact with other groups with jihadist ideas. Some of these, such as Omar el-Eulmi's followers, had previously been affiliated to the FIS during its peaceful political campaign, only to break away in 1992 when they found it incapable of taking power.[1] That same year this motley assortment of jihadists came together and formed the GIA.

Meliani at the Helm

Mansour Meliani's faction was one of the foremost Algerian paramilitary groups of the 1990s. Most of its members were Algerians who had gone to Afghanistan to take part in the jihad against the Russians and the communist regime they left behind. As the mujahidin began their advance on Kabul in 1991, these Algerians started looking for a way to return home and apply the jihadist ideas and combat experience they had acquired in the mountains of Afghanistan.

Admittedly, not all the Algerian fighters who returned took up arms against their government during the period of political pluralism which began in 1989. Some joined the FIS, participating in and occasionally even leading the demonstrations that took place in Algiers during the summer

---

1   Omar el-Eulmi was a radical Islamist ideologue and an activist in the Islamic Labour Union or Syndicat Islamique du Travail; he was killed in 1993.

of 1991, wearing traditional Afghan dress.[1] However, other Afghan veterans had no faith in either the Algerian regime's democratic credentials or in the FIS's agenda. They had come back convinced that the only way to establish an Islamic state was through jihad, not the ballot box. They were keen to put into practice what they had learned in Afghanistan, and they had no shortage of money or experience. But what they did lack was a religious figurehead, a well-known Algerian cleric whose support would lend weight to their ideas. Conscious of this, the first thing they did on their return to Algeria was make contact with clerics known to sympathise with the jihadist-Salafist cause. They included Abdelkader Chebouti, a leading jihadist known by his associates as 'the General' in recognition of his part in Bouyali's Armed Islamic Movement of the 1980s. Chebouti had played a prominent role in that group and was one of only three of its members to be sentenced to death, a distinction which enhanced his prestige in the eyes of Algeria's budding Islamists.[2] Although he took part in marches and rallies organised by the FIS between 1989 and early 1992, he never renounced his jihadist ideas. He is said to have called on others not to join the political process, which he regarded as a government ploy to silence the opposition. He was already secretly establishing cells in preparation for the inevitable confrontation with the regime he so distrusted.[3]

Contact between the Afghan veterans and Chebouti began during the FIS-led campaign of civil disobedience between May and June 1991, when its senior leaders were arrested. In making overtures to Chebouti, the Afghans may have envisaged him becoming their emir, but it is unclear whether they would actually have granted him this role had he responded positively. Abdullah Anas claims that the leading Afghan veteran, Qari

---

1   Semi-official Algerian figures put the number of the country's veterans of the Afghan jihad at 1,200 (according to an Agence France Presse report of 11 April 1993). The Syrian radical Islamist, Abu Mus'ab al-Suri, estimates that by the early 1990s 2,000 Algerians had fought in Afghanistan.

2   Meliani and Chebouti were sentenced to death in 1987 for an attack on an Algerian police academy two years earlier. In July 1990, following a pressure campaign by the FIS, the Algerian president, Chadli Bendjedid, pardoned them and the two men were released from prison.

3   See Yahya Abu Zakariya, *al-Haraka al-Islamiyya al-Musallaha fi al-Jaza'ir, 1978–1993* ('The Armed Islamic Movement in Algeria, 1978–1993'), (Dar al-Ma'arif li al-Matbu'at, Beirut, 1993), p. 74.

Saïd, thought Chebouti lacked the health and physical strength to lead the mujahidin, and that he therefore began seeking an alternative candidate.[1] In any case, the Afghan veterans were unable to persuade Chebouti to declare a jihad against the regime, despite his own commitment to the idea. There are two reasons why he may have rejected their advances: on the one hand he was still close to certain Salafist members of the FIS, who were still engaged in non-violent action and planning to stand in the elections scheduled for late 1991; and on the other, he was still secretly building up his own group, the Movement for an Islamic State (MEI), which would embark on paramilitary operations in February 1992, two months after the elections were cancelled.

The statements which Chebouti issued in 1992 help to shed light on his relationships with both the Afghan veterans and the FIS. On the eve of the FIS leaders' trial in June of that year, he released a statement which he called 'The Call to Jihad', addressed to the Algerian people:

> Your leaders have been imprisoned because they sought the good of the people, because they tried to address corruption and because they wanted an Islamic state, a state of truth and justice, of peace and prosperity. Those who have jailed them are the leaders of the conspiracy against Islam and Algeria, who have denied the public their choice [of leaders]. In these proceedings, it is the will of the people that is on trial, and the only crime that our leaders have committed is that of faithfully serving the people.[2]

If Chebouti's statement shows one thing, it is the deep respect which he still held for the leaders of the FIS. The Afghan veterans, in contrast, rejected them outright, convinced that their acceptance of democracy and multi-party elections was heretical.

Following his fruitless contacts with Chebouti, Qari Saïd approached another leading member of Bouyali's group: Mansour Meliani. It is unclear whether their discussions began before or after the failure of the talks with Chebouti, or in parallel with them. But what is certain is that

---

1 Abdullah Anas's reservations are discussed in Chapter Two.
2 See Chebouti's statement No. 5, 'A Call to Jihad' in Tawil's *al-Haraka al-Islamiyya al-Musallaha fi al-Jaza'ir, Min al-Inqadh ila al-Jama'a*, pp. 61–72.

Meliani remained friends with his old comrade Chebouti until Qari Saïd came between them. Chebouti had once been Meliani's emir and there are some, including Abdullah Anas, who say that the strength of their bond owed more to this hierarchical relationship than to friendship alone. Whatever its basis, their association only came to an end when the Afghan veterans intervened.

Meliani's acceptance of the Afghans' offer suited both parties: they got a leader with a reputation in Algeria, and he got his own independent group. It mounted its first attack in February 1992, after the elections had been cancelled, targeting the admiralty in Algiers; ten people, including seven members of the armed forces, were killed. However, some Algerian Islamists had wanted to declare war on the regime back in the summer of 1991, when dozens of their comrades were killed in clashes with the security forces following demonstrations in the capital. 'After the bloodshed in Algeria in June 1991, some of the brothers went to Afghanistan to rally the mujahidin to the Algerian cause,' says Mokhtar Belmokhtar, the GSPC's emir of Algeria's desert region.[1] 'Foremost among them was Brother Abderrahmane [Dahane, also known as] Abu Siham, emir of the Guemmar operation.[2] He did his best to persuade the brothers of the need to begin a jihad in Algeria, but they disagreed among themselves about the timing and the need for preparation. It was then that he [Dahane] made his famous remark: "We have come to light the flame of jihad: come with us and carry the torch aloft."'

---

1   From an interview with Mokhtar Belmokhtar published on the GSPC's website. This website is no longer active, but the full interview can still be accessed at the following link: http://www.alsunnah.info/r1?i=6710&x=guq4hze8. Belmokhtar was born in the central Algerian city of Ghardaïa in 1972. At the age of nineteen he went to Afghanistan, where he claimed to have received paramilitary training at various camps before returning to Algeria in late 1992.

2   In November 1991 Abderrahmane Dahane led an attack on an Algerian army barracks at Guemmar on the Tunisian border, killing several soldiers and mutilating their corpses before making off with weapons and ammunition.

The Role of Qari Saïd

While Meliani's leadership of the Afghan veterans was undisputed, the role played by Qari Saïd in the GIA has proven much more controversial over the years. The Afghans argue that he was key to the establishment of the GIA, and point to the part he played in persuading Meliani to lead them. However, the men who headed the GIA after Djamel Zitouni became the group's emir in 1994 have played down Qari Saïd's importance. In doing so, their aim seems to have been to inflate the Salafists' role in the GIA at the expense of the Afghan veterans. The GIA officially maintains that Qari Saïd had nothing to do with its creation, while conceding grudgingly that 'he may, at most, have encouraged people to join the group'.[1] They point out that the Afghan veterans headed by Meliani joined the GIA under Moh Leveilley's leadership in October 1992, some eight months after the Algerian security forces had detained Qari Saïd.[2]

Yet for all the GIA's attempts to belittle his role, Qari Saïd was undoubtedly a significant figure. In Afghanistan he had been one of the principal Algerian fighters under Ahmad Shah Massoud's command, and spent years in the north led by Abdullah Anas. However, his relationship with the latter cooled following a disagreement, leading Qari Saïd to leave Anas's group and join al-Qaʿida. He then ran a hostel for Algerian Islamists, located in the Hayatabad suburb of Peshawar and financed by bin Laden. Under Saïd's supervision the guesthouse became a GIA stronghold and a platform for criticising the strategy of the FIS, which some jihadists regarded as infidel for its participation in the political process. Nonetheless, even the more radical jihadists drew a distinction between the FIS's programme and its members, whom they did not condemn personally as unbelievers. This was a point of difference between the Afghan members of the GIA and the Takfiris[3], who condemned both the

---

1 ʿAbd al-Muʾmin al-Zubayr, *al-Sayf al-Battar fi Man Taʿana al-Mujahidin al-Akhyar wa Aqama bayna Azhur al-Kuffar* (meaning approximately 'The Sword Wielded Against Those Who Betrayed the Excellent Mujahidin and Lived Among the Infidels'), published by the GIA and distributed by its supporters in the UK in 1997, p. 12.

2 Ibid.

3 The Arabic term *takfir* means to condemn someone as an unbeliever. The

FIS agenda and its supporters as infidel. For its own part, the FIS lumped all its opponents together. This helps explain why the GIA was widely accused on its emergence in 1992 of being a Takfiri organisation, a charge the group vehemently denied.

The Libyan, Noman Benotman, witnessed the ideological disputes between the Algerians based at the hostels in Peshawar and how Qari Saïd took some of them off to set up his own guesthouse, the *Bayt al-Mujahidin*. This was the seed which would eventually grow into the GIA.[1] 'Most Algerians in Afghanistan were involved in fighting at the various fronts and did not belong to any particular movement,' says Benotman:

> The *Bayt al-Muhajirin* hostel where they used to stay in Peshawar had no specific affiliation either. But things started to change as a result of events back in Algeria and the signs of an imminent coup following the arrest of Abbasi Madani and Ali Belhadj [in June 1991]. When a group with jihadist ideas, led by Qari Saïd and Abou Leith [al-M'sili], disowned the FIS, there were problems in the *Bayt al-Muhajirin* and the supporters of this group were expelled. They went off and set up the *Bayt al-Mujahidin* in Hayatabad and Osama bin Laden paid their rent. Later on, they established themselves in one of the main hostels in Babi, a large village inhabited by Afghan emigrants and dominated by Sayyaf's Ittehad-e Islami.

Benotman admits that the people who joined Qari Saïd and Abou Leith were not a homogeneous, disciplined group: some of them regarded the moderate Islamists in Algeria in the same light as the regime itself, and even thought they should be targeted first, before the battle against the government began.

In 1991, having set up the *Bayt al-Mujahidin* with his associates, Qari Saïd travelled to Algeria to establish a jihadist paramilitary faction, agreeing with Meliani that the latter would act as its leader. He then returned to Afghanistan, where he put his group's affairs in order; he also appointed

---

implications are severe, particularly when applied to nominal Muslims: in Islamic law the traditional punishment for apostasy is death. Islamist extremist groups described as Takfiri are those that condemn their opponents, and in some cases entire societies, as infidel.

1   Noman Benotman in an interview with the author in the spring of 2006.

a deputy to send experienced Algerian fighters back home and meet new ones coming to Pakistan for training.[1] Qari Saïd then set off back to Algeria himself to oversee the formation of the GIA, but was arrested in February 1992, shortly after his arrival. However, two years later he would play an important part in re-establishing the GIA, following his escape with hundreds of others from the vast Tazoult Prison in March 1994. He was key to the discussions which led to the declaration in May of that year of a merger between the GIA, the MEI and a wing of FIS. Yet within months he would be killed by the security forces, alongside Khatir ben Mouhannad Boudali, the GIA's local commander in the eastern Algerian city of Constantine in November 1994.[2]

Qutbists

After Meliani was arrested in July 1992 the leadership of the GIA passed to his deputy, Dr Ahmad al-Wadd.[3] Al-Wadd belonged to another school of Afghan veterans who had been particularly influenced by the theories of Muhammad Qutb, brother of the late Egyptian Islamist intellectual, Sayyid Qutb. On their return from Afghanistan, Algerian exponents of these ideas had been especially active in the western provinces of the country, such as Tiaret and Sidi Bel Abbès.[4]

The GIA refuses to acknowledge that the Qutbists, or followers of Muhammad Qutb, constituted a distinct movement when they joined the GIA under Meliani. Instead, it regards them merely as ordinary Afghan veterans who returned to Algeria along with so many others and became involved in paramilitary activity. Hassan Hattab, a leading member of the GIA, concedes that Ahmad al-Wadd was part of the Qutbist group, but

---

1 Qari Saïd's brother, Qari 'Abd al-Rahim, like him a veteran of the Afghan jihad, remained in Afghanistan. Qari 'Abd al-Rahim currently lives in Algeria, where he was pardoned under an amnesty in 2006.

2 Some Islamists suspected that Qari Saïd had been liquidated by his fellow GIA members as part of moves to eliminate Afghan veterans from the group. The GIA itself has denied this.

3 Meliani was sentenced to death and executed in August 1993.

4 According to Noman Benotman, the Qutbists constituted the largest group of Algerians fighting in Afghanistan in the early 1990s.

claims that he 'repented, returned to the Salafist fold and renounced that movement.'[1] In any event, al-Wadd was himself detained soon after Meliani and locked up in the high-security Serkadji Prison in Algiers, where he was killed with almost a hundred other inmates during the mutiny which took place there in February 1995.

Moh Leveilley's Group

The first group from which the GIA was formed, led by Meliani, was relatively homogeneous, in that most of its members were Algerians who had returned from Afghanistan. In contrast, the second group was a conglomeration of small Salafist factions consisting mainly of young people from Algiers and neighbouring areas. Of these factions, the most prominent was that headed by Moh Leveilley.

Leveilley's group was active mainly in Algiers and its environs. Unlike Meliani's men, most of whom were steeped in theological works on the principles of jihad, the members of Leveilley's group were not known for their grasp of Islamic law. They did have a keen sense of the public's mood, however, and they enjoyed considerable popularity in Islamist circles in and around the capital, especially the areas of Boufarik, Blida and Médéa. Leveilley very nearly redrew the map of the paramilitary movement in Algeria altogether, and might have done so had he lived. He took part in a famous meeting of armed groups at Tamesguida (in the province of Blida) in late August and early September 1992. The meeting almost produced an agreement to unite the Islamist militias, but when the army attacked the participants both Leveilley and one of his senior aides, called Noureddine Boufara, were killed. Leveilley's death caused consternation among the groups which had taken part in the Tamesguida meeting, each of which suspected that the others had been infiltrated by the security services.

The GIA's first official emir, Abdelhak Layada, explains why the meeting

---

1 The former GSPC emir, Hassan Hattab, in an interview with the author, conducted through the group's media representatives in March 1998. At that point Hattab was still the GIA's emir of what it called the 'second zone' or Kabylie in northern Algeria.

at Tamesguida ended in failure and how the GIA subsequently emerged under his direction in the suburbs of Algiers:

> The GIA had already been active in 1992, but it didn't have a name.[1] There were three [main] groups: us [i.e. Moh Leveilley's group], Meliani's group [of Afghan veterans] and the group led by Abdelkader Chebouti and Saïd Makhloufi [the MEI]. These three groups used to liaise with one another and all their members were acquainted. However, they didn't merge, partly because some of the brothers had reservations about members of the other groups. Their misgivings didn't have to do with forming a single group; they were about someone assuming the leadership.

Layada explains that these reservations concerned Saïd Makhloufi, head of the MEI. Algerians who had volunteered to join the jihad against the Americans during the Gulf War of 1991 had complained, on their return to Algeria, of money going missing. They also spoke of certain documents in the possession of people who had facilitated their travel to Iraq. These men included Makhloufi and another prominent figure called Ali Ayya.

'In the summer of 1992 a meeting was held in Tamesguida [to unite the armed groups],' continues Layada:

> I attended the meeting, which went smoothly, without any disagreements. But I remember that the other people present included someone, who shall remain nameless, who told us all an outright lie: he claimed that Makhloufi wasn't with his group, but we later discovered that he was ... In any case, there wasn't an agreement on Chebouti being a national emir [of the united factions]. Instead it was agreed that both Chebouti and I would be co-emirs until we all met again. But that other meeting never took place. That same day both Muhammad Allal [Moh Leveilley] and Noureddine Boufara were killed; meanwhile, we went off somewhere else. What we didn't know was that before the Tamesguida meeting the security services had arrested two people who had been sent by Ashour Touati [one of the leaders of the FIS]. One of those people remains in prison to this day. The security services found out from them where the

---

1 Abdelhak Layada, also known as Abou Adlane, in an interview with the author in May 2007 in Baraki on the outskirts of Algiers.

meeting would be taking place. Chebouti sent someone to ask me to hold the meeting, but Muhammad Allal told me we had to meet at the top of a mountain, not at its foot. We duly met, performed the morning prayer and then went back down the mountain. But as we were returning there was a shootout with the security forces. About eight brothers were in the house when it was surrounded; they included Djafar al-Afghani [Mourad Sid Ahmed], who covered the brothers from inside the house so they could get away. If he hadn't, they'd all have died. The security forces were afraid to storm the place; instead they surrounded it and began throwing stones at the roof. Noureddine Boufara went out holding his machine gun, and they shot him dead. Then Djafar went out with his machine gun and began firing at the security forces, enabling the other brothers who were inside the house to get out. All of them escaped, including Muhammad Allal, who headed up into the mountains. If he'd followed the other brothers who escaped he could have got away like they did, but instead he took a route that he didn't know. The security forces were calling to him from a helicopter, using a loud speaker, but he refused to surrender. So they killed him.

According to Layada, it was after the Tamesguida meeting that the GIA was formally established with that name:

The group was founded in the suburbs of Algiers, but not in Baraki [where Layada himself lives]. I was the national emir; the other founders included Sid Ahmed Lahrani, Mourad Sid Ahmed, Ali Zouabri and Brahim Zekioui. In all there were about fifty of us involved in setting up the group; we used to visit one another and talk things over. It was after Muhammad Allal was killed in Tamesguida that we decided to call it the Armed Islamic Group, though the name had been suggested before; members of the FIS who were involved in founding the GIA also proposed eight or nine other names, but we rejected them. In fact, the name GIA came from Afghanistan, as there had been a group [of Algerians] there called the same thing. Abou Leith al-M'sili, one of the foremost Afghan veteran founders of the GIA, was that faction's emir in Afghanistan, and Gharbi Mourad [al-Afghani] was another member. But the GIA's first logo or 'seal' did not originate from Afghanistan – I saw it being designed myself. And there wasn't only one: the national emir had his own seal, as did the five other regional emirs.

Layada claims that Qari Saïd was indeed one of the Afghan veterans who helped launch the GIA project. However, his role was cut short because of his arrest in February 1992, several months before the GIA was founded.

Omar Chikhi, emir of the Lakhdaria Group and a leading GIA figure during the 1990s, tells a more detailed version of the GIA's foundation which differs in certain respects from Layada's account:[1]

> We were involved in an FIS-affiliated faction known as the Lakhdaria Group. We only began our paramilitary activity after the elections were cancelled in 1992. However, I had been in hiding since the summer of 1991, when there was a skirmish between us and the security forces. They wanted to remove the slogan 'Islamic Municipality' from the Lakhdaria town council and replace it with the motto 'By the People, For the People'. It was then that we started preparing for the armed struggle. The first thing we did was get in touch with Abdelkader Chebouti and Meliani, who was head of a group with its own Consultative Council, and which also began preparing for paramilitary action in 1991. I first met Meliani in person in 1992, after the elections were cancelled; he had come to an area near Lakhdaria looking for somewhere to base himself. I met him by chance in the mountains and he began telling us how he wanted to organise the armed struggle and bring the different factions together. He spoke to me at the time about his group and said he had a number of Afghan veterans who were preparing for a major paramilitary operation: to storm a military barracks, seize some weapons and distribute them to other factions. I had already met some of the veterans who used to come to see Meliani, such as Qari Saïd, Abdullah ben Massoud, Saad, Abou Leith al-M'sili and Mounir al-Gharbi. We also had contact with Abdelkader Chebouti and Muhammad Allal and his group.
>
> When the clashes with the security forces began there were various paramilitary groups operating in Algeria. They included the factions led by Chebouti, Meliani and Moh Leveilley, together with Abdelhak Layada and Ali Zouabri, Antar Zouabri's brother.[2] There

---

1 Omar Chikhi in an interview with the author in Algiers in May 2007. Lakhdaria, after which his group was named, is a town in Bouira Province, southeast of Algiers.

2 Antar Zouabri would become head of the GIA in 1997, leading it in an ever

was also an independent group led by Tawfik Hattab.[1] These were the main groups at the time. We tried to reconcile their different views, something that Hocine Abderrahim, head of the Islamic Labour Union, assisted us with.[2] Abderrahim helped me hold a meeting I had been trying to arrange between Chebouti, Leveilley and Meliani's groups; it took place in early 1992 in Zbarbar.[3] Muhammad Allal didn't attend, but sent someone in his place, and Abou Leith al-M'sili came [from Meliani's group of Afghan veterans]. However, there were disagreements between those present at the meeting and it did not produce any results.

After the failure of that meeting another gathering was held in Tamesguida, when Allal and a close associate of his called Noureddine Boufara were killed and Hocine Abderrahim's brother was wounded. I wasn't able to get to the place where the meeting was being held; afterwards I went to Baraki, where I met Djafar al-Afghani: he operated in the Lakhdaria area and we got on well. He introduced me to Abdelhak Layada and they told me what had happened at Tamesguida. Abdelhak said it could be difficult to reach an agreement with Chebouti's group [on the merger of their respective factions]; he asked whether I could contact Meliani's group and convince them to get together and talk. I agreed and duly got in touch with Meliani's faction, which at that time had almost disintegrated following successive attacks [by the security services]. Meliani himself had been arrested, as had Sid Ahmed Lahrani, one of the co-founders of the group; only its general co-ordinator, Mounir al-Gharbi, was left. I contacted him and put the idea [of a merger] to him, saying that we'd held several meetings but that none of them had been successful. Mounir told me he had no objection to uniting the groups, but that we had to talk. I suggested that we both go to see Abdelhak Layada and Djafar al-Afghani and put the issue to them. I managed to get Mounir to Baraki [on the outskirts of Algiers], where he spoke to Abdelhak

more extreme direction.

1   Hassan Hattab was the founder of the Salafist Group for Preaching and Combat (GSPC). His older brother, Tawfik, assassinated the former Algerian prime minister and one-time intelligence chief, Kasdi Merbah, in August 1993.

2   Hocine Abderrahim was head of the Islamic Labour Union or Syndicat Islamique du Travail (SIT), which was established by the FIS in 1991. He was executed for his alleged part in a bomb attack on Algiers Airport in August 1992.

3   Zbarbar is located in Bouira Province, southeast of Algiers.

and agreed to meet him again a week later. But in the meantime
Sid Ahmed Lahrani managed to escape from prison in Blida and
things became clearer [in Meliani's group]. The next meeting was
held in a house in Baraki, and this time eight people came: Lahrani,
Mounir, Khaled Sadjali, Layada, Ali Zouabri, Djafar al-Afghani,
Brahim Zekioui and me. That was when the GIA was established.
At the start of the meeting Lahrani said he had no objections to
unification or to whoever was to be the emir: the important thing
was to form a single group. 'We have to unite,' he said. If Chebouti's
group wanted to join too, it was welcome to do so, but if it didn't,
it was free to go its own way.

At that time Muhammad Allal's group was militarily the most
powerful, but Meliani's group was more organised and had a better
grasp of Islamic law. There was discussion of who would lead the
new group, but it was a civilised debate: no one raised their voices.
Ali Zouabri proposed Abdelhak [Layada] as the new emir, on the
basis that he was the oldest of us and well respected by everyone.
Sid Ahmed Lahrani said he had no objections to Abdelhak, and
that he would accept the others' choice of candidate. In the end
everyone agreed on Abdelhak. Then Lahrani said he should leave
the room, so that they could discuss his fitness for the job in his
absence. Abdelhak duly went outside and the people who knew him
well, such as Ali Zouabri, Djafar al-Afghani and Brahim Zekioui
(who was from the same area as Abdelhak) all spoke about him.
For our own part, we hadn't known him for long, but we said we
had nothing against him. Abdelhak was then called back in and
told that he had been chosen as the group's emir. He said very little,
only that he expected the others to stand by him. Lahrani, who was
formerly an imam in a mosque and known to be highly educated,
said that we should all pledge allegiance to Abdelhak as emir, so we
all swore obedience to him.

Then the question of what the group was to be called was raised.
People were unwilling to accept the word 'movement' for religious
reasons, because it's often used by the Shia. Lahrani said that they
had considered calling Meliani's organisation the Islamic Group and
that they had a logo, which they had designed in Afghanistan. It
was suggested that we call the faction a 'group' because of the saying
attributed to the Prophet Muhammad: 'A group of people from my
community shall continue to do good, and shall come to no harm
from those who oppose them.' Another version of this story quotes

the Prophet as saying 'a band of people', but we thought if we called
the group a 'band' people would think we were a gang of highway
robbers. Abdelhak said he had no objection to calling our faction
a 'group': the important thing was for us to unite, and provided the
name we had chosen was a legitimate one, we should set to work.

At the end of the meeting we all went our separate ways. At a
subsequent gathering attended by most of the same people, Abdelhak
allocated roles to the other members of the group. Djafar al-Afghani
was made emir for Algiers, Ali Zouabri emir for Blida Province,
Abou Younes el-Khan [Atiya Sayeh] emir for Médéa and Abdel
Aziz al-Afghani emir for Boumerdès Province. I was appointed
emir for Bouira Province, and Mounir el-Gharbi and Khaled Sadjali
were both chosen to liaise with Algerian Afghan veterans abroad.
Meanwhile, Lahrani was made responsible for questions of Islamic
law and began drafting the GIA's constitution.[1]

Layada's Leadership

Under Layada's direction the GIA stepped up its paramilitary activity and
clarified its ideology. He remained at the head of the group until 1993, when
Algerian intelligence succeeded in tracking him down to Morocco. It was
there that the GIA Consultative Council used to assemble, allowing the
group's leaders based in Algeria to meet their supporters from abroad. They
would also discuss ways to get weapons and reinforcements into Algeria
across some of the remoter stretches of the Moroccan border.

For the first time Layada has revealed how he was arrested when he
travelled to Morocco in 1993:

> I went there for several reasons. One of them was the fact that
> when Hasan II [the late king of Morocco] visited Algeria in 1990,
> the only political leader he met was Abbasi Madani [the head of
> the FIS]. When the situation here became critical [following the
> cancellation of the elections in 1992] we hoped that the king might
> be able to act as an intermediary [between the Algerian regime
> and the Islamists]. I went to Morocco in the hope of finding a
> solution, but that wasn't what people wanted at the time: if they

---

1   Lahrani was killed in 1993 in an exchange of gunfire with two policemen who
     had recognised him.

had, the whole situation could have been resolved in 1993. There I was, hoping that the Moroccans would mediate between us and the regime, and they sold me out to Algeria. 'You're worth your weight in gold,' they told me: those were the very words spoken to me by a senior Moroccan official. Khaled Nezzar [the former Algerian minister of defence] wrote in his memoirs that Hasan II mentioned my case to him as though it were comparable with the Western Sahara issue.[1] At that point I was not under arrest in Morocco; I was staying in a palace near Salé, and the people I met were senior to Driss Basri [then Moroccan Minister of the Interior and Hasan II's right-hand man]. The Moroccans made me all kinds of offers, but I refused to go along with them. Another reason why I went to Morocco was to meet some of my Algerian brothers who had started coming back from Afghanistan. There were many of them; we're not talking ten or twenty people: there was a whole army of them. They had arrived with the help of the Moroccans, who knew who they were the moment they stepped off the plane in Rabat. They had Pakistani visas and had arrived from Pakistan, where the authorities were putting pressure on the Islamists at [US President Bill] Clinton's request. Some brought their two-way radios with them; others were even carrying military equipment.

Following Layada's arrest in Morocco, the GIA leadership was assumed by Aïssa ben Ammar, who was promptly killed by the security forces a few weeks later in August 1993. After him, Djafar al-Afghani, an Afghan veteran who had fought in Khost in 1991, took over. He was in turn killed by the security forces on 26 February 1994, along with nine other GIA members, and was succeeded by Cherif Gousmi.[2]

The GIA mushroomed from the moment it was created in 1992. Most FIS members had been locked up, while those who had evaded arrest and fled to the mountains now lacked credibility in the eyes of the population. The field was thus left wide open for the GIA. After the wing of the FIS, led

---

1   The future of the Western Sahara has been a source of tension between Algeria and Morocco since the latter took control of most of the area from Spain in 1975. Thousands of Saharan refugees still live in camps in Algeria, which supports the Polisario Front seeking the Western Sahara's independence from Morocco.

2   Cherif Gousmi, also known as Abou Abdallah Ahmed, was killed in Algiers on 26 September 1994.

by Muhammad Saïd and Saïd Makhloufi's MEI, joined it in May 1994, the GIA's position as Algeria's pre-eminent paramilitary group was assured.[1]

Libyan Afghan Veterans Move to Algeria

The LIFG lost no time in finding out what was going on when the situation in Algeria erupted in 1992. It was aware of the part Algerian Afghan veterans had played in the formation of the GIA, but the size of the group remained unclear. Up until then the FIS had been the country's largest Islamist party and it was only with the merger of 1994 that the GIA became a household name.

Events in Algeria had direct repercussions on Libya, so it was only natural that the LIFG should show an interest in the shifting balance of power there. The first Libyans began arriving in Algeria in 1993, but not in collaboration with the GIA, which at that point was still only one among several factions operating in the country. These individuals included a member of the LIFG's Shura Council, known as Abu Mu'adh, and another Libyan called Muhammad al-Ghiryani (also known as Abu Wabisa). 'In early 1993 the Shura Council member, Abu Mu'adh, went to Algeria with Abu Wabisa, a member of the LIFG's military committee,' explains the former senior LIFG member, Noman Benotman.[2] 'Abdelmadjid el Djazairi, an Algerian commander in Jalalabad, had arranged their trip, but it was a failure, because they hadn't arranged it in advance with the GIA. Abu Mu'adh then went back to Afghanistan, while Abu Wabisa joined the MEI; he was killed in fighting in Algeria the next year.'[3]

In early 1994 a second delegation from the LIFG travelled to Algeria. Whatever Abu Mu'adh's advice to his associates had been, by this point the GIA was undisputedly the most powerful Islamist faction in the country: any foreign group wanting to send its members to Algeria would have to liaise with the GIA. This time the LIFG made sure to coordinate its visit

---

1 The meeting at which the merger was agreed took place on 13 May 1994. The proceedings were recorded on video and audio cassettes, which were circulated among Islamists in Europe; the author possesses copies of both.
2 Noman Benotman in an interview with the author in London in the spring of 2005.
3 Abu Mu'adh developed cancer following his return to Afghanistan.

with GIA members based in Khartoum, where the Libyans also had an office, in common with many other Arab jihadist groups to which the Sudanese regime had opened its arms.[1] The Libyan deputation was led by the senior LIFG leader, Salah Fathi bin Sulayman, also known as 'Abd al-Rahman al-Hattab. He was one of the founders of the LIFG and a member of its Shura Council; he was also well known among fighters in Afghanistan as the emir of his own base in Jalalabad, called the Hattab Centre.[2] He was accompanied to Algeria by Abdullah Umar, a middle-ranking LIFG field commander.[3] 'Abd al-Rahman al-Hattab spent several months in Algeria in 1994, making enquiries about the situation in the country and reporting back to the LIFG leadership what he had seen. "'Abd al-Rahman al-Hattab went to Algeria to find out about the state of the GIA leadership and spent six months there,' says Noman Benotman:[4]

> First he went to Algiers and the neighbouring areas, then he went on to visit the GIA's bases in remoter regions. Apart from his day-to-day reporting on the fighting that he witnessed and the GIA's general situation, his overwhelming impression was that the GIA leadership was disorganised and riven by disputes. He told me this himself. The GIA had a problem at the leadership level, and 'Abd al-Rahman did not know how they would end up. He also observed a lack of theological expertise or what he called 'religious depth' to the group. At the same time, he was amazed at the number of fighters that the GIA had, especially in areas near the capital: he said there were thousands of fully armed men, and that if they had been given orders to march on the city they could have taken it.

According to Benotman, al-Hattab met both the GIA's then leader, Cherif Gousmi, and Djamel Zitouni, who was introduced to him as the 'emir of the death squad'. It was Zitouni who succeeded Gousmi when the latter was killed in an ambush by the security forces in September 1994. The

---

1   The jihadists' activities in Khartoum are discussed in detail in Chapter Five.
2   Salah Fathi bin Sulayman, also known as 'Abd al-Rahman al-Hattab, was originally from Tripoli, where he studied engineering at the al-Fatih University. He was killed in 1998 during clashes inside Libya.
3   Abdullah Umar was killed in Algeria in early 1994, during Cherif Gousmi's leadership of the GIA.
4   Noman Benotman in an interview with the author in London in 2005.

'leadership problems' to which Benotman alludes concerned the struggles between the Salafist members of the GIA and the Afghan veterans in its ranks, as well as the tensions between the Salafist and the 'Djazarist' wings of the group.[1] However, al-Hattab could hardly have predicted the speed of the GIA's transformation after Zitouni took over the leadership. No sooner had he taken the helm than Zitouni began a purge of anyone who cast doubt on the legitimacy of his position. He was also quick to punish anyone he suspected of being less rigorous a Salafist than he and his fellow extremists, such as the group's *mufti*, Redouane Makador, demanded.

On the basis of al-Hattab's visit to Algeria, his discussions with the GIA leaders and his inspections of the group's camps and bases, the LIFG decided to send a third team to Algeria. This time the Libyan envoys were to head directly to where fighting was taking place and go into battle alongside the GIA. 'We dispatched fifteen of our members in 1994, all of whom had previously been in Afghanistan,' explains Benotman.[2] 'Some of them travelled first to Sudan and then went on to Algeria, while the rest took another route. None of them were leaders of the LIFG, but they were all well trained and had combat experience. One of them was known as Faruq; he was an unusual type of military commander who had taken part in numerous battles in Afghanistan. He was from Benghazi and used to carry around a Pika heavy machinegun of the kind that isn't given to ordinary fighters.'

Soon after the third group entered Algeria it disappeared off the radar. The LIFG leadership abroad was not immediately concerned: the men had gone to Algeria to fight and one or two casualties were only to be expected. News arrived confirming that one of the party, a man called Sabri Salih, had indeed been wounded in combat with the Algerian army, suffering injuries to both legs. But then there was silence: the LIFG never heard anything more about him, or about any of his fourteen comrades. With a mounting sense of unease the LIFG decided to send a fourth

---

1   The Djazarists, named after the Arabic name for Algeria, believed that Islam in the country had to be given a specific Algerian character; they also maintained that the armed struggle should be confined to Algerian territory. Formerly part of the FIS, this movement joined the GIA in the spring of 1994.
2   Noman Benotman in an interview with the author in 2005.

delegation to Algeria to look into what had become of the missing men. Al-Qa'ida was also anxious about what was going on; it appears to have been considering opening camps in Algeria in collaboration with the GIA, but the Libyans' disappearance worried bin Laden and other al-Qa'ida leaders. Eventually it was decided to dispatch a three-man delegation to Algeria, comprising both LIFG and al-Qa'ida members. It was headed by a member of the LIFG Shura Council, who shall be called Abdullah here;[1] he was accompanied by another senior figure called Abu 'Asim al-Libi.[2] The third member of the delegation was a Libyan al-Qa'ida member called 'Atiya 'Abd al-Rahman.[3]

As soon as the envoys arrived in Algeria they set about trying to find out from the GIA, and in particular its leader, Djamel Zitouni, what had become of the fifteen Libyans, who included a prominent veteran of the Afghan jihad called Abu 'Ujayla al-Rayis.[4] Abdullah, the head of the delegation, wrote messages back to the LIFG leadership in invisible ink: a mark of his distrust of the GIA leaders, who had argued with him on religious grounds when he got to Algeria. 'The GIA's members have a grossly distorted concept of Islam,' wrote Abdullah in one of his letters, according to Benotman. 'They are completely devoid of religion or morality.' He explained that the fifteen young men he had come to enquire after had vanished and that he had been unable to discover anything about their fate.

---

1   The man referred to in these pages as Abdullah currently lives in Europe and shall remain anonymous.

2   As this book went to print, Abu 'Asim al-Libi was still being held in Tripoli, having been handed over to the Libyan government by the Jordanian authorities in 2000.

3   'Atiya 'Abd al-Rahman went to Afghanistan to join the jihad and was a member of al-Qa'ida from the outset. His later role in conveying orders from the leadership to the Jordanian extremist, Abu Mus'ab al-Zarqawi, in Iraq is discussed in Chapter Twelve.

4   Abu 'Ujayla al-Rayis, also known as Sakhr, was a senior LIFG member who was wounded in fighting in Gardez in Afghanistan in 1991.

5

The Sudanese Interlude

Sudan in the early 1990s played a crucial role for opposition Islamist groups from across the Arab world. President Omar al-Bashir and his then ally, Hasan al-Turabi, adopted an open-door policy towards these movements, briefly turning Khartoum into a hive of Islamist activity, much as Peshawar had been during the 1980s.[1]

Arab veterans of the Afghan jihad did not use Sudan's hospitality merely for political ends; they also began preparing for conflict with their own countries' regimes. Some groups opened hostels for members who had fled abroad but found nowhere else willing to take them in. Others set up companies, some of which were involved in legitimate commercial business, while others were front organisations intended to mask the true nature of their employees' activity. Certain factions even opened paramilitary training camps on farmland which they purchased in various parts of Sudan. Some of these activities were concealed from Sudanese intelligence. But more often than not they were carried out either with the authorities' tacit consent or in direct collaboration with the Sudanese security services.

This period saw many Arab jihadists relocate from Afghanistan to Sudan. The years after Kabul fell to the mujahidin in the spring of 1992 were disastrous, both for the Afghans and for their Arab guests. No sooner had President Najibullah's communist regime collapsed than the mujahidin began fighting among themselves, destroying what little remained of the

---

1 Omar al-Bashir came to power on 30 June 1989 as the leader of a military coup known as the 'National Salvation Revolution'. Although the Islamist ideologue, Hasan al-Turabi, was among the politicians arrested after the coup, this was merely a ploy intended to obscure his role in helping to engineer it.

Afghan capital. On the whole, the Arab fighters managed to avoid being drawn into this internecine conflict. Yet it was clear that with the Soviet withdrawal from Afghanistan, the Arabs' role in the jihad had come to an end; there was little incentive for them to stay and watch the country torn apart in a power struggle between their erstwhile allies.

Yet despite all the destruction, perhaps the Arabs would have remained in Afghanistan had Sudan not extended its welcome to them. In the circumstances, it was an offer too good to refuse. Sudan's proximity to the countries the Afghan veterans had in their sights – above all Egypt, Libya, Algeria and the Gulf – gave it a strategic significance for them far greater than that of Afghanistan. And so, while small groups of Arab fighters did stay behind, the majority began moving to their new base on African soil.

This chapter examines how from 1993 Sudan replaced the Afghan-Pakistani border area as the main base for the Arab jihadists' new, or newly re-established, organisations.

Egyptian Islamic Jihad

Of all the Islamists based in Sudan during this period, by far the most active were the Egyptians. This fact doubtless owed much to the historical and geographical ties between their country and its southern neighbour. Between 1991 and 1993 numerous EIJ members moved to Sudan from their bases in Yemen and the Afghan-Pakistani border area, with Ayman al-Zawahiri leading the way. They then set about preparing to overthrow the Egyptian regime headed by President Hosni Mubarak.[1] In 1993 an investigation into the attempted assassination of the Egyptian Prime Minister, 'Atif Sidqi, revealed that EIJ was using the Yemeni capital, Sana'a,

---

1 When Ayman al-Zawahiri moved to Sudan, EIJ's emir, Dr Fadl, and several other leading members of the group were living in the Afghan-Pakistani border area. Other EIJ members preferred to base themselves in Yemen, where they enjoyed the protection of local tribesmen. They were also able to exploit the country's proximity to the Gulf, especially Saudi Arabia, where many Egyptian Islamists were secretly operating.

as a base.[1] It was in the aftermath of this exposure that most of the group's members finally decided to move to the relative safety of Sudan.

EIJ purchased farmland in remote areas of Sudan, where it opened training camps and drilled new recruits in the use of weapons and explosives. It also smuggled hundreds of men trained in its Afghan camps into Egypt, while supplying its cells there with arms and ammunition carried over the border by camels.[2] However, its plans were soon exposed. In 1992 the Egyptian security services arrested a number of men who had received weapons training at camps in Afghanistan. These individuals, who were members of EIJ and al-Gama'a al-Islamiyya, revealed under interrogation where they had been trained and who had sent them.[3] The authorities subsequently rounded up one Islamist cell after another until they had detained more than a thousand people, and in 1993 the suspects were put on trial in what became known as the 'Vanguards of Conquest' case. Many EIJ members blamed their leader, Dr Fadl, who remained in Pakistan, for the fact that their comrades had fallen into the hands of the Egyptian authorities. When he refused to come to Sudan to face his accusers, rifts within EIJ's ranks deepened; as crisis loomed, Ayman al-Zawahiri saw his opportunity, stepped in and took over the leadership of the organisation.

Al-Qa'ida

The Egyptians may have been the busiest Islamists in Sudan, but they did not have it all to themselves: Osama bin Laden and his fledgling al-Qa'ida were also on the scene. In the wake of the Gulf War of 1990–91, Bin Laden

---

1   See the minutes of the interrogation of the EIJ member, Ahmad Ibrahim al-Sayyid al-Najjar, from the Egyptian State Security Prosecutor's case No. 8/98; the Arabic text can be found at http://www.metransparent.com/old/texts/interrogation_minutes_najjar_to_qaida_1.htm. Al-Najjar claimed to have been tortured and it is possible that his statements were obtained under duress.

2   From Jamal Ahmad al-Fadl's testimony to the Manhattan Federal Court in New York in 2001. Al-Gama'a al-Islamiyya is believed to have cooperated closely with EIJ in smuggling arms and ammunition over the Sudanese border.

3   In October 1992 Egypt began prosecuting, by presidential decree, civilians accused of terrorist offences in military courts. Details of the cases in Arabic can be found at http://www.eohr.org/ar/articles/2006/pro404.shtml.

was placed under virtual house arrest in his native Saudi Arabia, where he had returned in 1990. It was only when he got to Sudan that he was able to build al-Qa'ida into a clearly defined organisation with its own hierarchy, weapons and financial resources.

However, bin Laden did not move directly from Saudi Arabia to Sudan.[1] The restrictions imposed on him back home proved unbearable after the freedom of movement to which he had become accustomed during his long years in Afghanistan. At the same time, he was appalled by the presence of what he saw as infidel Western forces on Saudi soil. Feeling unable to remain in the country any longer, bin Laden used one of his brothers' contacts with a Saudi official to pull strings and get out of the kingdom. He told his brother he had certain financial commitments in Pakistan and elsewhere that he had to see to: various debts that only he could settle, given the personal nature of the relationships involved. His brother fell for this story and explained the situation to an acquaintance in the Interior Ministry, persuading him to return Osama's passport with permission to make a single journey. Bin Laden seized his opportunity and left the country. The first thing he did on arrival in Pakistan was to write to his brother, explaining that he had no intention of coming back and apologising for the embarrassment this was bound to cause him.

Bin Laden did not remain long in Pakistan, apparently afraid of falling prey to the close cooperation between the Saudi and Pakistani security services. Instead he hurried to Afghanistan, where the situation, if comparatively safe from bin Laden's point of view, was nevertheless an unenviable one. The mujahidin factions were battling for control of Kabul, while at the same time squabbling among themselves over who was to be first to enter the beleaguered city: Hekmatyar's Hezb-e Islami or the Jamiat-e Islami led by Burhanuddin Rabbani and Ahmad Shah Massoud. Bin Laden is said to have attempted to mediate between them, but to no avail. He asked his Arab supporters not to get involved in the power struggle between the Afghan factions, but at the same time began to feel

---

1 See the report published by the London-based Islamic Observation Centre (IOC) in 1999 about bin Laden's relocation to Sudan, p. 4. The IOC's website address no longer works (www.marsad.net/arabic/ioc/bin.htm), but a copy of the report is retained by the author.

THE SUDANESE INTERLUDE 93

that there was no point in his remaining in the country. After discussing the situation with some of his closest associates, bin Laden decided to look for somewhere else where he could pursue his aims. That place was to be Sudan. The time bin Laden spent in Sudan was one of the most important periods of his life. Not only was he able to continue training his men in camps all over the country, his contacts with senior Sudanese officials allowed him to keep his finger on the pulse of events in the region, particularly in the Gulf, East Africa, Egypt and the Maghreb.

Bin Laden travelled to Sudan secretly in a private jet, accompanied by several of his associates; others followed by different routes. He arrived to a warm welcome from the Sudanese government. At that point he was not in need of any financial assistance: he remained in control of all his assets and was able to have some of his money and possessions transferred to Sudan without difficulty.[1]

With bin Laden's arrival in Sudan, al-Qa'ida began expanding its activities significantly. Most notably, it set up a large number of companies, the exact nature of whose activities would later prove highly controversial. Bin Laden's supporters maintain that employees of these firms were simply earning a living from perfectly normal jobs and knew nothing of the covert roles of some of their colleagues. Yet it is this clandestine element which is seized on by Western and Arab intelligence services alike, which regard these companies as fronts for al-Qa'ida's real activity.

The Role of the LIFG

Thanks to their overt activity in Khartoum, it was bin Laden and the leaders of the Egyptian groups who attracted most interest at the time. But the Sudanese capital was also a vital base for other Arab organisations, including the LIFG and the Algerian GIA.

'The LIFG leadership was based in Sudan from 1993,' says Noman

---

1   See the IOC's 1999 report on bin Laden, p. 4. While bin Laden did not engage directly in any paramilitary activity in Sudan, he was able to use his resources in a wide variety of investment projects, from road building to agricultural schemes. The best known was the so-called *Tariq al-Tahaddi* or 'Challenge Road', linking Khartoum and Port Sudan.

Benotman, who spent time in Khartoum himself between 1994 and 1995. 'But this had nothing to do with bin Laden's role there. In fact, we had first visited Sudan in 1988–89, when we went to test the water before the coup led by Omar al-Bashir. LIFG members visited Sudan often after that, without the group itself actually settling there. But we were keeping an eye on the country.'[1] The LIFG continued to monitor the situation in Sudan until 1993, when it decided the time had come for its leadership to move somewhere close to Libya. The fact that the group was preparing to get involved in Algeria and help the mujahidin fighting to bring down the regime there gave the LIFG a new sense of urgency. 'It was in early 1993 that the situation in Sudan stabilised and we established a "station" there, in the operational sense of the word,' explains Benotman. 'This meant that from then on we had secret safe houses and hostels in Sudan too. If an LIFG member decided to visit the country, there would be people to meet him at the airport, arrange his onward travel, organise his accommodation and provide him with the necessary documents.' Benotman stresses that 'there was no collaboration between the LIFG and the Sudanese security services. They knew we had a presence in the country, but we did not cooperate with them. On the contrary, sometimes friction between our members and Sudanese security officers would lead to a few of our guys being arrested and then later released.'

As proof that the LIFG did not collaborate with the Sudanese, Benotman explains how the group's members used to disguise the true nature of their activity in Khartoum:

> We operated in Sudan using non-Libyan identity documents. We used to say that we were from other parts of the Maghreb. For example, when the authorities asked us for details of the people living in our houses, we would show them Tunisian passports. On one occasion an officer asked one of the brothers his name. The brother handed the officer the passport he was carrying, before realising he had forgotten the name that was in it. When the officer pressed the brother to tell him his name, he clapped his hand to his head and said he'd forgotten. 'Aren't you so-and-so?' the officer asked him,

---

1 Noman Benotman in interviews with the author in London in the spring and summer of 2005.

taking a look at the passport. 'Yes, that's me,' the brother replied, and the officer believed him and left him in peace!

Between 1993 and 1995 the LIFG became increasingly active in Sudan. It was from there that the group sent fighters to Algeria and contacted cells operating inside Libya itself. However, when the situation in Libya erupted in the latter half of 1995, the Libyan security services discovered how the LIFG had been stirring up unrest from Sudan. Tripoli then began putting intense pressure on al-Bashir's regime to expel Libyan opposition figures operating from the country. Caving in, the Sudanese government began by asking bin Laden to expel Libyan members of his organisation from Sudan. Bin Laden complied, no doubt reluctantly, and provided Libyan al-Qa'ida members with money and passports to enable them to move elsewhere. Some headed to Europe, where they sought political asylum; others chose to leave al-Qa'ida altogether and join the LIFG, motivated by their desire to take part in what they saw as the jihad underway in Libya. The latter included Nazih al-Ruqay'i, also known as Abu Anas al-Libi, who would later gain notoriety when the Americans accused him of involvement in the 1998 bombing of their embassies in Nairobi and Dar es Salaam.[1]

Gaddafi's regime was not only concerned with the Libyan al-Qa'ida members based in Sudan. These people did represent a danger for Tripoli, despite their limited numbers; but the greatest threat was posed by the LIFG and its cells, not bin Laden and his organisation. Tripoli naturally demanded that Khartoum extradite the LIFG activists and provided the Sudanese with more than fifty names and aliases of Libyan nationals active on their soil.[2] Khartoum had not intended to comply with Libya's demands, but to escape the pressure from Gaddafi it asked the LIFG leaders to conduct their business outside Sudan. They had no choice but

---

1   Nothing has been heard of Abu Anas since he fled the UK at the end of the 1990s, to evade arrest for his alleged involvement in the 1998 US embassy bombings. The author understands from a credible source that Abu Anas was subsequently killed in Afghanistan, during fighting against the Northern Alliance. However, it has proven impossible to verify this claim, which may have been circulated by Abu Anas himself in order to throw the Americans off his scent.

2   Sudanese intelligence often knew Libyan activists' nicknames and aliases, but not their real names. It is also possible that their true identities were known only to a very few people within the Sudanese intelligence services.

to agree. Their departure came at a critical time for the LIFG, coinciding as it did with fierce fighting which had begun in June 1995 between the group's members inside Libya and the Libyan security services. Meanwhile, the elite fighters the group had sent to fight alongside the GIA in Algeria had gone missing.

To make matters worse, the GIA seemed indifferent to the fate of the Libyans who had come to help them. At the same time, the GIA made radical staffing changes at its office in Khartoum. This was the base the GIA used to liaise with other jihadist groups operating in Sudan, including al-Qa'ida, EIJ and the LIFG. And it was from Khartoum that the GIA used to dispatch volunteers to join the conflict in Algeria. The management changes at the GIA's Khartoum station reflected the group's efforts to assert itself as the sole representative of Algeria's jihadists. This increased self-confidence was in turn the fruit of its merger with the MEI and a branch of the FIS in 1994. The GIA sent two envoys to Khartoum to warn other Islamists what would happen if they sent any kind of assistance to the groups operating in Algeria without going through the GIA.

The GIA's representatives delivered their starkest warning to Osama bin Laden himself. He had been seeking assurances about the soundness of the GIA's ideology, particularly after hearing of the disagreements between the group's leaders and the Libyan Afghan veterans. He was also interested in opening training camps for fighters inside Algeria, in return for providing support to the GIA. However, the Algerians categorically rejected his proposal: they would not accept offers of help with strings attached.

According to Noman Benotman, the GIA's senior *mufti* or Islamic scholar, Redouane Makador, also known as Abou Bassir, visited bin Laden in Khartoum in late 1995. He spelled out the GIA's position in no uncertain terms: the GIA would kill anyone who offered help of any kind to any other group in Algeria. 'A Libyan al-Qa'ida member was present at the meeting between bin Laden and Abou Bassir,' says Benotman. 'Abou Bassir started ranting and raving and wagging his finger at bin Laden, as he sat there in his house in Khartoum. "No one is to get involved in Algeria without going through us," he said. "This is what will happen if they do," he said, drawing his finger across his throat. Then he stormed out.' The message was not lost on bin Laden.[1] But even he could not have predicted the ferocity with which the GIA would in due course turn on its brothers in arms.

---

[1] The former GIA member, Omar Chikhi, has told the author that he does not know of any visit paid by Abou Bassir to Bin Laden in Sudan.

6

Egyptians in Sudan:
A State within a State

The years in Sudan were a golden age for EIJ following its reestablishment in Afghanistan in the late 1980s. It was in Khartoum that Ayman al-Zawahiri consolidated his control of the group, finally taking over from Dr Fadl as its leader. In the process he appointed his closest associates to senior positions in the organisation, opened training camps in preparation for the imminent battle with the Egyptian regime and bolstered his relationship with Osama bin Laden.

Yet the relaunch of EIJ was not as easy as it might have appeared. Al-Zawahiri failed to reunite the group with al-Gama'a al-Islamiyya, the former ally with whose help it had assassinated President Sadat in 1981. The two groups had quarrelled as they served their prison sentences for their role in his murder. The result was that the two organisations – al-Gama'a al-Islamiyya, with its seat of influence mainly in southern Egypt, and EIJ, based mainly in Cairo and the north – split once again. It was a rift that al-Zawahiri could not overcome.

Despite its proximity to Egypt, al-Zawahiri also failed to use the EIJ's base in Sudan to deal a decisive blow to the Mubarak regime. Instead it was the Egyptians who gained the upper hand. Having infiltrated EIJ, they very nearly killed al-Zawahiri himself, and might have done so had the Sudanese intelligence services not tipped him off in time. On learning of the plot against him, al-Zawahiri arranged a kangaroo court to 'try' two youths accused of working for Egyptian intelligence. To the fury of the Sudanese, the boys were swiftly condemned and executed. It was a fateful decision: al-Zawahiri's conduct, allowing EIJ to operate as a state within a state, was to be one of the main reasons behind the closure of the EIJ's station in Khartoum.

The Revival of Egyptian Islamic Jihad

When EIJ regrouped in Afghanistan during the late 1980s, it chose Dr Fadl as its emir. Yet it was another doctor, Ayman al-Zawahiri, who provided the real drive behind the organisation.[1] Indeed, many of those who joined EIJ at this time and pledged allegiance to 'the doctor' assumed that they were swearing obedience to al-Zawahiri, not Dr Fadl. It was a mark of how quickly al-Zawahiri had established himself as the group's best known representative.

Nonetheless, EIJ was not the only Egyptian group in Afghanistan. Al-Gama'a al-Islamiyya also moved there, opening camps and beginning training new fighters to resume the jihad against the Egyptian regime, only a few years after most of its cells had been dismantled following Sadat's death. With the end of the Afghan jihad the Egyptians, like other Arab fighters, began looking for ways to go home, or at least somewhere nearby where they could begin planning operations. Sudan, governed by the Islamist double act of Omar al-Bashir and Hasan al-Turabi, was their preferred destination, and in early 1992 both EIJ and al-Gama'a al-Islamiyya began moving their members there. However, it was only in 1993 that the process of relocation gathered pace. There were two reasons for this apparent delay. Following the end of the Afghan jihad, the Pakistani government had carried out mass arrests of Arab fighters who had settled on the border with Afghanistan, particularly in Peshawar, Waziristan and Baluchistan.[2] The other reason had to do specifically with EIJ. After coming under pressure in Pakistan, the group had operated mainly out of Yemen, and it was from there that it had orchestrated two assassination attempts in 1993: one against the Egyptian Interior Minister, Hasan al-Alfi, and

---

1   Ayman al-Zawahiri graduated from Cairo University's medical school in 1974 and obtained a Masters degree in surgery four years later.

2   At this time the Pakistani government was led by Benazir Bhutto, who was prime minister from 1988 to 1990 and again from 1993 to 1996.

the other against the Prime Minister, 'Atif Sidqi.[1] When the investigation into the attempt on Sidqi's life revealed that EIJ leaders were based in Yemen, the organisation ordered its senior members to leave the county immediately and move to Sudan.

But the relocation was not plain sailing. EIJ was already in a state of turmoil following the arrest of hundreds of its members in Egypt and their trial in the 'Vanguards of Conquest' case. Meanwhile, as different camps within EIJ vied for control, the rank and file were urging the leadership to authorise paramilitary attacks like those the GIA was carrying out in Algeria almost daily, or like the operations that al-Gama'a al-Islamiyya was perpetrating in Egypt with similar frequency. As the situation within EIJ reached boiling point, the group's very existence appeared to be in jeopardy.

The former EIJ affiliate, Hani al-Siba'i, explains the growing anger within the group at this time and how Ayman al-Zawahiri ultimately turned it to his advantage.[2] Following the 'Vanguards of Conquest' arrests, differences broke out between two main camps within EIJ: one loyal to al-Zawahiri himself and the other allied to a jihadist leader called Ahmad Husayn 'Agiza:[3]

> Some people tried to reconcile Ayman and his group with those who wanted to break away. Al-Zawahiri had a band of supporters, such as his brother [Muhammad], who was based in the Gulf, as

---

1   Four people were killed and several others wounded in the attack on the Egyptian Interior Minister, Hasan al-Alfi, in August 1993; al-Alfi himself survived. The following November the Egyptian Prime Minister, 'Atif Sidqi, also survived an assassination attempt, which killed a young bystander. EIJ claimed responsibility for the attack on Sidqi, saying that it disproved the Egyptian government's assertion that it had destroyed the group.

2   Hani al-Siba'i in an interview with the author, serialised in *al-Hayat* newspaper 1–4 September 2002.

3   Ahmad 'Agiza, along with another Egyptian national named Muhammad al-Zari, were rendered from Sweden to Egypt on a US-government-leased jet on 18 December 2001. In 2004 'Agiza was convicted before a military tribunal of membership of an organisation seeking to overthrow the Egyptian government, and was sentenced to twenty-five years in prison. Al-Zari was released without charge in October 2003. See Human Rights Watch report Black Hole, 9 May 2005: http://www.hrw.org/en/node/11757/section/2.

well as many longstanding EIJ activists, members of the group's
legal committee and certain prominent figures, such as Muhammad
Salah, Tariq Anwar and Tharwat Salah. Ahmad Husayn 'Agiza had
the younger EIJ members on his side, but none of the old-timers. It
was Abu 'Ubayda al-Banshiri, among others, who tried to heal the
rift between the two sides; he organised a meeting between them
to try and calm things down.[1] The younger EIJ members demanded
that Dr Fadl come from Pakistan to sort things out, given that he
was the emir and people had a lot of respect for him. Many people
tried to persuade him to come to Sudan, but he wouldn't. The
disagreements between the EIJ members became very bitter; at this
point Abu 'Ubayda al-Banshiri also contacted Dr Fadl. A group
including Ahmad Husayn 'Agiza demanded that Dr Fadl resign,
because he was unwilling to take charge. Rumours were flying, as
the differences within EIJ became ever more deeply entrenched. Of
course, they told Dr Fadl that he had to come to Sudan, to which
he replied that he was resigning and they should pick another emir.
He said all this over the telephone, and Abu 'Ubayda informed the
rest of the group.

'The secessionists wanted Dr Fadl to resign because he was the biggest
obstacle in their path,' explains al-Siba'i:

> If he had come to Sudan, they'd have had to stop agitating: he was
> held in great esteem for his knowledge of Islamic law and it would
> have been impossible to defy him. But if they managed to get him
> out of the way, it would be easy for them to demand that other
> people resign too. Abu 'Ubayda made things simple for them when
> he said that Dr Fadl had tendered his resignation and left it to them
> to choose a new emir. At this stage EIJ was temporarily without a
> leader. Only someone who knows EIJ's structure can understand
> how serious this was: the position of emir and the members' oath
> of allegiance to him were absolutely fundamental to the group's
> identity and the way it functioned.

A meeting of the EIJ's Shura Council was hastily convened to address
this hiatus. According to the group's regulations, fifty-two members were

---

1   Ali Amin al-Rashidi, more commonly known as Abu 'Ubayda al-Banshiri,
    subsequently became a senior al-Qa'ida military commander.

supposed to attend. EIJ sent out summonses to all its senior leaders and stressed the importance of attending, fearing that unless they did so the secessionists would declare that they were the real EIJ. However, in the end al-Zawahiri's supporters managed to assemble enough of EIJ's leading figures from various different countries, who duly pledged allegiance to al-Zawahiri as the group's new emir.[1]

Al-Gama'a al-Islamiyya: Two Attempts at Unification

While EIJ was preoccupied with its internal divisions, al-Gama'a al-Islamiyya was carrying out almost daily operations inside Egypt, proving itself far more capable in paramilitary terms than its rival. The arrest of hundreds of EIJ activists in 1992 and 1993 may well have helped weaken the group, to the advantage of al-Gama'a al-Islamiyya. But the latter had always had a keener sense of the public's mood; it had also established a reputation for trying to put Islamic teachings into practice. All this had created a base of popular support which the more elitist EIJ lacked.

There is no question that many EIJ members were unhappy with the way in which al-Gama'a al-Islamiyya was hogging the media spotlight at the time. The group's operations received extensive coverage, particularly those in southern Egypt against foreign tourists, one of the mainstays of the national economy. EIJ disagreed with this strategy, but its reservations were not enough to prevent the two groups from considering a new merger. Yet ultimately the gulf between them, created by their different interpretations of Islamic law, was too wide for these efforts to succeed.

'There were two main attempts to unite the two groups,' explains Hani al-Siba'i:[2]

> The first took place in Pakistan, when certain well-intentioned people tried to bring about a rapprochement between them. EIJ had moved to Afghanistan before al-Gama'a al-Islamiyya; when 'Abd al-Fattah Isma'il, the first member of al-Gama'a al-Islamiyya

---

1 Al-Zawahiri's supporters included Abu 'Ubayda al-Banshiri, whom many people had wanted to assume the position of EIJ emir himself.

2 Hani al-Siba'i in an interview with the author, serialised in *al-Hayat* newspaper 1–4 September 2002.

to travel to Afghanistan, arrived there, he stayed with Ayman al-Zawahiri. Al-Gama'a al-Islamiyya was expanding at the time and made the most of this. Its senior leaders then included Abu Yasir [Rifa'i Taha] and Abu Talal [al-Qasimi].[1] Some people started asking why the two groups didn't unite, given their common hostility to the Mubarak regime. EIJ's response was, 'Fine, as fellow Muslims it's our duty to unite, but we'll have to discuss the conditions first.' The two groups were organised in different ways and each had things that the other would find unacceptable. This would require concessions on both sides, though not of any fundamental points. EIJ said they thought the best thing would be to get together a group of Islamic scholars. They duly nominated some, including 'Abd al-Razzaq 'Utayfi, and Sheikh al-Qa'ud, to mediate between them. Al-Gama'a al-Islamiyya insisted on retaining its name; EIJ said it had no objection: they would accept whatever the clerics decided was the most appropriate name for the combined organisation. EIJ's only stipulation for the merger was that the clerics' recommendations should be implemented. I heard all this from al-Zawahiri himself. Abu Talal was one of the most passionate advocates of the merger; he did his utmost to make it happen and prepared various draft agreements in preparation. He was told to consult the brothers [in al-Gama'a al-Islamiyya], but reported back to the doctor that they had rejected EIJ's terms.

'The other significant attempt to unite the two factions took place in Sudan in late 1994 or early 1995,' says Hani al-Siba'i:

Abu Yasir and Ayman al-Zawahiri in particular had been discussing it. At that time the leaders of al-Gama'a al-Islamiyya and EIJ got along fine whenever they met, possibly because they were going through much the same problems in those days. Some of the more dovish members suggested that the two groups merge, pointing to

---

1 Rifa'i Taha, also known as Abu Yasir, was head of al-Gama'a l-Islamiyya's *Majlis al-Shura* or Consultative Council. His increasing marginalisation after he rejected the group's non-violence initiative is discussed in Chapter Eight. The real name of the senior EIJ member, Abu Talal al-Qasimi, was Tala'at Fu'ad Qasim. After 'Abd al-Fattah Isma'il died in Afghanistan, Abu Talal married his widow. He was later granted asylum in Denmark. In 1995 he disappeared in Croatia; it has been alleged that he was abducted by US agents and handed over to the Egyptian authorities, but these claims have proven impossible to corroborate.

the good relationship that already existed between them. Abu Yasir for one insisted on it; Abu Talal was based in Denmark then, but was kept informed about what was happening. For the first time al-Gama'a al-Islamiyya put aside any preconditions, saying that it regarded the unification of the two groups as a sacred duty. There was a debate, during which each side identified the concessions it was prepared to make, and a proposal was drawn up showing what the combined organisation might look like. EIJ was divided. The hawks ruled out a merger with al-Gama'a al-Islamiyya, arguing that it might go back on its word or even split, with a breakaway faction later refusing to recognise the unification of the two organisations. In the EIJ hardliners' opinion, the main problem with al-Gama'a al-Islamiyya was the way it was divided between its imprisoned leaders, its members in Egypt and those based abroad. This situation made it much more difficult for the group to reach a consensus on a merger with EIJ; yet only once it had done so would it be possible to conclude an agreement with them. These were the objections raised by EIJ members who were unhappy about the prospect of a merger, not because they rejected the idea out of hand, but based on their experience of al-Gama'a al-Islamiyya.

'The doves in EIJ included Ayman al-Zawahiri. They argued that the best solution would be to create a new Shura Council, comprising members of the two groups, and then select a new emir for the merged organisation,' continues Hani al-Siba'i:

> But then arguments began about certain old theological questions, such as *wilayat al-darir* or 'the rule of the blind'.[1] What would happen to Omar Abdel Rahman: would he be recognised as emir or not? This was one of the important issues. Omar was both imprisoned [in the United States] and blind, two things which in EIJ's view disqualified him from the position of emir. There was also the question of 'the excuse of ignorance'. In al-Gama'a al-Islamiyya's view, if a person did something forbidden by Islam,

---

1 The leader of al-Gama'a al-Islamiyya was the blind Egyptian cleric, 'Umar 'Abd al-Rahman (often spelled Omar Abdel Rahman); the question of whether his disability rendered him unfit to head the group was hotly contested. He is currently serving a life sentence in the United States for his part in a plot to carry out attacks in New York.

that person was to be excused if they were ignorant [of the tenets of Islam]. However, EIJ argued that this issue was related to the very essence of Islam: the belief that there is no god but Allah and that Muhammad is His prophet. If someone did something sacrilegious, such as making a pilgrimage to the tomb of a holy person, making an offering to the dead or venerating a human being, they could not be excused such ignorance of the very basis of Islam. People were not to worship anything or anyone but Allah: that was the strict EIJ view. In contrast, al-Gama'a al-Islamiyya was not only prepared to excuse wrongdoing on the basis of ignorance, they thought that to dismiss this argument was itself heretical. This point was only one of the many differences between the two groups, including more practical matters such as financial arrangements and military strategy, which would have to be resolved if they were to unite.

'Finally, the date on which they'd agreed to discuss the merger came around,' says al-Siba'i:

EIJ's representative told me he'd never even dreamed they'd get as far as actually negotiating. EIJ brought along a list of conditions, including the status of Omar Abdel Rahman, the question of whether imprisoned members of the group could be emirs, the role of other expatriate members, the Shura Council and how the al-Gama'a al-Islamiyya's dissolution would be announced [if and when it merged with EIJ]. This was EIJ's attitude at the meeting. Al-Gama'a al-Islamiyya's representatives immediately trotted out a series of points they regarded as non-negotiable: Omar Abdel Rahman's position, the role of their members in prison, the status of their military organisation and their financial arrangements. 'How are we ever going to unite, then?' the EIJ representative asked. 'The merger of the two groups means all of you joining al-Gama'a al-Islamiyya,' they said. 'Full stop.'

'What happened at that meeting was astonishing,' says Hani al-Siba'i:

It was as if al-Gama'a al-Islamiyya didn't take the proceedings seriously, as though they thought that EIJ would simply be absorbed into their group and that would be that. Members of al-Gama'a al-Islamiyya behind bars, such as Karam Zuhdi and Najih Ibrahim, would retain their all-powerful status.[1] The group's members based overseas were also untouchable. What sort of merger was that? This was the second attempt to unite the two groups, and it left EIJ speechless.

Infiltration

Perhaps it was al-Gama'a al-Islamiyya's confidence in its theological views and the strength of its position compared with that of EIJ that led it to adopt such an inflexible attitude. It had been constantly escalating its attacks inside Egypt, whereas Ayman al-Zawahiri had conspicuously failed to orchestrate any at all. What is unclear is whether al-Gama'a al-Islamiyya's negotiating position had anything to do with one particular operation that it was planning: an attack which, if successful, would deal a devastating blow to the Egyptian regime. In June 1995 several Sudan-based members of the group ambushed Hosni Mubarak's motorcade in Addis Ababa, where he was due to attend a summit of the Organisation of African Unity. The Egyptian president survived the attack, however, and immediately returned to Cairo. When the Egyptians discovered the link between the attackers and Khartoum, Omar al-Bashir's regime came under intense pressure to surrender the culprits, culminating in a demand by the United Nations Security Council to that effect.[2]

As the Egyptian Islamists plotted their president's murder from Sudan, unbeknownst to them the Egyptian security services were only a hair's breadth away from their own leaders in Khartoum. Had it not been for the vigilance of Sudanese intelligence and its surveillance of Egyptian diplomats, they might well have succeeded in assassinating al-Zawahiri and other senior EIJ figures. Hani al-Siba'i describes how the Egyptian

---

1 Karam Zuhdi was head of al-Gama'a al-Islamiyya's Shura Council; he was imprisoned for his part in plotting the 1981 assassination of Anwar Sadat, but was released in 2003 after renouncing violence. Najih Ibrahim was Zuhdi's deputy and al-Gama'a al-Islamiyya's chief ideologue; he was also imprisoned for many years.

2 Mustafa Hamza, the leader of the plot to kill Mubarak, fled to Afghanistan, where he announced to the press that Sudan had had nothing to do with the conspiracy. The other prime suspects were Husayn Shamit and 'Isam al-Ghamri, whom the UN Security Council also demanded Sudan hand over.

security services infiltrated EIJ, leading to a game of cat-and-mouse between the two sides.[1] In early 1995, he claims, EIJ decided to end the armed struggle following the arrest of many of its members, the confiscation of its assets and the death of several of its senior leaders. Allah only requires His believers to do what they can, the group reasoned, and it could do no more. Yet in November of that year EIJ bombed the Egyptian embassy in Islamabad.

On 2 November 1995 EIJ issued a statement explaining its action. Among the reasons it gave was its desire to bring down what it called the 'collaborationist regime' in Egypt. It also alleged that the Egyptian government used its embassies to reach extradition agreements with other countries, such as the one it had signed with Pakistan; the latter was now persecuting the same Arab mujahidin who had defended Muslim honour in Afghanistan and was surrendering them to the Egyptian authorities. EIJ also claimed that Egyptian diplomats resorted to 'immoral methods' to spy on the mujahidin: EIJ had investigated several cases of such base practices and the time had come for the Egyptian Foreign Ministry to pay the price.[2]

In March 1996 Ayman al-Zawahiri published a treatise justifying the attack on the Islamabad embassy in terms of Islamic law.[3] Once again he reiterated the claim that Egyptian diplomats based at the embassy were in fact spies who used depraved methods to recruit agents, gather intelligence and direct attacks against the mujahidin. He alleged that in one case embassy staff had engaged in sexual intercourse with their agents to train them to entrap informers and collect information; EIJ had published the details 'to act as a lesson and a warning' to others. Moreover, EIJ would

---

1   Hani al-Siba'i in an interview with the author published in *al-Hayat* on 4 September 2002.
2   From a statement released by EIJ on 2 November 1995. The author has a copy of the statement in his archives.
3   The full title of al-Zawahiri's treatise was *Shifa' Sudur al-Mu'minin: Risala 'an ba'd Ma'ani al-Jihad fi 'Amaliyyat Islamabad* ('The Cure for Believers' Hearts: a Treatise Regarding Some of the Meanings of Jihad in the Islamabad Operation'). It was published by EIJ's *Dar al-Mujahidin li al-Nashr wa al-I'lam* in March 1996. The author has a copy in his archives.

not rest until it had avenged itself on 'all the criminal members of the diplomatic corps'.[1] The Islamabad operation was just the beginning.

Al-Zawahiri spared his readers the details of the Egyptians' alleged practices. However, these were spelled out in a 'case file' EIJ published on the interrogation and execution of two young men accused of spying for the Egyptian security services. These grisly events were the outcome of a long game of bluff and counter-bluff between EIJ and Egyptian intelligence. With the aim of duping the Egyptian authorities, EIJ had announced that al-Zawahiri would be travelling to Switzerland to give a press conference. Shortly before the conference was due to take place, the group released another statement claiming it was cancelled: EIJ, it claimed, had learned that the Egyptian intelligence services had surrounded al-Zawahiri's hotel and were planning to kill him. In actual fact, al-Zawahiri had never even left Khartoum. The Egyptians were well aware that the whole thing was a set-up, but nevertheless protested to the Swiss government for allowing al-Zawahiri into their country. The Swiss in turn said they had no record of his arrival.

Meanwhile, the Egyptians were hatching a plan of their own. Their intelligence services had recruited two teenage boys to spy on EIJ. One, called Mus'ab, was the son of a senior member of the group; the other was the son of an Alexandrian man with links to al-Qa'ida. Sudanese intelligence had been monitoring everything. They photographed Mus'ab getting out of a car thought to belong to his Egyptian handler and then alerted al-Zawahiri, passing him details of flats frequented by the boy. According to the file which EIJ published on the affair, Mus'ab was summoned and confronted with this information.[2] He duly confessed to working for the Egyptians, whereupon he was asked to repent and dispatched to a school for memorising the Qur'an. However, when Mus'ab refused to do as he was told, he was called back again; this time, instead of complying he went to his Egyptian handler and told him that EIJ knew all about the case. When the group questioned Mus'ab later, he gave them false information about the man he had met and EIJ realised that he was trying to mislead them. Meanwhile, Sudanese intelligence were still monitoring

1 Ayman al-Zawahiri, *Shifa' Sudur al-Mu'minin*, pp. 17–18.
2 The details published by EIJ included video footage of Mus'ab's interrogation.

developments; they again warned EIJ about the boy and asked the group
to move to new premises.

EIJ claims that Mus'ab continued to have dealings with the Egyptian
security services, who asked him to take a case packed with explosives
to an office where al-Zawahiri used to meet other EIJ leaders. However,
both Sudanese agents and EIJ members were still watching the boy;
when he went to collect the case, the Sudanese pounced and arrested
him. They then held him in custody, but EIJ insisted that he was one
of theirs and that as such it was their responsibility to question him.
Eventually they got their wish and took the boy away for what appears to
have been a brutal interrogation, along with the other teenager recruited
by the Egyptians. Both boys confessed, and were promptly condemned
to death and executed.

The boys' deaths sparked a crisis between EIJ and the Sudanese
government. Al-Zawahiri protested weakly that he had merely been
applying Islamic law, but even in Khartoum's eyes he had gone too far.
Accusing al-Zawahiri and his group of acting like a state within a state,
the Sudanese expelled them from the country. Vengeance, violence and
vanity had led to al-Zawahiri's exile from the country where, for three
short years, he and his associates had lived in relative safety.

7

Londonistan:
Jihadists in the Lion's Den

The year 1996 marked a turning point in the history of the alliances and divisions between the Islamist groups. In London, where many of them were based, the distinctions between Salafists and jihadists began to crystallise. At the same time, there were signs that in Britain, which had first opened its doors to them in the early 1990s, the Islamists had outstayed their welcome. The Syrian militant, Abu Mus'ab al-Suri, described London aptly as 'the lion's den'. He and others like him would have to take care not to be devoured.

By early 1996 relations between the LIFG and the GIA were going from bad to worse. The LIFG leaders were growing increasingly anxious about the fate of their fifteen comrades who had disappeared while fighting alongside the GIA in Algeria. For them, the future of the LIFG's relations with their Algerian counterparts hinged on finding out what had happened to the missing men. When the delegation they dispatched to Algeria failed to track down a single one of them, the LIFG leaders became increasingly suspicious that their fighters had been killed by the GIA itself. They duly began plotting their revenge.

Senior LIFG figures secretly made contact with London-based Islamists known to support the GIA. They included the Palestinian, Abu Qatada, the Syrian jihadist, Abu Mus'ab al-Suri, and various representatives of al-Zawahiri's EIJ.[1] The LIFG's aim was to persuade these prominent figures to pull the rug from under the GIA leadership, especially the group's head,

---

1 The real name of the radical Palestinian cleric known as Abu Qatada is 'Umar Mahmud Muhammad 'Uthman.

Djamel Zitouni. The GIA's ideology had become increasingly extreme since Zitouni had taken over the running of the group after the death of his predecessor, Cherif Gousmi, in September 1994. At the same time, the influence of Afghan veterans in the organisation had been steadily curbed. However, in their meetings with the GIA's supporters, the LIFG's representatives in London insisted that their efforts to put pressure on Zitouni remain secret for the time being. The LIFG did not want to do anything that might jeopardise attempts to rescue their fifteen missing members, if indeed they were still alive. At the same time, between late 1995 and mid-1996 the GIA's London-based supporters lacked a clear sense of the group's direction, not least because the Libyans who had gone missing had themselves been an important source of information.

London Opens its Doors

London began to attract a large influx of jihadists after the end of the Gulf War in 1991 and the escalation of violence in Algeria the following year. Some had fled their countries of origin; others had been unable to return home after the end of the Afghan jihad, fearing that they would be arrested. One of the leading Algerian activists at the time was Rachid Ramda, who came to Britain from Peshawar to act as the GIA's spokesman. The Egyptians operating from London included the lawyer, 'Adil 'Abd al-Majid 'Abd al-Bari, Hani al-Siba'i and Yasir al-Sirri, all of whom were affiliated to EIJ, as well as Muhammad Mustafa al-Muqri', who belonged to al-Gama'a al-Islamiyya. Meanwhile, the prominent Saudi Islamists in the city included Osama bin Laden's envoy, Khalid al-Fawwaz, the representative of the Saudi opposition body known as the Advice and Reform Committee.[1]

In addition to the jihadists affiliated to various groups, several independent Islamists were also active in London. Of these, by far the best known was the Palestinian, Abu Qatada, who succeeded in attracting a large following of North Africans, particularly Algerians. The jihadists did not initially base themselves in well known mosques, as the Egyptian,

---

1   Osama bin Laden established the Advice and Reform Committee in 1994 to publicise his activities.

Abu Hamza, would do later when he operated out of Finsbury Park Mosque in north London. Instead they rented sports halls, which they would turn into prayer centres on Fridays; of these, the best known was the Four Feathers Social Club off Baker Street in central London, where Abu Qatada used to lead prayer sessions for his acolytes.

The London-based jihadists used newsletters to promote their ideas, distributing them in the mosques and prayer halls that they frequented. They included one called *al-Ansar*, which supported the GIA; *al-Fajr*, published by the LIFG; and *al-Mujahidun*, which was issued by EIJ. These same groups also took advantage of the plethora of Arabic media outlets in London to convey their views regarding the ongoing and bloody struggles against the regimes in their home countries.[1] Many Arab states duly complained about their activities, but the British regarded the Islamists as political opposition groups and seldom took action against them, provided they operated within the law. Moreover, both the Conservative government and the Labour administration which succeeded it in 1997 were well aware that not they but the courts had the last say in the matter.[2]

Nonetheless, as the number of jihadists based in London grew in parallel with the rising tide of violence in their home countries, the British security services began to take a greater interest in them. Their aim was to map out the organisations and their leaders, open a channel of communication with them, find out their objectives and identify to what extent their activities constituted legitimate political opposition or terrorism. None of this was easy, particularly at a time when developments were moving at a pace with which the authorities could barely keep up.

It was late 1995 when the willingness of the British to accept the consequences of the jihadists' presence was first tested. Ironically, it was

---

1 Numerous Arabic media organs were based in the United Kingdom during the 1990s. They included the newspapers *al-Hayat*, *Asharq al-Awsat*, *al-Quds al-'Arabi* and *al-'Arab*; the magazines *al-Wasat* and *al-Majalla*; and the television channel MBC.

2 In the mid-1990s the British government tried to deport the Saudi dissident, Muhammad al-Mas'ari, to the Caribbean island of Dominica, but was forced to back down following a High Court ruling that it had circumvented the UN Convention on Refugees. Al-Mas'ari was subsequently granted Exceptional Leave to Remain.

events over the Channel in Paris which occasioned this. Ever since Djamel Zitouni had taken over the leadership of the GIA in late 1994, the group had been pursuing an increasingly fanatical agenda. No longer content with murdering intellectuals, journalists, foreigners, politicians, civil servants and army conscripts, the GIA had now started openly targeting civilians with no apparent link to the conflict. Sometimes it did so under the pretext of their 'un-Islamic' behaviour, such as smoking, drinking alcohol or failing to perform their prayers: in the eyes of the GIA, such failure to abide by Islamic strictures deserved punishment by death. Other people it condemned for their indirect links to the security services: in February 1995, for example, the group issued a notorious fatwa justifying the slaughter of the mothers, wives and daughters of members of the security forces. *Al-Ansar* published an edict by Abu Qatada supporting the GIA's position, arguing that it was permissible to kill the wives of Algerian security personnel because they themselves attacked Islamists' female relatives. This statement focused attention sharply on the London-based jihadists. It provoked outrage in Islamist circles, especially among Algerian opponents of the GIA, and alarmed Western intelligence services, which were becoming increasingly concerned about Abu Qatada, his activities and his contacts.[1]

The Paris Bombings

For Zitouni, the intensity of the violence in Algeria was not enough: he was determined to take the fight outside the country's borders and strike at the French on their own soil.[2] In the summer of 1995 his wish

---

1   The author interviewed Abu Qatada in 1995; he was the first journalist to do so. Abu Qatada defended the GIA and its operations, while maintaining that he himself was a mere 'student of Islamic law' and not the Algerian group's *mufti*.

2   On 24 December 1994 GIA members hijacked an Air France jet at Boumedienne International Airport in Algiers. It was the first indication of the group's desire to internationalise the conflict. The hijackers wanted to fly to Paris, but the pilot persuaded them to land in Marseilles, where commandos stormed the plane. It is claimed that the hijackers had intended to crash the aircraft into the Eiffel Tower.

was fulfilled, as the Paris Metro was hit by a series of bomb attacks. Such a momentous development had obvious implications for the freedom of movement of GIA supporters abroad, especially in Britain. Soon after the bomb attacks began in Paris, the French security services tracked down and arrested several of the suspected culprits. It was not long before they discovered their connections to both Algeria and Rachid Ramda, who was involved in publishing the *al-Ansar* newsletter in London and had spent time on the Afghan-Pakistani border with Qari Saïd, one of the GIA's founders. On the basis of this information, the French swiftly sought to extradite Ramda from the UK to face trial in France for complicity in the Paris Metro attacks.[1]

The bombings had scarcely begun when an issue of the *al-Ansar* newsletter appeared with an image on the front cover showing the Eiffel Tower being blown apart, its shattered pieces forming the letters 'GIA'. Abu Mus'ab al-Suri claims that this was not an official claim of responsibility by the group for the Metro attacks.[2] 'It was I who drew the famous image of the exploding Eiffel Tower,' he said later, 'but I did it after the attacks took place, not before. It was [only] intended as a symbol of what had happened.' In fact, Abu Mus'ab was well aware that the GIA had been behind the attacks, though he had not been involved in them himself. While he was not close to Djamel Zitouni, he had enjoyed such a good relationship with previous GIA leaders that he had even given them policy advice. 'From 1993 I corresponded privately with the group's emir,' he says:

---

1 Rachid Ramda was finally extradited to France from the UK in late 2005, after ten years of legal wrangling during which his defence lawyers argued that he could not receive a fair trial in France. They also cast doubt on the confessions which the French had obtained from other suspects in the case, who had implicated Ramda. In the spring of 2006 Ramda was convicted of criminal association with a terrorist organisation and sentenced to ten years in prison. He lost his appeal against his sentence in October 2009.

2 From a statement released by Abu Mus'ab al-Suri, entitled 'A Message to the British and Europeans and their Governments Regarding the London Bombings of July 2005'. A copy of the statement is retained by the author. It can also be found in Arabic at http://www.metransparent.com/old/texts/abu-mussab_assuric_communique_fulltext_pdf.pdf.

I advised him to strike deep inside France, to punish it for backing the military dictatorship [in Algeria]. I told him it could be useful to provoke France into making an explicit statement of the support which hitherto it had only provided covertly: this would rally the entire Muslim nation to the Algerian jihad, just as they had rallied to the Afghan jihad before. I was in such close contact with the GIA leader [Cherif Gousmi] that once, to our delight, he sent us some traditional Arabic sweets that he had looted from an Algerian army depot. We distributed them to the GIA's supporters in the UK.[1]

The British authorities tended to reject Arab countries' extradition requests on the grounds of their human rights records, suggesting that any evidence against UK-based Islamists might have been obtained through torture. When the French sought to have Rachid Ramda handed over, the British could hardly dismiss their demands for the same reasons. However, the security services were concerned that the arrest of the young Algerian could provoke the GIA to target the UK in retaliation. Seeking to pre-empt such an eventuality, officers from the British counter-terrorism community sent a verbal message to the GIA's supporters explaining why they were taking this action. British law, they said, was designed to protect everyone in the UK, including refugees; at the same time, the executive could not interfere in the work of the judiciary: Ramda's arrest was purely a matter for the courts and had nothing to do with the government. The British outlined their policy on terrorism, from the left-wing Palestinian groups of the 1970s to the campaign waged by the IRA: never to negotiate with terrorists and never to give in to their demands. At the same time, the British stressed that theirs was a free country: they were willing to protect Arab opposition groups operating on their soil, no matter what the complaints of Middle Eastern regimes, provided they did not break the law. However, if they overstepped that mark, they would have to face the consequences, which could include imprisonment or deportation. This message was conveyed to the GIA by someone close to their supporters in London. The reply came from the GIA's leader, Djamel Zitouni himself. Zitouni allegedly offered not to harm British interests, provided the British left the GIA

---

1 Ibid.

and its supporters alone. The British, needless to say, have never admitted receiving any such communication.[1]

It is now known that the British security services adopted a multi-pronged approach to preventing the GIA's attacks from spreading from Paris to London. In 1996 MI5 opened a direct channel of communication with leading jihadists in London, including Abu Qatada and Abu Mus'ab al-Suri, explaining their concerns about the prospect of such a development. Abu Qatada promised to use his influence to calm down his Algerian supporters and stop them doing anything to threaten the UK, since it had taken them in and given them shelter.[2] He claims to have met MI5 officers in June and December 1996, and then again in February of the following year. In the first meeting, Abu Qatada claimed, as a spiritual leader, to have considerable influence over the Algerian community in London; he was confident he could use his authority to prevent any terrorist reprisals if Rachid Ramda were extradited to France. He also said that a decision had been taken in Algeria not to carry out any attacks against the UK. In their second meeting, Abu Qatada and his interlocutors discussed the splits within the GIA caused by objections to Zitouni's leadership. Abu Qatada said he had no wish for Islamists to begin settling scores in London and indicated that he could report on anyone who might harm the UK's interests; an MI5 officer present at the meeting says he sensed that Abu Qatada was close to offering to assist their investigations into Islamist extremism.[3] At the third meeting, Abu Qatada claimed that the Islamists over whom he had any influence posed no threat to the UK and that he did not intend to bite the hand that fed him.

---

1 Omar Chikhi, who was close to Zitouni at the time, has said that he knows nothing of the letter, but admits that it could have been sent without his knowledge.

2 See the ruling of the Special Immigration Appeals Commission (SIAC), which in 2004 considered Abu Qatada's appeal against his imprisonment (SIAC File No. SC/15/2002 of 8 March 2004; see: http://www.siac.tribunals.gov.uk/Documents/outcomes/documents/sc152002qatada.pdf). Abu Qatada was being held under a law allowing the detention of foreigners whom the Home Office considered to pose a threat to British national security or whose presence it deemed to be 'not in the public interest'.

3 Ibid.

Abu Mus'ab has also spoken about his meetings with the British security services in the aftermath of the Paris Metro bombings:[1]

The British made it quite clear to us that we were entitled to all the rights and freedoms enshrined in the British Constitution. At the same time, they had to be sure that the activities of other countries' intelligence services trying to hunt us down in the UK would not lead to bloodshed on British soil. They were also keen to prevent disputes between Islamist groups from spilling over into violence and to stop any dissident Islamist groups from targeting the UK itself. Furthermore, as a member of the European Union and a signatory to international conventions, the British would not allow jihadists to use their territory as a base from which to attack other countries. It was for these reasons that they had us under surveillance and sometimes brought us in for questioning. Meanwhile, the jihadists themselves, who shared many of the same principles and objectives with one another, sought to coordinate their response to the British government through their lectures and publications, all of which were monitored closely by the British security services. There were several points we wanted to make clear to them. One was that we supported the armed struggle underway in our own countries and the wider Islamic world, which was being carried out in accordance with [internationally recognised] human rights: our brothers in Bosnia [for example] were resisting a war of genocide which had been condemned by the United Nations. Those of us who were based in the UK did not support paramilitary operations beyond the borders of our own countries, nor were we involved in any action of this kind in Europe or elsewhere. We called on our fellow jihadists to preserve the safe havens where they had settled in Europe, such as the UK: to do so was manifestly in our own interests. At the same time we explained to our supporters what room for manoeuvre we did have, so as to ensure that they did not overstep its limits. Our activities in the UK were all in accordance with that country's freedom of speech: all we were doing was publishing material and working with the media. On the one hand, we had certain principles, which we would never betray. And yet, on the other hand, we were well aware that we were only living in the UK with the consent of

---

1   Abu Mus'ab al-Suri, *A Message to the British and Europeans*.

the British government, and the moment they no longer wanted us there they could tell us to get out.

Islamists in Uproar

Meanwhile, a steady stream of reports was emerging from Algeria about Djamel Zitouni's increasingly deranged conduct. Instead of concentrating on the fight against the Algerian security forces, his ever more savage acts of violence were dragging the GIA into confrontation with other Islamist groups.

The first really alarming piece of news concerned the murder of Muhammed Saïd and Abderrazak Redjam, the leaders of the branch of the FIS which had merged with the GIA in May 1994. FIS members reported in December 1995 that both men had been killed along with several of their supporters the month before in an ambush laid by 'GIA extremists'.[1] Word of the killings spread among the Islamists like wildfire, partly because of Muhammad Saïd's standing as the leader of Algeria's Djazarist movement. GIA supporters in London, centred mainly around Abu Qatada, were working on a new issue of the *al-Ansar* newsletter at the time. They got in touch with their designated GIA contact in Algeria and asked for an explanation of the reports about the deaths of Saïd and his associates. Several days later the GIA's official answer finally came through: Saïd and Redjam had died as 'martyrs' in an ambush laid by the Algerian army. With huge relief, *al-Ansar*'s editors rushed the explanation into print.[2]

However, no sooner had the newsletter come out than the London cell received a shocking update from the GIA leadership: in fact it was the GIA that had liquidated Saïd and Redjam, because they had been plotting an internal GIA coup aimed at derailing its 'Salafist agenda'. This was an allusion to the fact that both men had remained committed to political pluralism, despite joining the GIA in 1994. The GIA leadership promised

---

1   See the edition of *al-Hayat* published on 11 December 1995. The murders took place south of Algiers, between Bougara and Blida.

2   See the issue of the *al-Ansar* newsletter published on 14 December 1995. Tawil, *al-Haraka al-Islamiyya al-Musallaha fi al-Jaza'ir*, pp. 224–225.

to provide details of interrogations proving the 'guilt' of Saïd and Redjam in conspiring against Zitouni and his supporters, including Antar Zouabri. In the meantime, the GIA leaders demanded the publication of their statement claiming responsibility for the killings. *Al-Ansar*'s editors had little choice but to agree.[1]

The Salafist-Jihadist Divide

The GIA's claim of responsibility for the murders of Saïd and Redjam not only split the movement within Algeria, it also divided the group's supporters abroad. The jihadists, led by the heads of the LIFG and EIJ, together with Abu Mus'ab al-Suri, were doing everything in their power both overtly and in secret to undermine Zitouni's leadership. Yet the Salafists, who consisted mainly of Algerians who had coalesced around Abu Qatada and another Palestinian known as Abu al-Walid, were reluctant to take such a step. Discussions between the two camps continued until June 1996, when the jihadists extracted an agreement from the Salafists to withdraw their support for Zitouni. Within days Abu Qatada, Abu Mus'ab al-Suri, EIJ and the LIFG had all issued statements condemning the GIA leader and his increasingly barbaric conduct.

The debate which took place around this time also divided the jihadists themselves into two main groups: those loyal to Abu Qatada and those sympathetic to Abu Mus'ab al-Suri. Since 1994 the two men had been the main source of legal guidance for the GIA, providing theological justifications for the group's fight against the Islamic Salvation Army, formed in 1994 from the Armed Islamic Movement (MIA), remnants of the MEI and a variety of smaller groups, all of which had refused to merge with the GIA at the time.

The London-based jihadist leaders had waited six months before denouncing Zitouni, hoping to receive the confessions that would prove Muhammed Saïd and Abderrazak Redjam's 'guilt', and which the GIA had promised to send them. The GIA's supporters eventually claimed that they had gone missing en route in the Sahel. Disgusted by this preposterous excuse, the Libyans demanded that the other jihadists take a firm stand

---

1   See issue 131 of the *al-Ansar* newsletter, published on 11 January 1996.

against Zitouni. In 1995 the LIFG's leaders had already informed EIJ, Abu Qatada and Abu Mus'ab al-Suri of their problems with the GIA, after their comrades had gone missing in Algeria. Now the GIA was telling the LIFG's members in London that the three-man delegation (Abdullah al-Libi, Abu 'Asim al-Libi and 'Atiya 'Abd al-Rahman) which came to Algeria to find out what had happened to the missing 15 men, had in fact been killed after running away to join a GIA splinter group led by Mustafa Kartali in the mountains of Larbaâ, south of Algiers.

The LIFG member, Noman Benotman, describes the series of meetings between his group and the other jihadist leaders in London that culminated in their condemnation of Zitouni in June 1996:[1]

> The LIFG had become convinced in early 1996 that the GIA was a corrupt organisation that had been infiltrated by the Algerian intelligence services. Initially we simply stopped expressing support for them in the *al-Fajr* newsletter. We also ceased publishing their statements; every time we'd find an excuse, claiming we'd received them too late and that the newsletter had already gone to print. We took this step for a reason: ever since Zitouni had taken over the GIA leadership we'd suffered at the hands of the group. We'd heard nothing from the fifteen LIFG members who went to Algeria, or the delegation we had sent to find out what had become of them. But that delegation had sent us secret messages when it first arrived in Algeria, warning us about the GIA. Its members had a weak grasp of Islam, they said, and were involved in 'deviant' practices. We should do everything we could to get our men out of the country.

The head of the joint LIFG-al-Qa'ida delegation, the LIFG Shura Council member called Abdullah in these pages, had written from Algeria saying that despite his best efforts he had been unable to see the missing men. Every time he asked the GIA about one of them, he would be told that the man in question was away fighting in another part of the country. The longer this went on, the more suspicious he became, until eventually Abdullah warned the LIFG against getting any more bogged down in the

1   Noman Benotman in interviews with the author in the spring and summer of 2005.

Algerian quagmire.[1] It was the messages from Abdullah which prompted the LIFG to begin preparing to withdraw its support from Zitouni. However, the situation became even more complicated when the Libyan delegation reported that they had had a blazing row with the GIA. The Libyan envoys had demanded their passports back so that they could leave Algeria, but the GIA leaders had refused to return them. No more was heard from the delegation after that. The LIFG was therefore afraid of the potential consequences for its members if it adopted an openly hostile stance towards Zitouni.

Benotman claims to have spoken to the LIFG leader, Abu Abdullah al-Sadiq, the moment the Libyan delegation's messages began arriving:

> I told him that we had to prepare to take a stand against the GIA. Eventually we received a strongly-worded letter from Abdullah saying that no one knew what had become of the fifteen missing men and that they might have been killed. I told al-Sadiq then that he had to tell people in London what had happened, so that we could adopt a collective position [towards the GIA], rather than taking a stand on our own. That was how we came to tell Abu Qatada, Abu Mus'ab, the EIJ representative and the Palestinian, Abu al-Walid, what we intended to do, on condition that they didn't say a word to anyone else.[2] We asked each of them to think things over; in the meantime, as the group most directly affected by what was going on, we undertook to inform the others what was happening in Algeria, based on the coded messages we were receiving from our contacts inside the country. We agreed with the others that none of them would comment on the situation publicly, least of all Abu Mus'ab al-Suri. However, matters were made more difficult when Abdullah [the head of the Libyan delegation in Algeria] and his two companions managed to escape from the place where they were

---

1   It was the senior LIFG figure, 'Abd al-Rahman al-Hattab, and not the man referred to in these pages as Abdullah, who had arranged for the fifteen LIFG members to go to Algeria. Al-Hattab himself spent time there supervising the deployment of his comrades to various GIA bases. He then returned to Sudan and later fought against the security services in Libya, before being killed in 1998.

2   The EIJ representative, who currently lives in Europe, shall remain anonymous.

being held by Hassan Hattab.[1] We then heard that the GIA thought
it had killed them inadvertently in an attack on Mustafa Kartali's
group [a splinter group from the GIA] in Larbaâ.

However, when it transpired that the three Libyans were actually still alive,
the LIFG stepped up its efforts to take a stand against the GIA. 'Several
meetings were held in the course of a few days,' says Benotman:

> One of them was a plenary session, attended by about fifteen people,
> but the main meetings were always between five individuals: 'Abd al-
> Rahman al-Misri,[2] Abu al-Walid, Abu Mus'ab, Abu Qatada and me.
> Later we were joined by Abu al-Mundhir [al-Sa'idi], on his return
> from Saudi Arabia. These gatherings were the scene of detailed
> discussions of Islamic law. Some of those present thought that the
> GIA's conduct did not warrant withdrawing our support from the
> group. They pointed out that it had united most other [Algerian]
> groups under its banner and that it was the only faction capable of
> taking on the Algerian regime. However, others rejected this view,
> arguing that what had happened to the Libyans and others, coupled
> with the GIA's increasing fanaticism under Zitouni, were sufficient
> grounds for sidelining the group's current leadership. It became clear
> during these discussions that Abu al-Walid was largely sympathetic
> to the GIA's views. Abu al-Walid divided Algerian society into three
> categories. On the one hand were the mujahidin, whom he regarded
> as pious and pure. On the other was the Algerian government,
> which he condemned as infidel. And in the middle there was a
> third category, consisting of collaborators with the government,
> civil servants and the rest of Algerian society. In Abu al-Walid's
> view, when a jihadist group emerged and began fighting, everyone
> in the third category would side with either the government or
> the mujahidin. The jihadists' polarising effect would thus cause
> the middle class to disappear altogether. But Abu Mus'ab al-Suri
> thought Abu al-Walid was just posturing to enhance his standing in
> the Algerian community, particularly once Abu Qatada withdrew
> his support for Zitouni's leadership.

---

1   At this time Hassan Hattab was the GIA's emir of what the group called the
    'second zone' or Kabylie in northern Algeria.
2   The man referred to here as 'Abd al-Rahman al-Misri is subject to legal
    proceedings in Europe and shall therefore remain anonymous.

According to Benotman, these meetings also saw some heated arguments between Abu Mus'ab and Abu Qatada: eventually it became difficult to persuade them to sit in the same room together. However, the GIA's attitude took even Abu Qatada by surprise. 'He had known many of the fifteen Libyans [who had disappeared in Algeria] since the days of the Afghan jihad; some of them had even studied under him. And in the past Abu Qatada had trusted the Algerians in London too. But when they told him that the GIA regarded the Libyans as having "gone astray" in Islamic terms, he did not believe them: he knew the LIFG weren't heretics.'

Benotman describes the meeting in London at which the jihadists discussed withdrawing their support from Zitouni:

> We met to talk about taking a joint decision and to draft our respective statements. A delegation went to see Abu Qatada to persuade him to issue one as well. Abu Mus'ab stayed away from the meeting, because he wasn't on speaking terms with Abu Qatada; he also wanted to issue his statement a day earlier than everyone else. However, the others refused to accept this and insisted that the statements all come out at the same time, which in the event is what happened. Four statements were issued in the name of the LIFG, EIJ, Abu Qatada and Abu Mus'ab. At the previous meeting, Abu al-Walid had also agreed to withdraw his support from the GIA, but the next day he changed his mind.[1] He argued that he was not sufficiently well known as a GIA supporter, unlike Abu Qatada and Abu Mus'ab, and that he did not represent any particular group such as the LIFG or EIJ. Many Algerians, including people who also knew the missing Libyans, were influenced by the position which Abu Qatada took. But it was hard for them to abandon the group which they had supported, and for which they had paid such a heavy price.

---

1   Abu Mus'ab al-Suri claims that he went to see Abu al-Walid the day after the four statements were published. 'Abu al-Walid stood by his front door and told me, "You've done more than just release some statements: you've caused a catastrophe." Then I saw all the visitors he had and I realised what was going on. He had become a spiritual leader for the pro-GIA Algerians.' See Abu Mus'ab al-Suri's statement entitled *Mukhtasar Shihadati 'ala al-Jihad fi al-Jaza'ir* ('A Summary of My Account of the Jihad in Algeria'). The author retains a copy of the 75-page Arabic document, which is dated 1 June 2004.

Operation Challenge

From then on the jihadists' base in London became less and less significant. At the same time, a new haven was opening up to them in Afghanistan, as the Taliban extended their control over the country. Within months of the jihadists' disownment of Zitouni and the closure of the *al-Ansar* newsletter, a new Egyptian Islamist known as Abu Hamza al-Misri was seeking to rally the London-based Algerians who remained loyal to the GIA. He provided them with an important platform by allowing them to operate from his mosque in Finsbury Park in north London. The Algerians soon turned it into a stronghold of their own and used it as a base to resume publication of *al-Ansar*, this time under the supervision of Abu Hamza himself. However, the experiment did not last long. In early 1998 Antar Zouabri, Zitouni's successor as leader of the GIA, issued a statement condemning the entire population of Algeria as infidels; it was a decision which Abu Hamza had been assured would never be taken when he agreed to back the GIA and to publish its statements.[1]

Things continued in much the same vein until September 1998, when the British security services rounded up numerous Islamists in what was known as 'Operation Challenge'. The arrests, which took place in the wake of the bombing of the US embassies in Nairobi and Dar es Salaam the previous month, included some of the most prominent activists suspected of having links to EIJ and al-Qa'ida.[2] In London, for so long a 'den' where the jihadists had felt secure, the British lion was beginning to bare its fangs.

---

1 Abu Hamza told the author this himself. Meanwhile Abu al-Walid's supporters tried to persuade him to take Abu Qatada's place. However, when Abu Hamza withdrew his backing from the GIA, Abu al-Walid did likewise and moved to Afghanistan.

2 The Islamists arrested in the UK in late 1998 included Khalid al-Fawwaz, Osama bin Laden's representative in London, and two leading EIJ members called 'Adil 'Abd al-Majid 'Abd al-Bari and Ibrahim 'Aydarus.

8

Setbacks: Jihad in Decline

The year 1997 saw the collapse of the jihadists' plans across North Africa as they failed to bring down Gaddafi's regime, the military junta in Algeria or Egypt's 'last pharaoh', Hosni Mubarak. The Islamists' only option was to retreat and do some soul-searching, in the hope of learning from their mistakes and trying again at a later date. Yet even here the different nationalities differed in their approaches. The Algerians sought to regroup inside their country, where they founded a new organisation on the ruins of the GIA, which they called the Salafist Group for Preaching and Combat. The Libyans chose to reorganise in Afghanistan, the original birthplace of their faction, while the Egyptians split between two divergent paths. On the one hand, EIJ also withdrew to Afghanistan to lick its wounds, while remaining more determined than ever to bring down the Egyptian regime through violent jihad. In contrast, al-Gama'a al-Islamiyya completely reassessed its own ideology, concluding that it had been wrong to take up arms against the government and announcing a comprehensive ceasefire.

Algeria

It was in Algeria that it first became clear that the jihadists were running into trouble. The GIA reached the zenith of its power in early 1995, but soon squandered its gains, suffering a series of reversals under Djamel Zitouni's leadership. Before taking up the reins of the GIA, Zitouni had worked as a butcher in the suburbs of Algiers: an omen, perhaps, of the direction in which he would take the group. He had also taken part in various attacks on the Algerian security forces, demonstrating his 'courage' through his willingness to kill.

Two operations in 1993 and 1994 allowed Zitouni to demonstrate his eligibility for the GIA leadership. One was an attack on a French embassy compound in Algiers, while the other involved an assault on some coastguards. Zitouni's experience in the GIA had certainly prepared him for a violent role: under Cherif Gousmi he had headed the death squad known as the Green Battalion or *al-Katiba al-Khadra'*. Made up of the GIA's best trained, most ruthless cadres, the battalion guarded the GIA emir and was the unit from which his successor was traditionally chosen. It was therefore natural that Zitouni should aspire to take over from Cherif Gousmi on the latter's death in September 1994.

The more moderate Djazarist members of the group sought to appoint one of their own number, Mahfoud Tadjine, at least as a provisional leader until a permanent replacement could be chosen. But Zitouni would not hear of it. 'Zitouni became emir through a stitch-up,' says Ali Benhadjar, the leader of a GIA splinter group called the Islamic League for Preaching and Jihad:[1]

> He wasn't a senior member of the GIA or even one of its leading activists. He made his name suddenly, through two operations: one against the French embassy [housing complex] in Aïn Allah and the other against some coastguards, when he seized a *Dushka* machine gun.[2] Word soon got around within the GIA that it was Zitouni who was responsible [for the coastguard attack], while the media reported that he had killed some policemen in the assault on the embassy. That's why his name came up [as a possible GIA leader] when Gousmi was killed. But some of the GIA's Shura Council members were up in the mountains at the time; they put forward Mahfoud Tadjine's name as an acting emir until the entire

---

1   Ali Benhadjar in an interview with the author conducted in Médéa, south of Algiers, in March 2002. His group, the Islamic League for Preaching and Jihad, is known by its French acronym LIDD. He claimed to have heard this account of Zitouni's selection as GIA emir from the latter's aide, Bachir Turkman. Bachir was later killed, possibly by Zitouni himself.
2   In August 1994 an attack took place on a French embassy housing complex in the Aïn Allah suburb of Algiers; three French paramilitary gendarmes and two consular officials were killed. The media attributed this attack to Zitouni.

council could meet and either confirm his appointment or select someone else. However, Zitouni's supporters objected and came out in force, very nearly sparking a conflict up in the mountains. They said that they refused to accept Tadjine as their emir, because he was a Djazarist and a member of the Movement for the Renewal of Civilisation.[1] Other people located at the same base sided with them, and together they managed to impose Zitouni as their choice of emir. [Abu Bakr] Zerfaoui [a leading member of the GIA at the time] was widely respected for his grasp of Islamic law; he asked how people with no such knowledge themselves could choose an emir, when they were unqualified to do so. Zitouni replied that he and his supporters had no need for such experts; when they wanted their opinion, they would ask for it. 'So you don't need theologians on the very council which elects the emir?' asked Zerfaoui. 'That sounds to me like secularism.' Zitouni became the GIA emir through a conspiracy.

It was under Zitouni's leadership that the GIA began its rapid descent into the abyss. This was the result of several factors, the most important of which was undoubtedly his condemnation of whole swathes of Algerian society as unbelievers. At the same time, Zitouni also denounced many of his fellow Islamists for what he saw as their lack of commitment to Salafist ideology. Meanwhile, the GIA had been penetrated by the Algerian security services, which manipulated the group's leaders and sowed suspicion among them. But most of the blame for the GIA's collapse must go to Zitouni himself. He killed the FIS leaders who had pledged allegiance to his predecessor, Cherif Gousmi, and then turned on the Libyan Afghan veterans who had come to Algeria to fight alongside the GIA. As if this were not enough, Zitouni also brought France into the conflict by orchestrating the Paris Metro bombings of 1995 and early 1996. These sudden and dramatic shifts in policy were to split the ranks of the GIA and drive some of its cadres into open revolt against Zitouni's leadership.

Yet there had been warning signs of Zitouni's fanatical tendencies back in Cherif Gousmi's time, as Ali Benhadjar admits:

---

1   The Mouvement pour le Renouveau Civilisationnel was founded by the Algerian intellectual, Malek Bennabi (1905–1973), who sought to reconcile Algerian nationalism with Islamism. His ideas had a profound influence on the FIS.

I went to the mountains around Cheria [in northeastern Algeria] and met the emir [Cherif Gousmi]. This was in 1994, before the merger [with the FIS and the MEI] and before Zitouni took over the leadership. I asked him about the constant stream of statements coming out of the GIA and the way that it was fighting all over the country simultaneously: was this a well planned way to go about a war? I said I thought we were opening up new fronts in the conflict unnecessarily. I also asked him about the GIA's statements concerning things like Algeria's schools and Sonatrach.[1] At the time we felt that these statements were taking us in new directions where no sensible person would have gone. We believed they were part of a plan to undermine and splinter the GIA, dissipating its energies by involving it in too many things at once and eventually turning the whole population against it.

The Army Regains the Initiative

The principal beneficiary of the splits within the GIA was the Algerian government. The army launched a campaign to seize back the initiative that it had lost when the conflict broke out in 1992, carrying out large-scale attacks aimed at 'cleansing' the mountains of central Algeria. It was these areas, particularly to the south and west of the capital, which the GIA regarded as 'liberated' territory, and where its leaders based themselves.[2]

By 1996 Zitouni and his cohorts had lost the battle. However, they did not immediately recognise the signs of their own defeat and continued to behave as if the GIA were still Algeria's pre-eminent paramilitary group. This status, Zitouni believed, gave the GIA's emir the right to attack anyone

---

1   On 6 August 1994 the GIA announced that teachers and pupils were 'strictly forbidden' to attend schools and that those who ignored the warning would be subject to 'dissuasive' sanctions. According to Algerian government figures, in 1994 some 142 teachers were murdered, and 813 schools and 26 vocational training centres were ransacked or destroyed throughout the country. Sonatrach was the Algerian national petrochemicals company, whose staff and installations the GIA also threatened to attack.

2   November 1995 saw the first presidential election in Algeria since Chadli Bendjedid stepped down in early 1992. The polls, which were won by General Liamine Zéroual, received a high public turnout and marked a significant psychological turning-point in Algerian politics.

who dared disobey him. Yet everything Zitouni did turned more and more people against him, until eventually the GIA became isolated and unable to function, least of all in areas controlled by GIA splinter groups. In July 1996 Zitouni met a fitting end, gunned down in an ambush laid by breakaway members of the GIA who did not even realise who he was. 'Zitouni's killing was not premeditated,' says Ali Benhadjar, who controlled the area where Zitouni died:

> When we [Benhadjar and his sympathisers] rebelled and left the GIA, it was *they* who declared war on *us*. We simply disassociated ourselves from the GIA's actions. But they began targeting our bases in the mountains around Médéa, forcing us to counter-attack. We had to defend ourselves, even if that meant going after them on their own territory just as they had attacked us on ours. They used to ambush us when we were en route to our bases, so we began doing the same to them, fighting them on their own ground. Otherwise we'd have ended up surrounded. That was how we came to be laying an ambush for the GIA when Zitouni happened to come along. We didn't realise this at the time; my men killed him along with a few other people, then stripped the bodies of their weapons and identity documents. It was only when we looked at their papers that we saw they weren't just ordinary fighters. That night we heard on the radio that Zitouni and two of his aides had been killed in the area, and we realised we'd got him.[1]

Zitouni's death only served to push the GIA towards ever greater excesses. He was succeeded by Antar Zouabri, commander of the Green Battalion; and no sooner had he taken over the helm of the GIA than he began to surpass his predecessor's bloodstained record.[2] It was under Zouabri that the GIA declared the entire Algerian people infidels, paving the way for acts of wholesale carnage in which thousands of ordinary civilians died in 1997 and 1998.[3]

---

1 Ali Benhadjar in an interview with the author in Algeria in 2002.
2 Antar Zouabri, also known as Abou Talha, was emir of the GIA from 1996 until February 2002, when he was killed by the Algerian security forces in Boufarik, south of Algiers. He was succeeded by Rachid Oukali, also known as Rachid Abou Tourab.
3 The most horrific massacres in Algeria took place between 1997 and 1998. For

Before setting upon the population at large, Zouabri first saw to
Zitouni's unfinished business with the Libyan Afghan veterans. They
had helped deprive the GIA of the backing of London-based jihadists, and
now they had to pay the price. One of the Libyan veterans who fought
alongside the GIA and later fell out with Zitouni was Abu 'Ujayla al-Rayis,
also known as Sakhr al-Libi; the former LIFG member, Noman Benotman,
explains what happened to him:

> When Cherif Gousmi was head of the GIA, the group's military
> leader was Abou Ali al-Afghani, who had spent time in Kandahar.
> He was killed early on in the Algerian jihad, leaving behind a widow
> and children. While Sakhr al-Libi was staying with the GIA, he
> received $1,000 [from someone outside Algeria]; he took $100
> or $200 for himself and gave the rest to Abou Ali al-Afghani's
> brother to pass on to Abou Ali's family. However, Abou Ali's brother
> reported this to Zouabri, prompting the GIA leaders to speculate
> that Sakhr was an agent, trying to bribe members of the GIA. They
> thought it was an attempt to penetrate the group. They fetched Sakhr
> and demanded that he confess to being an agent, even though he
> had been fighting alongside the GIA and had enjoyed the respect
> of its members since Gousmi's time.[1] This incident sparked a row
> among GIA members [over whether Sakhr was an agent]. Zouabri
> was behind it all ... They subjected him to the most horrific torture,
> even ripping out a metal rod that had been implanted in his hand
> [in an earlier surgical operation to treat a war wound]. What they
> wanted was revenge on the LIFG.[2]

---

a list of attacks and the numbers of victims see: http://www.algeria-watch.de/
mrv/2002/bilan_massacres.htm. The massacres provoked suspicion about the
involvement of the Algerian security services, either directly or indirectly, through
manipulating the extremist groups or turning a blind eye to their activities. The
Algerian government has repeatedly denied any such connection.

1 Noman Benotman maintains that the GIA leader, Cherif Gousmi, gave Sakhr
   al-Libi a pistol as a mark of his esteem.
2 Noman Benotman in interviews with the author in the spring and summer of
   2005. Benotman claimed to have heard the account of Sakhr's death from Abou
   Khaled al-Djazairi, a former leading member of the GIA.

The LIFG's official obituary for Sakhr differs somewhat from Benotman's account of his death. 'After a long journey of preaching and jihad,' runs the rather florid tribute:

> which took him from Libya to Afghanistan and then on to Algeria, Sakhr had a date with martyrdom, albeit not perhaps in the form which he had expected. When signs of the GIA's deviance began to emerge, Sakhr sought permission from the group's emir to travel to the east of the country, where he knew certain good and honest mujahidin. Such was Sakhr's standing that the emir granted his request. However, he received news en route that the emir [Zitouni] had been killed and that they [the GIA] had pledged allegiance to Zouabri as the new emir. Sakhr spoke to some of his trusted associates about this, saying that Zouabri was ignorant, corrupt and unfit to lead the group. Certain people repeated his remarks to Zouabri, who summoned him back. On his return they tortured him, trying to force him to say things that they could use to tarnish his reputation, and then they murdered him.[1]

Antar Zouabri himself spoke about his differences with the LIFG in the first interview that he gave as GIA leader, some two months after taking over from Zitouni. He presented the disagreement as a difference of opinion over theological matters, not a clash of personalities, and made no mention of Sakhr al-Libi.[2] 'The LIFG sent a delegation to see us. They met the GIA's [then] emir, Abou Abderrahmane Amine [Zitouni], as well as the group's legal committee. As they discussed various issues, it became clear that the LIFG was Salafist only on paper; in practice there was nothing remotely Salafist about it.'

The Strategy of the GIA's Opponents

As the GIA tore itself apart, other jihadist groups in Algeria were setting out on markedly different paths. The AIS, together with various other factions that had broken away from Zitouni's leadership, entered into

---

1 From the LIFG's obituary of Sakhr, of which the author possesses a copy, downloaded from the Libyan group's official website (no longer active).
2 Tawil, *Al-Haraka al-Islamiyya al-Musallaha fi al-Jaza'ir*, pp. 264–5.

negotiations with the Algerian regime. Meanwhile, other groups sought to unite in a new alliance that would remain true to the GIA's original manifesto.[1]

Senior members of the AIS, led by Madani Mezrag, secretly made contact with the Algerian authorities. A series of meetings followed with a high-ranking Algerian intelligence officer in the AIS stronghold of Jijel in the east of the country.[2] These difficult and complex talks went on for months, though the appalling carnage taking place in Algeria at the time no doubt spurred on both sides to reach an agreement. In a three-page communiqué issued in September 1997, Mezrag announced the total cessation of AIS operations. The group's aim, he said, was to pave the way to a 'just solution' to the conflict in Algeria, while protecting the country from those seeking to harm it. The AIS also hoped 'to expose the enemy behind these horrible crimes and isolate the criminal, extremist and perverted remnants of the GIA and the enemies of Algeria and Islam who back them.' With the assistance of the Algerian security services, Merzag succeeded in attracting other GIA splinter groups to his peace initiative, such as Ali Benhadjar's faction in Médéa and Mustafa Kartali's group based in Larbaâ. The Algerian authorities reciprocated by releasing several leaders of the FIS, the AIS's political wing, or placing them under house arrest instead of keeping them in prison.[3]

Meanwhile, other jihadists who had abandoned the GIA in Zitouni's time were seeking to join ranks and seize control of the GIA from Zouabri. Foremost among them was Hassan Hattab, until recently the GIA's commander of what it called Algeria's 'second zone', who had refused to accept Zouabri as Zitouni's successor. Hattab, from a family of radical jihadists,[4] joined ranks with other GIA commanders in eastern Algeria,

1   The GIA consistently rejected any compromise with the Algerian regime; its slogan was 'No dialogue, no truce and no reconciliation'.
2   The architect of the negotiations with the AIS was Major General Smaïn Lamari, then head of the Directorate of Internal Security within Algeria's military intelligence service, the Département du Renseignement et de la Sécurité.
3   The FIS leaders kept under house arrest rather than in prison included Abbasi Madani and Abdelkader Hachani. The latter was assassinated in 1999.
4   Hassan Hattab's older brother, Mouloud, was involved in Mustafa Bouyali's Mouvement Islamique Armé in the 1980s. In 1992 he joined the Movement for

including Amari Saïfi, Nabil Sahraoui and Abdelmadjid Dishu.[1] At first the men continued to operate under the name GIA, seeking to rectify the group's strategy by stressing that they would not target civilians. But it was futile trying to distinguish themselves from Zouabri while continuing to use the same name as his group. When he claimed responsibility in the name of the GIA for the appalling massacres of 1997 and 1998, his rivals knew that they had to do more to set themselves apart. Their response was to create a new organisation: the Salafist Group for Preaching and Combat (GSPC).

Libya: The LIFG's Dilemma

The LIFG's situation in Libya was no easier than that of its Algerian counterparts. From 1996 the group came under intense pressure at every level. In Algeria, the GIA had killed the fighters whom the LIFG had sent to prepare for an advance on Libya. In Sudan, where the LIFG had based itself since the early 1990s, the regime had tired of the plots which its jihadist guests kept hatching against their own governments. Unable to withstand the international pressure which these conspiracies inevitably provoked, the Sudanese finally asked the LIFG to leave or face extradition to Libya. As if all this were not enough, in Libya the Benghazi Hospital incident and the subsequent siege of the LIFG's hideout on the

---

an Islamic State (MEI) founded by Abdelkader Chebouti; two years later he was killed by the Algerian security forces. Hassan Hattab's brother, Abdelkader, belonged to an Islamist paramilitary group on the outskirts of Algiers; he was killed by the security forces in 1998. Meanwhile, Hassan's brother, Toufik, was accused of involvement in the assassination of the Algerian former prime minister, Kasdi Merbah, in 1993. Toufik was killed by the security forces in 1994.

1   Amari Saïfi was nicknamed Abderrazak 'el Para', meaning 'the paratrooper'. He was captured by Chadian rebels in 2004 and handed over to the Algerian authorities later that year. Abdelmadjid Dishu, also known as Abou Moussab Abdelmadjid, had a reputation for his knowledge of Islamic law; he was killed in 1999, probably by fellow Islamists. Nabil Sahraoui, also known as Abou Ibrahim Mustapha, was involved in the conflict in Algeria from 1992. In 2003 he assumed the leadership of the GSPC, only to be killed by the Algerian security forces the following year.

outskirts of the city had forced the group into the open in June 1995. The LIFG was well aware that it was not yet ready for a showdown with the security forces. However, once convinced that it had been discovered by the authorities, there seemed little to be gained from remaining a clandestine organisation.

The LIFG soon unleashed a series of attacks on the Libyan security forces around the country. Of these, the most significant were four clashes which took place in the mountains near Darnah in eastern Libya, where hundreds of Afghan veterans held out until they were defeated by a combination of aerial bombardment and thousands of army reinforcements. The Libyan armed forces' numerical superiority and more sophisticated weaponry made it inevitable that they would prevail; all the Islamists could hope for was to escape with some of their assets still intact. Following their most serious defeat at Wadi al-Injil, twenty kilometres west of Darnah, the LIFG made what it called a 'tactical withdrawal', abandoning the area to Libyan regular forces.[1]

Many LIFG members had thought all along that their conflict with the security forces was weighted hopelessly against them. However, some LIFG leaders believed they had sufficient men to seize control of certain parts of the country and declare them 'liberated territory', from which they could launch sorties into other areas. The LIFG leadership considered detailed proposals for occupying parts of the Libyan desert in this way, but eventually called off the plan, concluding that it would have been suicidal: with few places to hide, their fighters could all too easily have been surrounded and then destroyed by the Libyan air force.[2]

According to Noman Benotman, opinion within the LIFG was divided along two lines. One camp thought that since the regime had discovered so many of the LIFG's members, supporters and hiding places, the group's remaining men overseas had a duty to return to Libya and join the armed struggle. Others believed this would be self-destructive, giving the security forces the chance to finish off the LIFG altogether. Moreover, even if all the LIFG's fighters abroad were able to return home, the group's members

---

1 See the LIFG's statement no. 4, issued on 25 March 1996.
2 Noman Benotman in interviews with the author in the summer and autumn of 2005.

inside Libya could never accommodate them. At a meeting of LIFG leaders in Khartoum, advocates of the former view put forward a battle plan. They proposed infiltrating Libya via its border with either Chad or Sudan and then 'liberating' the oasis town of al-Kufra in the southeast of the country; this would then serve as a launch pad from which to take control of the rest of Libya. Benotman himself believes that the LIFG could have carried out the al-Kufra plan; the problem would have been how to defend the town once it had been taken, particularly if the Libyan air force were called in. When it came to a vote on the proposal, the LIFG leaders were evenly split. Four were in favour of dispatching all the LIFG's fighters to Libya and launching attacks from the south; the other four wanted to instruct their members in the country to withdraw, doing everything possible to avoid confrontation with the security forces: anyone who disobeyed these orders should be expelled from the group. This was Benotman's preferred option, while the LIFG's emir inside Libya, 'Abd al-Rahman al-Hattab, headed the group's more belligerent leaders. However, the LIFG's commander-in-chief, Abu 'Abdallah al-Sadiq, held the deciding vote, and cast it against carrying out the plan of attack.[1]

Targeting Gaddafi

In early 1996 the LIFG began to look beyond its hit-and-run attacks on the Libyan security services and devise a strategy for getting rid of Colonel Gaddafi himself.[2] Days before the fighting at Wadi al-Injil, an LIFG cell carried out an assassination attempt against the Libyan head of state in the coastal city of Sirte. Although the attack failed, it had momentous consequences. To the acute embarrassment of the British government it emerged that the UK's intelligence services had been in contact with people

---

1   Noman Benotman in interviews with the author in the spring and summer of 2005 and the summer of 2006. Abu al-Mundhir al-Sa'idi, the LIFG's head of Islamic law, did not attend the vote.

2   The LIFG spokesman, Omar Rashed, has said that the group did not expect Gaddafi's death to bring down his regime. However, it hoped to exploit the ensuing power struggle within the government to advance its Islamist agenda. See: http://www.almuqatila.com/interviews/rashidfajrhi.htm. The website is defunct now, but the interview is in the author's collection.

allegedly plotting to murder the Libyan leader. The LIFG was even more embarrassed by claims that these conspirators were members of the group and that they had been paid by the British. Amid the flurry of allegations and innuendo, the truth of what really happened is not easy to discern.

On 6 March 1996 the LIFG released a statement announcing that three of its members had been killed following an unsuccessful attempt to assassinate Colonel Gaddafi in Sirte. Gaddafi had been delayed en route to an official visit, the statement explained; the LIFG members had therefore called off the operation, but had run into the security forces as they left the scene. In the ensuing firefight, people on both sides had been killed.[1] The leader of the would-be assassins, a veteran of the Afghan jihad called 'Abd al-Muhaymin, had managed to escape the scene. The LIFG's claim of responsibility for the assassination attempt would later be linked to another plot, about which British intelligence had apparently known since 1995.[2] The former MI5 officer, David Shayler, told the press that his country had not only been aware of a plan to murder Gaddafi, it had actually funded the conspirators using taxpayers' money.[3] Shayler did not name the LIFG as the group which his counterparts in MI6 had paid to kill the colonel in early 1996. However, he did indicate that 'Islamist extremists' had been involved. When the LIFG claimed responsibility for the Sirte operation, the press naturally concluded that the LIFG was the group in question, particularly given that several of its leaders were based in London at the time.[4] However, the LIFG insisted that its operation to

1   The LIFG members killed by the Libyan security forces included Fathi al-Qat'ani, Muhammad al-Fituri and Anwar al-Jami'i.

2   Anglo-Libyan relations had yet to recover from their serious deterioration in the mid- to late 1980s. The causes included the murder of the police officer, WPC Yvonne Fletcher, outside the Libyan embassy in London in 1984; Tripoli's support for the Provisional IRA; British assistance to the US aircraft which attacked Libya in 1986; and the bombing of Pan Am Flight 103 over Lockerbie in Scotland in 1988, in which 270 people died.

3   David Shayler made his allegations in 1998, almost two years after leaving the British Security Service (MI5). He was subsequently convicted of breaching the Official Secrets Act and sentenced to a short period of imprisonment. His claims about the plot to assassinate Gaddafi were not examined during his trial.

4   The most senior LIFG figure based in London at this time was the group's head of Islamic law, Abu al-Mundhir al-Sa'idi.

kill the Libyan leader had nothing to do with the reported plot linked to British intelligence.[1]

The Collapse of the Libyan Jihad

Whether or not the British were involved in the plot to kill Gaddafi, the years 1996 and 1997 were disastrous for the LIFG. In that short period the Libyan security services managed to dismantle most of the group's cells and liquidate many of its senior leaders. In July 1996, the security forces rounded up numerous suspected Islamists throughout Libya. They then carried out a large-scale aerial bombardment of the LIFG's strongholds in eastern Libya, to pave the way for regaining control. Sensing that it was nearing defeat, the LIFG ordered its members to avoid armed clashes with the regime. In October 1996 the group issued a statement saying that its current policy was not to escalate the military situation. 'Sometimes certain difficulties prevent operations from being carried out,' the statement noted coyly, in an attempt to present its move as a short-term strategic decision.[2]

'Until mid-1996 the LIFG was trying to protect its members inside Libya,' explains Noman Benotman. 'When it became clear that the regime was on the front foot, the LIFG decided to try to save as many of its fighters as it could. It ordered all its senior members to leave the country immediately or face expulsion from the group. To those who remained in Libya, it issued instructions not to go on the offensive: they were only to defend themselves if they came under attack by the regime.'[3] Nonetheless, the LIFG continued its attempts to target Colonel Gaddafi, in the hope that by removing him it might bring down the regime as a whole. In November 1996 an LIFG member threw a hand grenade at Gaddafi in the town of Brak in central Libya, but the grenade failed to detonate and the Libyan leader was unharmed.

Although the LIFG continued to engage in intermittent skirmishes

---

1 See statement No. 15, dated 3 December 1999.

2 From an interview conducted by the international Arabic newspaper, *al-Hayat*, with LIFG spokesman, Abu Bakr al-Sharif, and published on the LIFG website in October 1996. See issue 12292 of *al-Hayat*, dated 21 October 1996.

3 Noman Benotman in an interview with the author in London in the summer of 2005.

with the regime, its activity was diminishing day by day as it came under sustained attack by the Libyan security forces. In October 1997 the group suffered a serious setback with the death of Salah Fathi bin Sulayman, its most senior field commander in Libya.[1] In the summer of the following year, the security forces destroyed the remnants of the LIFG in eastern Libya. The group had no choice but to suspend operations altogether, withdraw to reflect on its mistakes and find a new base for its leaders. They initially headed to Istanbul, where the LIFG opened a bureau and held a meeting of its Shura Council in 1998. Those present at the meeting discussed the group's recent setbacks, but were unable to agree to a formal end to hostilities. According to Benotman it was the LIFG's military chief, known as al-Zubayr, who was most insistent on calling a halt to its operations inside Libya:[2]

> Based on the information that he had at the time, al-Zubayr demanded at the 1998 Shura Council meeting that the LIFG cease fighting in Libya. The effects on the group of the conflict with the regime were becoming clear, and our room for manoeuvre was shrinking alarmingly. He argued that to go on fighting would only lead to more arrests and more deaths, losses that could not be justified. There had to be an immediate cessation of operations. I recall him saying, 'If the aim is to wage jihad, we don't necessarily have to fight in Libya: anyone who still wants to fight and seek martyrdom should go to Chechnya.'[3] Nonetheless, the LIFG did not declare a formal ceasefire until 2000, by which time the group's leaders had relocated to Taliban-controlled Kabul.[4]

1   In October 1997 the LIFG announced that Salah Fathi bin Sulayman, one of its founders and a member of the group's Shura Council, had been killed along with three other LIFG members on 23 September 1997 near Darnah in eastern Libya.

2   The real name of the LIFG military commander known as al-Zubayr was Mustafa Qunayfidh.

3   In 1999 al-Zubayr was extradited from Turkey to Libya, where he was still imprisoned at the time of writing.

4   Noman Benotman in an interview with the author in 2006. Benotman says that in 2000 the LIFG Shura Council decided unanimously to halt paramilitary activity in Libya for three years, after which they would decide whether to extend the ceasefire.

Egypt: Defeat and Division

The jihadists' experience in Libya and Algeria was paralleled by events in Egypt during the same period. EIJ had observed a ceasefire since 1995, as a result of the repeated blows it had suffered at the hands of the country's security services.[1] However, al-Gama'a al-Islamiyya continued its attacks, particularly against the Egyptian tourist industry. In 1996 the group carried out its largest operation to date, attacking a group of tourists at the Europa Hotel near the pyramids of Giza, killing eighteen people. The foreigners it had mistaken for Israeli tourists were in fact Greek pensioners: a grave error, even by the group's own standards.[2]

Meanwhile, from behind bars the heads of al-Gama'a al-Islamiyya, led by Karam Zuhdi and Najih Ibrahim, were completely rethinking the theological basis of their armed struggle. It was this process of revision which led the group's leaders to call a unilateral ceasefire in July 1997.[3] However, only four months later a massacre in Luxor threatened to split the group in two, with one wing committed to the leadership's non-violence initiative and the other intent on continuing attacks. On 17 November 1997, six of the group's militants disguised as members of the security forces headed to the Temple of Hatshepsut at Deir el-Bahri, on the opposite bank of the Nile from the town of Luxor. Stabbing and shooting indiscriminately, the men killed a total of fifty-eight foreign tourists and four Egyptians.[4] All six assailants were themselves killed by the security forces in the aftermath of the attack.

The repercussions of the atrocity were felt not only in Egypt's tourist industry, on which millions of Egyptians depend for their livelihoods; it

---

1 In mid-1995 EIJ plotted to attack tourists in Cairo's Khan al-Khalili Bazaar, the only operation the group is known to have attempted in Egypt that year. Two of the conspirators, Ahmad Ibrahim al-Sayyid al-Najjar and 'Adil al-Sudani, were later executed for their part in the conspiracy.

2 The attack on the Europa Hotel near Cairo took place on 18 April 1996.

3 Al-Gama'a al-Islamiyya renounced violence in a dramatic fashion during the trial of some of its members in July 1997, when one of the accused suddenly read out a prepared statement. For details in Arabic of the group's retraction of its violent ideology see: http://www.murajaat.com/trajuaat_akra.php.

4 The Egyptians killed in the Luxor massacre included three police officers and a tourist guide.

also threatened to sabotage the non-violence initiative launched by the leaders of al-Gama'a al-Islamiyya earlier in the year. Rifa'i Taha, head of the group's Shura Council overseas, issued a statement claiming responsibility for the Luxor attack, while the group's media spokesman, Usama Rushdi, openly condemned it. In what became a very public row between the two men, Usama Rushdi was backed by the group's leaders imprisoned in Egypt.[1] Meanwhile, Rifa'i Taha sought the support of its blind emir, Omar Abdel Rahman, who remained incarcerated in the United States. Omar's legal adviser, an Egyptian activist called Ahmad 'Abd al-Sattar, managed to smuggle in Taha's messages to him using Omar's American lawyer, Lynne Stewart. Omar Abdel Rahman initially backed Rifa'i Taha and issued a statement which was seen as retracting his support for the group's leaders imprisoned in Egypt. However, such was his influence that these same leaders promptly contacted him themselves to persuade him not to withdraw his support for their ceasefire.[2]

Ultimately Rifa'i Taha was more committed to violent jihad than to his status within al-Gama'a al-Islamiyya.[3] Still refusing to accept the leadership's peace strategy, he handed over responsibility for the Shura Council to Mustafa Hamza, who had led the 1995 assassination attempt against Hosni Mubarak in Addis Ababa. In so doing, Rifa'i Taha became increasingly marginalised within al-Gama'a al-Islamiyya, a process that was sealed when the group's leadership outside Egypt endorsed the non-violence initiative on 28 March 1999. Facts on the ground had already shown that this power struggle had been resolved in favour of the group's veteran leaders: in 1998

---

1   At this time Usama Rushdi was living in the Netherlands; he subsequently moved to the UK. Rifa'i Taha was then based in Iran.

2   In 2002 Umar 'Abd al-Rahman's lawyer, Lynne Stewart, his legal adviser, Ahmad 'Abd al-Sattar, and an interpreter called Muhammad Yusri were charged in connection with facilitating the blind cleric's communications. All three were convicted in 2005 of obstruction of justice and conspiracy to provide material support to terrorism.

3   Rifa'i Taha explored his ideas about the legitimacy of armed attacks, including the murder of Egyptian Coptic Christians, in a book called *Imatat al-Litham 'an Dhurwat Sanam al-Islam* ('Unveiling the Pinnacle of Islam'). The book was published in London in 2001 by the IOC; the centre's director, Yasir al-Sirri, was subsequently investigated for incitement of violence. In 2002 the charges against him were dropped.

Islamists perpetrated only two attacks in Egypt.[1] The following year, only one attack was carried out: not by Islamist groups this time, but by the security forces, who killed four senior members of al-Gama'a al-Islamiyya while attempting to arrest them in Giza on 7 September. The dead men included Farid Kidwani, whom the Egyptian security services regarded as the de facto leader of the group's military wing. Yet even his death did nothing to undermine al-Gama'a al-Islamiyya's ceasefire, which remains in force to this day.

---

[1] The two terrorist attacks in Egypt in 1998 both took place in the central governorate of Minya. Four members of the security forces were killed in the first attack, which was carried out in February 1998. In the second attack, which occurred the following August in a village near Mallawi, a Copt and a Muslim were killed. During the same period the security forces killed eighteen suspected militants in Minya. See issue 410 of the Egyptian newspaper *al-Ahram Weekly* at http://weekly.ahram.org.eg/1998/410/eg4.htm.

9

The Return to Afghanistan

As the jihad in Algeria and Libya ended in failure, and both Sudan and Britain closed their doors to Islamist militants, the jihadists began looking for a new refuge. But by now their options were severely limited. From the mid-1990s Bosnia was no longer the jihadist magnet it had been earlier in the decade, when fighters flocked there to protect the Muslim population from Serbian attack.[1] The Dayton Peace Accords signed by the warring parties in November 1995 stipulated that foreign combatants were to leave the country. The Bosnian government duly thanked the jihadists for their assistance and then showed most of them the door.[2] They now had two main options: to move to Chechnya, where local separatists and Russian forces had been fighting since 1994, or to Afghanistan, where the mujahidin factions were still locked in a power struggle with one another.[3]

In 1996 the Taliban were virtually unknown to the Arab veterans of the conflict. However, as they burst out of their stronghold in the southern city of Kandahar and defeated the other mujahidin factions one by one,

---

1   The date of the outbreak of civil war in Bosnia is disputed. Many maintain that the conflict began on 6 April 1992, when the European Community recognised Bosnia as an independent state and Serb snipers opened fire on an anti-war demonstration.

2   The General Framework Agreement for Peace in Bosnia and Herzegovina, commonly known as the Dayton Peace Accords, was signed near Dayton, Ohio in November 1995. Under the terms of the agreement the Bosnian government asked Arab mujahidin to leave its territory. However, some chose to stay and were granted Bosnian citizenship.

3   There were of course other conflict zones where jihadists could fight, such as the Philippines or Tajikistan. However, Chechnya and Afghanistan attracted most aspiring holy warriors.

the Taliban's star began to rise. Within a few years they had extended their control over all of Afghanistan but a small patch in the north, where an assortment of factions clung on.[1] Struck by the Taliban's prowess, the Syrian militant, Abu Mus'ab al-Suri, was instrumental in convincing his associates to side with them against the other Afghan factions.[2] One of the first people to make their way back to Afghanistan was Osama bin Laden. His destination was Jalalabad, the capital of the eastern Afghan province of Nangarhar, where he had friends and allies from the days of the jihad against the Russians. This chapter examines how the jihadists who followed bin Laden's example regrouped beneath the shelter of Taliban rule.

Bin Laden's Relocation

By early 1996 bin Laden knew full well that President al-Bashir of Sudan regarded the Afghan veterans on his soil as an insufferable nuisance. Sensing that his Sudanese hosts could no longer tolerate his presence in the country, bin Laden arranged to leave Khartoum before he was kicked out.[3] The first thing he did was contact two old Afghan mujahidin friends, Yunus Khalis and Jalaluddin Haqqani, both of whom were influential figures in the Jalalabad area: Afghanistan at this time was still carved up between various warlords.[4] Having arranged new accommodation in Hadda, near

---

1   The United Islamic Front for the Salvation of Afghanistan, commonly known as the Northern Alliance, comprised the Jamiat-e Islami, led by Burhanuddin Rabbani and his military commander, Ahmad Shah Massoud, Hekmatyar's wing of the Hezb-e Islami, the Ittehad-e Islami of Abdul Rabb al-Rasul Sayyaf and the forces under the Uzbek leader, Abdul Rashid Dostum.

2   Abu Mus'ab was a former companion of Osama bin Laden and had worked as a trainer in al-Qa'ida's camps during the early 1990s.

3   The account of Bin Laden's move to Afghanistan is based largely on information published by the IOC in 1999; many of the details have proven to be accurate. IOC report (last accessed on 3 February 2003 on the IOC website at www. marsad.net/arabic/ioc/bin.htm). The website is now defunct, but the author has a copy of the statement in his collection

4   Yunus Khalis broke away from Gulbuddin Hekmatyar's leadership in 1979 and established his own wing of the Hezb-e Islami, which was named after him. He was based in Nangarhar Province in southeastern Afghanistan. Jalaluddin Haqqani was second-in-command of Yunus Khalis's wing of the Hezb-e Islami.

Jalalabad, bin Laden prepared to leave Sudan clandestinely. He flew from Khartoum to Jalalabad via the United Arab Emirates in a private jet. Yunus Khalis and Haqqani were both waiting for him on his arrival.[1]

As soon as bin Laden reached Afghanistan, he wrote to the country's warlords reaffirming his promise not to meddle in their disputes. Since 1992, Gulbuddin Hekmatyar's Hezb-e Islami had been trying to take Kabul, where the Jamiat-e Islami led by Burhanuddin Rabbani and Ahmad Shah Massoud had dug themselves in. However, the struggle for control of the capital had exhausted the two factions; when the Taliban genie escaped from its bottle in Kandahar, neither had the strength to resist it. In September 1995 the Taliban defeated Ismail Khan, known as the 'Lion of Herat', and seized control of his stronghold in western Afghanistan. As the Taliban proceeded to advance on Kabul, Hekmatyar and Massoud quickly resolved their differences, and in March 1996 formed an alliance to defend the capital from their common enemy. But it was of little use: six months later the Taliban took Kabul as their opponents hurriedly abandoned the city, adopting a remote corner of northern Afghanistan as their base. Although isolated, the United Nations continued to treat Rabbani and his associates as Afghanistan's legitimate government. It was a decision which deprived the Taliban of international recognition, even though they controlled more than 90 per cent of the country.

It was just as the Taliban were consolidating their grip on power that many Arab jihadists were looking for a new haven. However, at this point the Taliban were virtually unknown to most of them: it was the Syrian activist, Abu Mus'ab al-Suri, who first took a serious interest in them. He put forward a theological defence of the movement and justified both fighting alongside the Taliban and emigrating to areas under their control. His arguments were key to persuading many Arabs who wanted to take part in jihad to support the Taliban, overcoming religious scruples about siding with one Islamist faction over another.

---

1 The Americans had known Bin Laden was preparing to leave Khartoum, but it was only two days after the event that they learned from the Sudanese that he had actually gone. See 'The Final Report of the National Commission on Terrorist Attacks upon the United States', widely known as 'The 9/11 Commission Report' (New York, 2004), p. 109.

Abu Mus'ab could sense that the jihadists were no longer welcome in Britain and that they would be well advised to leave the country quickly.[1] He himself travelled to Afghanistan in 1996 and wrote a detailed study on the Taliban, in which he extolled their virtues as he saw them. The text, which was distributed in London with the help of EIJ's press office, appears to have been well received. The EIJ activist, Ahmad al-Sayyid al-Najjar, told Egyptian investigators how Abu Mus'ab introduced the Taliban movement, of which he wholeheartedly approved:

> He described it as a religious Salafist movement led by a group of theology students with a good, clear manifesto. Abu Mus'ab also explained the movement's paramilitary activity and defended some of the policies for which it had been criticised, such as its rejection of women's education and the way that it had closed down schools and forced men to grow their beards. Abu Mus'ab argued that the Taliban only intended to put a stop to education until the curricula had been changed, and to forbid women to work until suitable jobs had been created for them. This was a temporary phase; as such, he claimed, EIJ's own policies were fully in accordance with the Taliban's strategy.[2]

Abu Mus'ab conducted another recce to Afghanistan in April 1997, as a result of which he decided to move there permanently. This he did in August of the same year. Before packing his bags, however, Abu Mus'ab arranged for CNN and the UK's Channel Four to interview bin Laden. Both interviews were organised through the Islamic Conflict Studies Bureau, which Abu Mus'ab had opened in London in early 1997, and both were prompted by bin Laden's desire to resume his propaganda activity. In June 1996, soon after the al-Qa'ida leader moved to Afghanistan, an attack had taken place on a US housing complex in Khobar, in eastern

---

1 The British authorities began restricting the movements of jihadists on their soil when it emerged that some of them might have been connected to the Paris Metro bombings of 1995. This subject is discussed in greater detail in Chapter Seven.

2 See the records of Ahmad al-Sayyid al-Najjar's interrogation on the Middle East Transparent website: http://www.metransparent.com/spip. php?page=article&id_article=2098&lang=ar. Last accessed on 5 November 2009. A copy of the report is retained by the author.

Saudi Arabia.[1] Bin Laden appears to have had no connection to the attack, but he issued a statement soon afterwards declaring a 'jihad to expel the infidels from the Arabian Peninsula'. The proclamation, signed in his own name 'from the mountains of the Hindu Kush', marked the official start of his campaign to drive the Americans out of the Gulf and the wider Islamic world.[2]

Relations with the Taliban

Bin Laden did not remain under the protection of Yunus Khalis for long. In July 1996 the city of Jalalabad, where bin Laden and his supporters were living, fell to the Taliban, only two months before they took Kabul. However, bin Laden's situation did not change immediately, as both Yunus Khalis and Jalaluddin Haqqani had decided to join the Taliban. Needless to say, it was not long before the movement contacted bin Laden himself. The Taliban leader, Mullah Omar, sent a delegation to reassure bin Laden that the movement would continue to protect him, just as Khalis and Haqqani had done. However, Mullah Omar's envoys also politely requested that bin Laden cease his media activity, alluding to the television interviews he had given earlier in the year.

In late 1996 or early 1997 bin Laden moved from Jalalabad to the Taliban stronghold of Kandahar, again at Mullah Omar's bidding. This followed news that tribesmen on the Afghan-Pakistani border, acting as hired mercenaries, were planning to carry out a raid on the area where he was living, with the aim of abducting and perhaps killing him. Bin Laden's relocation was made easier by the fact that in September 1996 the Taliban had taken control of Kabul, through which he travelled on his journey to

---

1 Nineteen people died in the attack on a housing complex in Khobar in eastern Saudi Arabia. The Americans believe that a group with links to Iranian intelligence calling itself Hizballah al-Hijaz, or the 'Party of God in the Hijaz', was behind the bombing. Tehran denies any such involvement.

2 Bin Laden sent agents to examine ways of attacking embassies and other Western facilities in East Africa. Al-Qa'ida fighters also played a role in training and assisting the Somalis who killed nineteen American troops in Mogadishu in early October 1993, leading the US to withdraw from the United Nations-sponsored Operation Restore Hope in Somalia.

southern Afghanistan. On his arrival in Kandahar, Bin Laden asked to see Mullah Omar, with whom he had corresponded but never met. Islamists who were present at the meeting maintain that the atmosphere was amicable. Mullah Omar welcomed bin Laden and reiterated his assurances that the Taliban regarded him as a guest whom they would be honoured to protect. He went on to outline the Taliban's situation and the challenges facing them in their impending battle with the remaining Afghan factions, including the Uzbeks and Tajiks in the north. It might be best, Mullah Omar said, if bin Laden eased off his campaign in the media for the time being, though this was of course a request and not an order. Bin Laden replied that he had already decided to freeze his propaganda activity.[1]

However, within months bin Laden was busy contacting clerics within the Taliban movement and others based in Pakistan. Between late 1997 and early 1998 he persuaded about forty of them to issue a fatwa backing his call for the expulsion of 'infidel forces' from the Arabian Peninsula. Bin Laden appears to have had two main aims in this. One was to mobilise Muslim clerics against the Americans based in the Gulf. The other was to obtain their blessing for his activities in Afghanistan, in the hope of resuming his propaganda activity and strengthening his position in Mullah Omar's eyes.

Ideology in Flux

This period saw a fundamental transformation in al-Qa'ida's thinking. Bin Laden and those around him, especially EIJ, had asked themselves why their aspirations for the Middle East had come to nothing. They concluded that defeating the Arab regimes currently in power would be impossible as long as they continued to enjoy the support of the United States. Bin Laden and his associates therefore decided that they had to draw the US into a conflict with the Islamists; this would force Arab governments and the religious establishments of the region to defend the Americans, which would in turn destroy their legitimacy in the eyes of

---

1   See the IOC report in 1999, last accessed on 3 February 2003 at www.marsad. net/arabic/ioc/bin.htm. The website is now defunct, but the author has a copy of the statement in his collection.

the public. This analysis represented a radical shift in jihadist ideology. Hitherto, Islamist groups had sought above all to combat what they regarded as apostate Muslims, whom they labelled the 'near enemy'. Now the priority was to fight the 'far enemy', or what they called the 'original infidels' of America and the West.

At first, only bin Laden's ally, Ayman al-Zawahiri, appears to have endorsed this shift in his thinking. Nonetheless, on 23 February 1998 bin Laden announced his new policy to the world, with the formation of the 'World Islamic Front for Jihad against Jews and Crusaders'. Within months he would show what this meant in practice, as the American embassies in Nairobi and Dar es Salaam were bombed on 7 August 1998.

Bin Laden had wasted no time in reorganising his group following his return to Afghanistan in 1996. He had immediately conducted a comprehensive review of al-Qaʻida, looking particularly closely at its structure and strategy. Abu Hafs al-Misri was put in charge of the organisation's military committee.[1] This appointment did not come as a surprise, given that Abu Hafs had been deputy to his predecessor, Abu ʻUbayda al-Banshiri. Nonetheless, it appears to have strengthened the hand of those al-Qaʻida members keen to carry out attacks on the United States and its allies. Abu Hafs himself had a history of conflict with the US dating back to 1992 and 1993, when he had trained al-Qaʻida cells in Somalia to fight American troops there. He had subsequently gone on to plan bomb attacks on American installations around the region.

Abu Hafs's second-in-command was another Egyptian called Sayf al-ʻAdl, a former colonel in the Egyptian armed forces who had joined al-Qaʻida from EIJ. Another senior figure in the group's military committee was Abu Khalid al-Misri, an Egyptian who belonged to both al-Qaʻida and EIJ. He had been known for his ability to drive and repair tanks during the Afghan jihad, when he had lost one of the fingers of his left hand in fighting against the Soviet forces.[2] These appointments were symptomatic of bin

---

1 Muhammad ʻAtif, also known as Subhi Abu Sitta, and Abu Hafs al-Misri, succeeded ʻAli Amin al-Rashidi, who was himself more widely known as Abu ʻUbayda al-Banshiri. The latter was drowned in a ferry accident in Lake Victoria on 21 May 1996.

2 Abu Khalid al-Misri was extradited to Egypt from Yemen in 2004.

Laden's growing reliance on Egyptians to run his organisation, and this is known to have provoked numerous disputes within the group, as Arabs of other nationalities resented the Egyptians monopolising senior positions. However, the grumbling in the ranks does not appear to have bothered bin Laden, who had complete trust in his Egyptian aides. 'We are doing this for God,' he is reported to have said once in Peshawar, 'and there must be no complaining. If a commander assumes responsibility for running a guesthouse or giving training, it is because he is qualified to do the job. He is responsible for his actions and we must have confidence in him.'[1]

Al-Zawahiri

Just as bin Laden depended increasingly on EIJ members to run al-Qa'ida's military wing, so too was his relationship with the group's theorists growing stronger. This was particularly true of bin Laden's ties to the EIJ leader, Ayman al-Zawahiri. Their association dated back to the days of the Afghan jihad in the 1980s; it had deepened in the early 1990s, when they were both based in Sudan, and had continued when both men subsequently moved back to Afghanistan.

Al-Zawahiri had initially been unenthusiastic about the idea of returning to Afghanistan. Instead he had travelled to Chechnya in 1996 to support the jihad against the Russians there, with the knowledge of only bin Laden and a handful of senior EIJ members. The trip very nearly ended in disaster when al-Zawahiri and his companions were arrested in Dagestan for entering the country illegally.[2] For six months not even EIJ's upper echelons knew what had happened to their leader. Envoys sent by bin Laden are alleged to have tried to bribe the Dagestani security services to release the men, while pointing out the triviality of their offence. Whether or not bin Laden's representatives were involved, the Dagestani authorities failed to identify their prisoners, who had been travelling on

---

1   See Jamal Ahmad al-Fadl's testimony to the Manhattan Federal Court in New York in 2001, pp. 322–324. The transcript of the testimony can be accessed from www.findlaw.com, case No. S(7) 98 Cr. 1023.

2   Al-Zawahiri was accompanied by two senior EIJ members called Mahmud al-Hinnawi and Ahmad Salama Mabruk.

false passports, and eventually decided to let them go. It was only then that al-Zawahiri moved back to Afghanistan.[1]

Settling in Afghanistan gave al-Zawahiri a chance to reflect on the reasons why his group, like all other jihadists in the Arab world, had failed to realise its ambitions. It was this soul-searching which led him to consolidate his alliance with bin Laden and establish the World Islamic Front with him in early 1998. Prior to the official announcement of the front's creation, bin Laden had sent envoys to various countries calling on other jihadist groups to join the new venture. Those they approached included the leaders of the LIFG, who rejected bin Laden's overtures. 'The plan to create the World Islamic Front for Jihad against Jews and Crusaders was put to us, just as it was to all the other jihadist groups,' explains Noman Benotman. 'We rejected the proposals of our own free will, saying that the plan was incompatible with our own strategy and doomed to failure.'[2]

Bin Laden was not about to give up, despite being snubbed by the LIFG and others. The formation of the new front was formally announced on 23 February 1998, at a press conference held by bin Laden, al-Zawahiri and Abu Hafs al-Misri at al-Qa'ida's camp in Khost. At the same time, bin Laden issued a fatwa declaring it the religious duty of all Muslims to kill Americans – civilians and military personnel alike – and plunder their possessions. The edict was signed by bin Laden himself, al-Zawahiri, Rifa'i Taha (head of al-Gama'a al-Islamiyya's Shura Council), Mir Hamza (head of Pakistan's Association of Muslim Clerics or Jamiat Ulema-e-Pakistan) and Fazlul Rahman (the leader of the Jihad Movement of Bangladesh).

Bin Laden's announcement caused uproar almost the moment it was published, not only within the American security services but also among other Islamist movements. Many thought the declaration of war on the Americans merely on the grounds of their nationality indefensible in terms of Islamic law. Just as importantly, they saw it as a strategic error that would

---

1 Ahmad Salama Mabruk travelled to Azerbaijan, where he was later detained and deported to Egypt in 1998. Al-Hinnawi decided to settle in the Caucasus, where he remained until 2005 when he was killed in Chechnya. See the 20 April 2005 edition of the international Arabic newspaper *al-Hayat*.

2 Noman Benotman in an interview with the author in London in 2006.

provoke the US to devote greater resources to fighting Islamist movements, particularly those under the umbrella of the World Islamic Front. In what was the first sign of dissent within the organisation, Rifa'i Taha had to issue a clarification stating that although he had signed bin Laden's fatwa, al-Gama'a al-Islamiyya was not bound by it.[1] Ayman al-Zawahiri had similarly omitted to consult other EIJ leaders before endorsing the formation of the World Islamic Front, to their consternation. However, unlike Taha, whose relationship with the heads of al-Gama'a al-Islamiyya was already strained, al-Zawahiri had his own group largely under his control. His opponents, those Shura Council members mainly based at that time in Yemen, were in no position to mount a coup against him, however cavalier his attitude towards them had been.

A Shift in Strategy

The sea change in bin Laden's thinking undoubtedly took some jihadists outside Afghanistan by surprise. However, those close to him at the time maintain that it was the logical outcome of his long exposure to al-Zawahiri's ideas. When bin Laden first went to Afghanistan in the 1980s, his outlook, like that of so many young Saudis eager to fight the Russians, was shaped by both the Muslim Brotherhood and the official Wahhabi-Salafist school of his home country. However, the more contact he had with the leaders of the jihadist groups, the more their influence over him increased. This process gathered pace after he passed responsibility for training at his camps in Afghanistan to Egyptian EIJ members and other jihadists, such as Abu Mus'ab al-Suri. Their books, lectures, methods and arguments all imbued the young al-Qa'ida members with their ideas. Having taken root among the group's rank and file, it was not long before jihadist ideology gained sway over bin Laden himself.

Having embraced jihadist dogma, bin Laden became one of its leading

---

1   Al-Gama'a al-Islamiyya had launched its non-violence initiative in mid-1997; this is discussed in greater detail in Chapter Eight. Sources close to Rifa'i Taha have told the author that he was not in Afghanistan the day the formation of the World Islamic Front was announced. However, he had previously given his consent when urged to add his name to its list of founders.

exponents, as the al-Qa'ida strategist, Abu Mus'ab al-Suri, has observed.[1] He had also been influenced by the Saudi government's attitude towards the liberation of Kuwait in 1990–91 and the presence of American troops in the Arabian Peninsula. Later, while based in Sudan, bin Laden had gone from regarding the Saudi regime as flawed but legitimate, to denouncing the government and its official clergy and calling for radical reform of both. 'When Osama was expelled from Sudan and returned to Afghanistan,' writes Abu Mus'ab al-Suri, 'he was surrounded by people who favoured confrontation on an international scale with America and its allies. Through a combination of the jihadists' influence and his own assessment of the international situation, Osama concluded that jihad against the apostate regimes [of the Islamic world] would inevitably entail conflict with America.'

Bin Laden could hardly tackle Saudi Arabia's powerful clerics head on, as Abu Mus'ab points out. He therefore chose to attack the American presence on Saudi soil, hoping 'to force the Saudi regime to defend the Americans, leading it to lose credibility in Muslim eyes. Then, when the religious establishment came to the defence of the government's position, it too would lose popular support.' Convinced that the demise of the US would bring Arab regimes tumbling down with it, bin Laden began focusing his efforts on the Americans, calling on others to attack 'the head of the serpent' rather than its Middle Eastern tail.

Plans to Capture bin Laden

The United States had been monitoring bin Laden's increasing activity in Afghanistan from late 1997, but had not yet adopted a clear strategy on how to deal with him. In the autumn of 1997 the CIA's bin Laden unit had drawn up a preliminary plan for Afghan tribesmen to abduct him and hand him over for trial in America or an Arab country. In early 1998 the CIA received the blessing of the US administration to proceed. At the same time the US Department of Justice was preparing a case against bin Laden, with the aim of securing his conviction. In June 1998 a Federal Grand Jury in New York issued a sealed indictment accusing Bin Laden of

1   Abu Mus'ab al-Suri, *Da'wat al-Muqawama*, pp. 713–14.

'conspiracy to attack defense utilities of the United States', charges which were made public the following November.

The Americans felt sure that Bin Laden was planning to take some kind of action against them, but they did not know what or where. Aware that the core of his organisation was made up of Egyptians, they decided to start by rounding up EIJ members in the Balkans, particularly Albania, in cooperation with the local intelligence services. Several senior members of the group, most of whom had been living under assumed names, were extradited to Egypt.

The American campaign undoubtedly dealt a blow to al-Zawahiri's group in Europe, but it was far from a decisive defeat. Conscious of this, EIJ issued a statement in early August 1998 threatening to retaliate for the Americans' action 'in a language which they understand'. Days later the nature of that response became clear: two massive explosions on 7 August 1998 which destroyed the American embassies in the Kenyan capital Nairobi and the Tanzanian capital Dar es Salaam.

Bin Laden Defiant

On 20 August 1998 the Americans retaliated by firing cruise missiles at al-Qa'ida's camps in Khost in Afghanistan. Yet all this achieved was some minor damage to a mosque: not one senior al-Qa'ida member perished in the assault. The ineffectiveness of the response handed bin Laden a valuable propaganda tool, allowing him to appear to have emerged victorious from his first clash with the United States. As he set about plotting further strikes, his supporters launched a campaign to recruit would-be jihadists and to persuade them to enrol in the training camps springing up in areas under Taliban control. Yet Mullah Omar's movement was in a precarious position: it was only the support of bin Laden and his fighters in September 1998 which helped it avoid defeat and possible collapse.

Between 1997 and 1998 the Taliban tightened their grip on Herat in western Afghanistan, the southeast of the country and then Kabul. Soon the only territory beyond their reach would be a strip of land from the Panjshir Valley to the far north of Afghanistan, on the border with Tajikistan, as well as the predominantly Shi'ite areas of Bamiyan, west of

Kabul. In 1997 and then again the following year the Taliban fought two battles at Mazar-e Sharif, finally inflicting a heavy defeat on the Uzbek leader, Abdul Rashid Dostum. In so doing, the Taliban avenged themselves for the events of May 1997, when they had lost hundreds of fighters in a failed attempt to take the city.[1]

During the Taliban's bloody conquest of Mazar-e Sharif in August 1998, eight Iranian diplomats and a journalist were murdered at the Iranian Consulate General. In response, Tehran announced plans to carry out military exercises on Iran's border with Afghanistan. This growing tension coincided with the US missile strikes on al-Qa'ida's camps in Afghanistan. At the same time, the Taliban were facing increasing international isolation because of their refusal to hand over bin Laden to the Americans in connection with the embassy bombings.

Abu Mus'ab al-Suri witnessed developments in Afghanistan during this period. 'From a military perspective,' he says, 'the massing of Iranian troops on the border prompted the Taliban to redeploy a large number of their forces to the southwest':

> Meanwhile, the threats coming from Tajikistan, Russia and Uzbekistan, and the announcement of military manoeuvres led the Taliban to move another substantial portion of their fighters to the north, which remained unstable. When the Shia in Bamiyan began agitating and Iran started airlifting supplies to the Hizb-e Wahdat, the Taliban diverted a third division of their forces to the area.[2] The Taliban's deployment of its forces to these flashpoints created breaches in their defences around Kabul, especially to the north of the city, close to the front lines with the forces led

---

1   In May 1997 General Abdul Malik Pahlawan, one of Dostum's deputies, turned against him and allied with the Taliban, prompting Dostum to flee to Uzbekistan. Later that month the Taliban entered Mazar-e Sharif unopposed; both Pakistan and Saudi Arabia swiftly recognised them as the legitimate government of Afghanistan. However, when the newborn alliance between Pahlawan and the Taliban came under strain, hundreds of the latter's forces were massacred in the city. These were the events which the Taliban would brutally avenge in August the following year.

2   The *Hizb-e Wahdat-e Islami-ye Afghanistan* or Islamic Unity Party of Afghanistan, was formed in the late 1980s under Iranian auspices from several Shi'ite factions.

by Ahmad Shah Massoud and Abddul Rabb al-Rasul Sayyaf. It was as if the international community were colluding with the Afghan opposition to help them seize back control of Kabul and undermine the Taliban's position in the north ... In early September [1998] Massoud and Sayyaf's forces began attacking the defences north of Kabul at two strategic points, one of which was a mere 15 kilometres from the centre of the capital. These defences were undermanned and ill-equipped, as a result of the Taliban's recent redeployments. The attacking forces managed to seize a number of the hills overlooking the main routes into the city. Fighting between them, the Taliban and the latter's mujahidin allies reached a climax two days later, with the Arab fighters and their allies holding out until Taliban reinforcements arrived. As the new troops filled the breaches in Kabul's defences, the attack on the city crumbled and Sayyaf's troops withdrew, having suffered heavy losses. Five Arabs were martyred, as were twenty of their Taliban and other associates. It had been one of the greatest traumas Kabul had suffered since the Taliban had taken the city two years earlier.[1]

While all this was going on, the LIFG was trying to bring about a reconciliation between the Taliban and the other Afghan factions with which the Libyan group still enjoyed cordial relations. According to Noman Benotman, between 1999 and 2000 the LIFG leader, Abu Abdullah al-Sadiq, contacted Sayyaf, in whose camps the LIFG had first been formed in the early 1990s. Al-Sadiq tried to persuade Sayyaf to cooperate with the Taliban, but to no avail: Sayyaf remained loyal to the Northern Alliance. He was intensely hostile to the Taliban, while the Taliban themselves had no time for Sayyaf or the role that he had played in the jihad against the Soviet occupation. Benotman claims that Abu al-Mundhir al-Sa'idi, the LIFG's head of Islamic law, subsequently contacted Gulbuddin Hekmatyar, leader of the Hezb-e Islami, in an effort to persuade him to side with the Taliban. However, like Sayyaf before

---

1 Abu Mus'ab al-Suri, *Afghanistan wa al-Taliban wa Ma'rakat al-Islam al-Yawm* ('Afghanistan, the Taliban and the Battle of Islam Today'), Kabul, Markaz al-Ghuraba' li al-Dirasat al-Islamiyya, 1998, pp. 4–5.

him, Hekmatyar rejected the proposal: both men were convinced that the Taliban were mere puppets of the Pakistanis.[1]

America Holds Back

As bin Laden backed the Taliban against its rivals and plotted new attacks on American targets, he was seldom off the CIA's radar. Together with senior figures in the Clinton administration, the agency considered carrying out renewed strikes against al-Qa'ida's camps in Afghanistan. However, some military leaders argued that they were little more than 'jungle gyms', rather than large installations that could be destroyed by military means.[2] They also maintained that attacking bin Laden might serve merely to increase his popularity. In 1999 the Americans had at least two opportunities to get rid of bin Laden, but they failed to seize either of them. The first was in February, when bin Laden was reported to be staying at a hunting camp in southern Afghanistan. The other was in May, when the CIA received information about his presence in Kandahar.[3] Not until September 2001 did the CIA consider launching another attack on bin Laden.

---

1 Noman Benotman in an interview with the author in London in 2006.
2 The 9/11 Commission Report, p. 120.
3 Ibid., pp. 137 and 140.

10

The Approach to 9/11

Bin Laden used the three years between the US embassy bombings and the attacks of 11 September 2001 to consolidate his alliances in Afghanistan. Although he failed to win over the known jihadist groups operating in Algeria (such as what was left of the GIA and the GSPC), Libya (the LIFG) and Egypt (al-Gama'a al-Islamiyya), he did manage to bring independently operating jihadists into his World Islamic Front. They included 'Abd al-Rahim al-Nashiri, who would mastermind an attack on an American warship, and Khalid Sheikh Muhammad, who first thought of using hijacked aircraft to attack the United States. In June 2001 bin Laden merged his organisation with al-Zawahiri's EIJ, forming a new entity which they named *Qa'idat al-Jihad*, the 'Jihad Base'. This chapter examines the relationship between al-Qa'ida and the other jihadist groups sheltered by the Taliban, and bin Laden's plans to attack the Americans on their own soil.

The Millennium Plot

Within two years of the US embassy bombings, al-Qa'ida was getting ready to launch new and bigger attacks on the Americans and their interests around the world. And it was not alone: other factions had also embraced al-Qa'ida's idea of a jihad against the United States. These groups, to use the American terminology, were associated with al-Qa'ida, rather than formal members of bin Laden's organisation: what might be called al-Qa'ida's 'brothers in arms'.

The year 1999 saw a fresh influx of aspiring jihadists into Afghanistan. Not all of them had come to train in al-Qa'ida's camps, but it was nonetheless al-Qaʻida that proved most successful at recruiting them. The organisation used its highly effective propaganda machine to trumpet its ability to strike at the Americans, while all the latter could do in retaliation was launch a few cruise missiles and inflict minor damage on the odd training camp. Al-Qaʻida also used its supporters in the Gulf to promote the merits of the Taliban, their success in establishing security in the areas under their control and, above all, their strict application of Islamic law. All of this was bound to appeal to pious young Arabs from the Gulf, and many duly responded by going to Afghanistan to fight alongside the Taliban, though not necessarily with the intention of joining al-Qaʻida. But al-Qaʻida nonetheless kept a close watch on new arrivals in Afghanistan, and as they passed through the training camps it would seek to recruit them.[1]

Various plots were being hatched to attack American targets at the turn of the new millennium. Although motivated by the same ideology and focused on attacking the same enemy within the same timeframe, these plans do not appear to have been coordinated. In the event, not one of them succeeded: two were foiled by the American and Jordanian security services, while another was thwarted by a technical error. Together they have become known as the Millennium Plot.

The conspiracy was first detected in Jordan, where, in late November 1999, a telephone call was intercepted between a well-known Islamist called Khadr Abu Hoshar and a Palestinian known as Abu Zubayda.[2] The latter was one of the main people responsible for putting up volunteer fighters at hostels and safe houses in Pakistan and then sending them to the Khaldan

---

1   Al-Qaʼida even sought to recruit members from independent training camps, such as the one at Khaldan run by the Libyan, Ali Muhammad al-Fakhiri, more commonly known as Ibn al-Sheikh al-Libi. The latter was captured on the Afghan-Pakistani border in 2001 and handed over to the Americans. He has identified as the source of claims made by the United States before its invasion of Iraq of a connection between al-Qaʼida and Saddam Hussein's regime. He was later returned to Libya, where he died in prison, allegedly committing suicide in May 2009.

2   See The 9/11 Commission Report, pp. 174–5. Zayn al-ʻAbidin Muhammad Husayn, also known as Abu Zubayda al-Filastini, was an aide to the Khaldan training camp supervisor, Ibn al-Sheikh al-Libi. Abu Zubayda was detained in Pakistan in 2002 and handed over to the United States; at the time of writing he was being held at Guantanamo Bay.

camp in Afghanistan to undergo training. During their conversation, Abu Zubayda said that 'the time for training is over', which Jordanian intelligence interpreted as an indication that attacks were imminent. The Jordanians immediately arrested a number of Islamists, including Abu Hoshar, and charged them with conspiracy to carry out explosions. Of the twenty-eight defendants, twenty-two were sent to prison; the remaining six were sentenced to death.[1]

At the same time that the Jordanians were disrupting these attacks, the Americans stumbled across explosives and detonators in a car belonging to an Algerian called Ahmed Ressam. Ressam had entered the US from Canada by ferry, arriving on 14 December 1999 at Port Angeles in the northwest state of Washington. He was discovered during a routine search by customs officials of cars coming off the boat. It subsequently emerged that he had undergone military training at the Khaldan camp, that he had links to Abu Zubayda and that he had come to the United States with the intention of attacking Los Angeles Airport in California.[2]

Evidence submitted for a review of Abu Zubayda's 'combatant status' at Guantanamo Bay includes statements from Ahmed Ressam. He is quoted as saying that he had studied for the Los Angeles attack in April 1998 at the Khaldan camp, one of 'many' such facilities run by Abu Zubayda. The latter was 'an associate' of bin Laden, 'equal ... and not subordinate' to the al-Qa'ida leader. Ressam claimed that Abu Zubayda had known of his intention to carry out an attack in the United States, although not precisely where or when.[3] Abu Zubayda himself admitted asking Ressam to obtain Canadian passports, but rejected Ressam's claim that their purpose was to enable Ressam and others to enter the United States to carry out attacks. Abu Zubayda maintained that the Khaldan camp existed for 'training Muslim brothers for defensive jihad', by which he meant the sacred duty

---

1   The convicts sentenced to death for their part in the plot included Abu Hoshar himself and a Palestinian-American called Ra'id Hijazi, who had previously worked as a taxi driver in Boston.

2   In 2005 Ahmed Ressam was sentenced to twenty-two years in prison in the United States.

3   From a summary of the evidence for the Combatant Status Review Tribunal for Zayn al-'Abidin Muhammad Husayn, also known as Abu Zubayda, dated 19 March 2007. See: http://www.defenselink.mil/news/ISN10016.pdf.

of every Muslim to defend the territory of Islam from invaders. He did not support 'what Osama bin Laden and al-Qa'ida were promoting, which was and is a doctrine of offensive jihad.'[1]

If Abu Zubayda is to be believed, Ressam's plot to attack the US can only be linked to al-Qa'ida indirectly, something which was also true of the terrorist group dismantled by the Jordanian authorities. The 9/11 Commission Report concluded that the Jordanian cell was only loosely affiliated with al-Qa'ida, and that while its members had 'sought approval and training from Afghanistan, and at least one key member swore loyalty to bin Ladin ... the cell's plans and preparations were autonomous.' Ressam's connections to al-Qa'ida were 'even looser': although he had been recruited and trained by a network affiliated to the group, 'Ressam's own plans were, nonetheless, essentially independent'.[2]

A third plot around this time did have direct links to the al-Qa'ida leadership, but was no more successful than the other two. This time it was not the vigilance of the security services which proved the conspiracy's undoing, but a technical error by the perpetrators. A decision had been taken to launch an attack on the American destroyer, the USS *The Sullivans*, while it was moored at Aden. The attack was to be carried out by ramming a boat packed with explosives into the side of the ship on 3 January 2000. In the event, the boat capsized and sank under the weight of the explosives.

On 12 October 2000, two years and two months after the US embassy bombings, a small boat loaded with explosives collided with the American destroyer, the USS *Cole*, in Aden, tearing a huge hole in the side of the ship that almost sank it. The attack, in which seventeen US sailors were killed, was a harbinger of what bin Laden was planning against the Americans. However, according to the United States, its real mastermind was a veteran of the Afghan jihad called 'Abd al-Rahim al-Nashiri.[3] The Saudi-born

---

1   From Abu Zubayda's own statement at his Combatant Status Review Tribunal in 2007. See: http://www.defenselink.mil/news/transcript_ISN10016.pdf.

2   The 9/11 Commission Report, p. 180.

3   Al-Nashiri was arrested in the United Arab Emirates in 2002 and handed over to the United States; the story of his involvement in al-Qa'ida rests mainly on statements he made subsequently. However, al-Nashiri later claimed that his confessions had been extracted under torture and they must therefore be treated

al-Nashiri claims to have left his home country in the late 1990s, after the authorities there discovered a plot to smuggle missiles over the border from Yemen. He made his way to Pakistan and then on to Afghanistan, where he became close to bin Laden, who had himself recently arrived from Sudan. Their relationship appears to have grown stronger after the US embassy attacks in 1998, perhaps because the first suicide bomber to target the American mission in Nairobi was al-Nashiri's cousin, Jihad Muhammad Ali al-Harazi (also known as 'Azzam). A second man involved in the attack, a Saudi called Muhammad Rashid Dawud al-'Awhali, survived the operation. He later told American investigators that al-Nashiri had helped him obtain a forged Yemeni passport which he used to travel to Kenya.[1] Whatever al-Nashiri's connection to the US embassy bombings, it was only with the attack on the USS *Cole* that his alleged role in al-Qa'ida came to light. The Americans maintain that he bought the boat that was used to attack the ship, and claim that he asked Jamal al-Badawi, a Yemeni convicted of coordinating the operation, to film it. Bin Laden braced himself for American retaliation of the kind that had followed the embassy attacks. But the response never came.[2]

Khalid Sheikh Muhammad

Meanwhile, bin Laden was making progress with a much larger conspiracy to launch an attack on American soil. The plan was not his own brainchild, but that of Khalid Sheikh Muhammad. Like al-Nashiri before him, Khalid was not originally a member of al-Qa'ida. It was only when he accepted

with caution. See: http://www.defenselink.mil/news/transcript_ISN10015.pdf.

1 Al-Nashiri denies the claim by al-'Awhali (whose name is also written Muhammad Rashed Daoud al-Owhali) and says he only learned the identities of the Nairobi attackers from the media. However, al-Nashiri does admit that he may have met al-'Awhali.

2 For his own part, al-Nashiri has admitted receiving regular payments from Osama bin Laden, but claims that they were for 'fishing projects' in the Gulf. He also concedes that he gave a boat to two men, but maintains that he intended it as a fishing vessel and that they attacked the USS *Cole* without his knowledge. He says that he heard about the attack by chance in Afghanistan, where he had returned two months before it took place.

that he would need help to carry out his plot to hit American targets using hijacked aircraft that he decided to join bin Laden's organisation.[1]

Khalid Sheikh Muhammad grew up in Kuwait in a religious family of Baluch origin, from the area straddling the border between Iran and Pakistan. In the 1980s he studied in the United States, before joining the Arabs who provided support to the Afghan mujahidin between 1988 and 1992. In that year he also fought alongside the mujahidin in Bosnia and collected donations for them. After his nephew, Ramzi Yousef's, failed attempt to blow up the World Trade Centre in New York in 1993, Khalid worked with him on a new conspiracy, this time in the Philippines. The plan, which became known as the 'Bojinka plot', envisaged blowing up at least twelve aircraft simultaneously. However, when this scheme also ended in failure, both Khalid and Ramzi fled Manila. Khalid made his way to Qatar, but on 7 February 1995 his nephew was arrested in Pakistan and deported to the United States, where he is currently serving a life sentence.

In 1996, having discovered that the Americans were planning to arrest him, Khalid fled Qatar and went to Afghanistan. There, for the first time, he presented bin Laden with proposals to train pilots to attack buildings in the United States. The al-Qa'ida leader invited Khalid to join his organisation there and then. However, it was another two years before bin Laden would be persuaded of Khalid's plan and, at the insistence of the al-Qa'ida military commander, Abu Hafs, would give Khalid the green light to proceed.[2] Khalid says that it was then that he accepted bin Laden's invitation to join al-Qa'ida, and that he swore an oath of allegiance 'to conduct jihad of self and money and also of *hijra*'.[3] He also moved his

---

1   In his statement to his Combatant Status Review Tribunal, Khalid Sheikh Muhammad said he had been Media Operations Director for the so-called al-Sahab Foundation. This was the propaganda arm of al-Qa'ida which used to send video recordings of bin Laden to al-Jazeera and other media outlets.

2   See The 9/11 Commission Report, p. 149.

3   From Khalid Sheikh Muhammad's statement at his Combatant Status Review Tribunal at Guantanamo Bay in March 2007; the English words are Khalid's own. By *hijra* Khalid means his willingness to migrate anywhere in the world for his cause. For the transcript of the proceedings see: http://www.defenselink.mil/news/transcript_ISN10024.pdf.

family to Kandahar, where he was put in charge of the *Bayt al-Shuhada'*
guesthouse, where the team that was trained to hijack aircraft in the US
would later stay.[1]

In early 1999 Khalid Sheikh Muhammad, bin Laden and Abu Hafs
met at the airport complex in Kandahar and drew up a list of potential
targets. They included the White House, the US Capitol, the Pentagon
and the Twin Towers of New York's World Trade Center. According to
The 9/11 Commission Report, bin Laden wanted to destroy the White
House and the Pentagon. Khalid himself was keen to strike the World
Trade Center, because of its place at the nerve centre of the American
economy, and perhaps also to complete the mission his nephew, Ramzi,
had failed to accomplish in 1993.

Ambition Checked

While the plans for 9/11 continued to evolve, changes underway in
Afghanistan inevitably left their mark on the country's Arab guests.
Between 2000 and 2001 the Taliban established control over more than
90 per cent of Afghan territory. As they sought to consolidate their grip
on power, the status of the plethora of jihadist groups in the country
had to be addressed. The Taliban reportedly asked the Arabs to join
ranks under bin Laden's leadership, although, for reasons which remain
unclear, this idea did not come to fruition. Many Arabs chose to pledge
allegiance to the Taliban leader, Mullah Omar, and the self-styled Islamic
emirate of Afghanistan over which he presided. But others preferred to
remain independent, even if in practice many of them too had close links
to the Taliban.

Yet Arab attitudes towards the fledgling Taliban state were a source
of intense controversy in jihadist circles. Some maintained that anyone
who chose to live under Taliban rule was obliged to obey their orders. But
others believed that the Taliban had ceased to have any legitimate authority
when they tried to limit the jihadists' aspirations. At marathon meetings
in Kandahar in April and May 2000, bin Laden and other jihadist leaders
discussed obedience to the Taliban and the danger of doing anything to

---

1 The Arabic name, *Bayt al-Shuhada'*, means 'House of the Martyrs'.

undermine Mullah Omar's rule. The al-Qa'ida leader outlined his own future plans, hoping to win over his peers to the alliance that he and al-Zawahiri had established in 1998.

'Many of those present demanded that bin Laden cease using Afghanistan as a base from which to launch operations,' says Noman Benotman, who attended the talks:

> Of all the groups, the LIFG was the most outspoken. I myself called on bin Laden to stop, in the presence of Abu al-Mundhir al-Sa'idi, among others. Our argument was that attacking the US from Afghanistan would undermine the Taliban state and bring it under unbearable [international] pressure. We said all this to bin Laden's face in Kandahar; al-Zawahiri, Abu Hafs al-Misri, Abu Hafs al-Mauritani and various other senior figures were there too.[1]
>
> When the LIFG's turn came to speak, I said we had to face the fact that the jihadists' strategy of military confrontation in the Arab world had failed. This didn't go down well. But when we listed the reasons for this failure, no one uttered a word of disagreement. One of the Egyptians argued that rather than failing, we just 'hadn't achieved our aims'. I told him it amounted to the same thing: as a jihadist movement we'd failed to achieve our strategic objectives for many reasons, some of which weren't even military. Our modus operandi, the cultures of the different groups, the way we engaged with wider society, even the nature of our message and how we communicated it through the media: all these things were bound up with our lack of success. The jihadist groups had become parallel communities of their own, closed off to the outside world and isolated from mainstream society. And honestly, bin Laden was convinced.
>
> Next, Abu al-Mundhir al-Sa'idi spoke about things from a theological perspective. If we accepted that the Taliban were a legitimate government and that we enjoyed their protection, could we, as Muslims, break their laws, defy their orders or disregard their policies? Or were we obliged to offer them our obedience – provided they ordered us to do nothing wrong – even if we hadn't formally pledged allegiance to them? In our view, anyone who regarded this as an intolerable imposition should leave Afghanistan. It was

---

1   Mahfouz Ould al-Walid, also known as Abu Hafs the Mauritanian, was an al-Qa'ida expert in Islamic law.

obvious during those meetings that we had the strongest argument of everyone there. Bin Laden duly promised to stop launching military operations from Afghanistan, because of the risk they posed to the Taliban. But there was one operation, he said, for which preparations were almost complete, and which he could not abandon under any circumstances. Nevertheless, once it was over there would be an end to his operations from Afghanistan. Those were his words. In retrospect, he was clearly referring to 11 September.[1]

Meanwhile, the Taliban continued their attempts to bring the Arab community under their control. They began by placing the Arabs' training camps under their supervision; some, such as the one at Khaldan, they closed down altogether. In eastern Afghanistan they forbade the Arabs to launch mortars from their training grounds, after local shepherds complained of having almost been killed by shellfire. They also brought foreign groups under the command of a 'Brigade 21', led by the Uzbek, Juma Namangani, to the chagrin of some Arabs who resented the authority of a foreigner.[2]

During their last two years in power, the Taliban officially recognised some fourteen jihadist organisations and camps based in their territory.[3] According to Abu Mus'ab al-Suri, the largest group of foreign fighters were the Uzbeks, who were intent on exporting the jihad to Uzbekistan in collaboration with the Taliban. Both their emir, Tahir Yuldashev, and his deputy, Namangani, pledged allegiance to Mullah Omar, but their relations with al-Qa'ida were less cordial.[4]

---

1   Noman Benotman in an interview with the author in London in 2006.

2   *Da'wat al-Muqawama al-Islamiyya al-'Alamiyya*, p. 787. Abu Mus'ab al-Suri claims to have suggested forming a non-Afghan division to Mullah Omar, who followed his advice in mid-2001. He claims that the brigade consisted of almost 3,000 men, who were fighting in northern Afghanistan when the attacks of 11 September 2001 took place. According to Abu Mus'ab, Namangani was killed shortly afterwards in an American air strike near Mazar-e Sharif.

3   *Da'wat al-Muqawama al-Islamiyya al-'Alamiyya*, pp. 727–29. These organisations did not include the various Pakistani groups, which had their own special arrangements with the Taliban government.

4   Tahir Yuldashev first founded a radical Islamist group called Adolat in Uzbekistan in the early 1990s, following the collapse of the Soviet Union. In 1996 he announced the formation of the Islamic Movement of Uzbekistan along with

Yuldashev had felt snubbed by bin Laden at their first meeting back in 1998; they subsequently went their separate ways, but in 1999 an incident threatened to spiral into armed conflict between their followers. Two Uzbeks susceptible to Salafist ideas left Yuldashev's group and went to stay at al-Qa'ida's guesthouse in Kabul. When Yuldashev discovered what had happened, he ordered his men to pursue the two youths and bring them back by force. His followers duly rammed their way into an al-Qa'ida camp using a couple of pickup trucks and made off with their former comrades. When a furious bin Laden threatened reprisals, Mullah Omar himself was obliged to intervene to defuse the situation.

The smaller groupings in Afghanistan included the East Turkestan Islamic Movement (ETIM), a band of militant Uighur separatists from the Chinese province of Xinjiang. The group pledged allegiance to Mullah Omar and stopped all paramilitary activity against China (which the Taliban could ill afford to upset), as requested. Other foreign jihadists were less obliging: small groups of Kurds and Turks continued to operate secretly from Taliban-held territory. Of the Arab groups in Afghanistan, the two largest were al-Qa'ida and the LIFG. Bin Laden had pledged allegiance to Mullah Omar, and the LIFG was also committed to supporting the Taliban, while continuing to prepare for jihad against Gaddafi's regime. Ayman al-Zawahiri's EIJ likewise remained focused on overthrowing the Egyptian government, and Palestinian and Jordanian fighters, led by Abu Mus'ab al-Zarqawi, harboured similar ambitions.[1] The Algerians and Tunisians were also getting ready to relaunch their campaigns in their respective countries, and yet another North African faction, the Moroccan Islamic Combatant Group (GICM), used Afghanistan as a place to train its militants.

By early 2001 bin Laden had won over only a fraction of these jihadists to his cause: most remained focused on combating the regimes in their home countries, not the US.[2] However, in June 2001 bin Laden scored a

---

Juma Namangani, the IMU's military commander. Yuldashev is reported to have been killed in a US air strike in August 2009.

1   The Jordanian, Abu Mus'ab al-Zarqawi, whose real name was Ahmad Fadil Nazzal al-Khalayila, would gain notoriety after the overthrow of the Taliban, when he moved to Iraq. His career there is discussed in Chapter Twelve.

2   Bin Laden's efforts to attract supporters from the Gulf received a boost in

major propaganda coup when his own group and al-Zawahiri's EIJ agreed to merge, renaming their combined forces *Qa'idat al-Jihad*, the 'Jihad Base'.[1] Yet even this was the fruit of a struggle which almost cost al-Zawahiri his position. 'The so-called merger did not mean the total unification of the two factions,' explains the former EIJ affiliate, Hani al-Siba'i:

> It meant al-Zawahiri and a handful of other EIJ leaders joining bin Laden.[2] Other senior EIJ figures refused to go with them, including al-Zawahiri's second-in-command, Tharwat Salah [Shihata]. He believed that EIJ should concentrate on overthrowing the Egyptian government, and that to expand the conflict to include the United States was far too risky a strategy. Yet he could see that EIJ was changing: it was no longer the group he had known. The whole basis of the jihad was shifting and the battle against the Americans was moving to the fore. Eventually Tharwat and his sympathisers decided to stay put, while al-Zawahiri and his cohorts went off to join bin Laden; this was how things stood when the Americans went on the offensive in late 2001. By that time all that was left of EIJ were some members behind bars in Egypt and a few scattered remnants in the mountains of Afghanistan.[3]

Two days before the attacks of 9/11, al-Qa'ida sent a couple of Tunisians posing as journalists to northern Afghanistan, ostensibly to interview Ahmad Shah Massoud, the military commander of the Northern Alliance. As filming was underway, they detonated an explosive charge hidden inside

---

March 2001, when the Taliban destroyed the monumental statues of Buddha in the Afghan province of Bamiyan. Bin Laden's supporters, who regarded the sixth-century figures as idolatrous, argued that their obliteration enhanced the Taliban's legitimacy and that of fighting alongside them.

1   For the sake of simplicity, the merged entity will henceforth be referred to as al-Qa'ida.

2   The other senior EIJ figures included Nasr Fahmi Nasr Hasanayn, also known as Muhammad Salah, and Tariq Anwar al-Sayyid Ahmad. Muhammad Salah was implicated in the attempted assassination of the former Egyptian interior minister, Hasan Abu Basha, in 1987; in 1999 he was sentenced to death *in absentia* in Egypt. Tariq Anwar al-Sayyid Ahmad, one of EIJ's most senior military commanders, is believed to have planned the 1995 bombing of the Egyptian embassy in Islamabad.

3   Hani al-Siba'i in an interview with the author published in *al-Hayat* on 4 September 2002.

their television camera, killing Massoud and one of the assailants. The other attacker was killed by Massoud's bodyguards. For years Massoud had been an obstacle in the Taliban's path, preventing them from extending their control over the whole of Afghanistan. By assassinating him, al-Qa'ida may thus have intended to do the Taliban a favour. But it is also possible that they wanted to pre-empt the response to 11 September 2001 by removing the one commander capable of posing a military threat to the Taliban and their allies. Thirteen years earlier, Arab jihadists had staged a mock 'trial' of Massoud in Pakistan. Now, at last, al-Qa'ida had succeeded in carrying out his death sentence. Admittedly, Massoud had himself conspired against al-Qa'ida: on the eve of his death, the new US administration was still deliberating whether to cooperate with him against bin Laden.[1] In the event, al-Qa'ida acted first.

---

1   In late 1999 the Americans contacted Ahmad Shah Massoud to discuss the possibility of his helping them to get rid of Bin Laden. See The 9/11 Commission Report, pp. 142–143.

11

Hellfire

In proceeding with the attacks on New York and Washington, bin Laden defied both his Afghan hosts and his opponents within al-Qaʻida itself. Yet the retaliation the attacks provoked affected not only him and his organisation, but all jihadists, regardless of whether they had backed the operation. In describing the price they paid for bin Laden's action, some jihadists have spoken of 'hellfire' unleashed by the Americans. It was a reaction that would destroy an entire generation of fighters and the self-styled Taliban emirate which had opened its doors to them. Never again would the jihadists find a haven like it.

Perhaps bin Laden had assumed that the Americans would retaliate merely by firing a few missiles at his camps in Afghanistan, as they had done following the 1998 US embassy bombings. Alternatively, he may have expected that, as in 2000, when al-Qaʻida attacked the USS *Cole*, the Americans would not react at all. Or he may have known full well that they would bring their entire military might to bear on Afghanistan, and hoped to drag them into the same quagmire that had proven so fatal to the Russians in the 1980s. Whatever bin Laden's calculations, the response to 11 September 2001 would force jihadists everywhere to define their stance on his holy war against the US.[1]

---

1 In an address to Congress on 20 September 2001 President Bush delivered a similar challenge to countries around the world. 'Every nation in every region now has a decision to make,' he said. 'Either you are with us, or you are with the terrorists.'

Preparing for the Backlash

There are firm indications in detainees' statements that bin Laden was expecting some form of American military intervention after 11 September. The Palestinian, Abu Zubayda, has claimed that bin Laden divided responsibility for various Afghan cities between al-Qa'ida commanders in anticipation of an attack.[1] Abu Zubayda himself was involved in buying and storing weapons, arming individuals and planning ambushes as part of bin Laden's military preparations, though it remains unclear whether these began before or after 11 September.[2] Bin Laden learned the intended date of the attacks a fortnight before they took place from their coordinator, Ramzi Binalshibh, and promptly ordered the evacuation of al-Qa'ida's training camps in Afghanistan. 'I was staying at the general guesthouse when a bus arrived from the camp with at least forty-five trainees on board,' says the former al-Qa'ida member, Muhammad al-Tamimi.[3] 'When we asked why they'd left the camp, they told us that it had been closed down on bin Laden's orders, because the date of the martyrdom operation was approaching. Everyone based at the camp was to head to Kandahar or Kabul or disperse into the mountains, to avoid becoming an easy target for any military strike. This was a fortnight before the operation was carried out.'[4]

Following the attacks themselves, CIA agents travelled to Afghanistan

---

1 Abu Zubayda claimed at his Combatant Status Review Tribunal in Guantanamo Bay that the leading Egyptian jihadists, Ahmad Hasan Abu al-Khayr and Abu Hafs al-Misri, were central to Bin Laden's defensive plans. However, the division of responsibilities between them remains unclear. See: http://www.defenselink. mil/news/transcript_ISN10016.pdf.

2 From the minutes of the Combatant Status Review Tribunal for Zayn al-'Abidin Muhammad Husayn, also known as Abu Zubayda, dated 19 March 2007. The details of Abu Zubayda's activities following 9/11 are drawn from diary entries he is alleged to have written.

3 From an interview with Muhammad al-Tamimi published in the Arabic newspaper al-Hayat on 20 September 2006; see: http://www.daralhayat.com/ archivearticle/115152. The 'general guesthouse' that he refers to was a hostel in Kandahar intended for new arrivals to the area.

4 'Martyrdom operation' was the term used in al-Qa'ida's camps to refer to the planned attack on the US, although only Bin Laden and his innermost circle knew how and where it would be carried out.

to begin coordinating directly with opponents of the Taliban. They included Pashtun tribes in the south of the country and leaders of the Northern Alliance. The latter, who had only just lost their military commander, Ahmad Shah Massoud, were no doubt thirsty for revenge.[1] More importantly, the Alliance was now united with the Americans by a common interest in bringing down the Taliban regime in Kabul.

The American military assault on Afghanistan commenced on 7 October 2001. After a month of non-stop aerial bombardment, the Taliban's defences in the north of the country collapsed. From then on the Afghan cities fell one by one into the hands of the Americans and their allies. In provinces with a mainly Tajik, Uzbek or Hazara population there was scarcely any resistance: the local inhabitants were glad to see the back of the Taliban. Even in Kabul, the Taliban and al-Qa'ida appear barely to have had time to pack their bags before the city fell on 13 November 2001. Al-Qa'ida may have been taken by surprise both by the speed of their allies' collapse and the outburst of popular hostility on the streets of the capital, where anyone who looked like an Arab suddenly came under attack.

The first serious blow to al-Qa'ida directly came in mid-November 2001, when its military commander, Abu Hafs al-Misri, was killed.[2] It is unclear whether his death influenced bin Laden's decision to withdraw from Kandahar to Tora Bora in eastern Afghanistan, but in practice he had few other options left.[3] Muhammad al-Tamimi has described leaving Kabul on 12 September 2001 and moving to Tora Bora, where bin Laden's bodyguard, Abu Yusuf al-Qannas, was in charge. The rugged, inaccessible terrain provided the area with a kind of natural fortification: al-Tamimi and his associates had to make their way on foot or by donkey, although most of the animals were used to transport arms and ammunition.[4]

Al-Tamimi's account suggests that bin Laden may have been hoping

---

1 Al-Qa'ida is suspected of having orchestrated the attack, although responsibility has not conclusively been proven.

2 Abu Hafs al-Misri had consolidated his relationship with Bin Laden earlier in 2001 by marrying his daughter to the al-Qa'ida leader's son, Muhammad.

3 Mullah Omar is also believed to have left Kandahar on 7 December 2001, as the former Taliban stronghold fell to Afghan opposition forces.

4 From the interview with al-Tamimi published in *al-Hayat* on 20 September 2006. Tora Bora is located in the eastern Afghan province of Nangarhar.

for a showdown with the Americans akin to the Jaji engagement with Russian forces back in 1987. Tora Bora was a natural choice for the al-Qa'ida leader, who knew the area like the back of his hand from the days of the jihad against the Soviets. On his return to Afghanistan from Sudan in 1996, bin Laden had settled in nearby Hadda, outside the provincial capital, Jalalabad, where he also had close ties to leading members of the community. But bin Laden's intimate knowledge of Tora Bora was of little advantage in the face of the Americans' overwhelming firepower. Between late 2001 and early 2002 his forces were thoroughly routed, and when his senior commanders later attempted to regroup inside Pakistan, they came under pressure from that country's security services as well. Nor was Abu Hafs al-Misri the only prominent member of the organisation to die in the American onslaught. Ayman al-Zawahiri's own family was caught up in the aerial bombardment of jihadists withdrawing from Khost between late November and early December 2001.[1] It was a period that was to mark the beginning of the end for al-Qa'ida as a coherent organisation capable of coordinating operations overseas.

In November 2001 Ibn al-Sheikh al-Libi, the former head of the Khaldan camp, was arrested in the Afghan-Pakistani border area. In March of the following year his former assistant, Abu Zubayda, was captured in a raid in Faisalabad in Pakistan. On 13 September 2002 the Pakistani authorities landed an even bigger fish in Karachi: Ramzi Binalshibh, the coordinator of the 9/11 attacks. Five months later, Pakistani and American intelligence thought they had identified Khalid Sheikh Muhammad's hiding place. However, when they stormed the flat in question, the person they found cowering inside was Muhammad, the son of al-Gama'a al-Islamiyya's spiritual leader, Omar Abdel Rahman.[2] Nonetheless, the noose around Khalid Sheikh Muhammad was rapidly tightening. He was finally captured

---

1   Khalid Sheikh Muhammad has confirmed that al-Zawahiri's wife and three of his children died in a US air strike; see the minutes of his Combatant Status Review Tribunal at Guantanamo Bay in March 2007: http://www.defenselink. mil/news/transcript_ISN10024.pdf. The former senior EIJ member, Nasr Fahmi Nasr Hasanayn, was also killed at this time. The merger between the original al-Qa'ida and EIJ earlier in 2001 makes it impossible to identify how, if at all, members of the two groups were affected differently by the aftermath of 9/11.

2   The Americans had detained another of Omar Abdel Rahman's sons, called

by the Pakistani intelligence services on 1 March 2003, after they tracked him down, with CIA help, to an apartment in Rawalpindi, near Islamabad. Within two months the Pakistanis had gone on to detain Tawfiq bin 'Attash, a leading accessory to the 11 September attacks and a mastermind of the USS *Cole* operation.[1]

Khalid Sheikh Muhammad was replaced as al-Qa'ida's third-in-command by a Libyan known as Abu Faraj al-Libi, according to the Americans and the Pakistanis.[2] His compatriot, Noman Benotman, claims that Abu Faraj had been a member of al-Qa'ida from its inception in the late 1980s. He continued to work closely with bin Laden throughout the 1990s, although he chose to remain in Afghanistan when the al-Qa'ida leader moved to Sudan in 1992. When bin Laden returned to Afghanistan four years later, Abu Faraj became one of al-Qa'ida's top field commanders; he did not immediately take on any major responsibilities, but strengthened his ties to bin Laden by marrying the daughter of one of his bodyguards.[3] After the arrest of Khalid Sheikh Muhammad in 2003, Abu Faraj's name seemed to crop up in almost every Pakistani counter-terrorist investigation. In 2004 the Pakistani authorities discovered that Abu Faraj was implicated in assassination attempts against their president, Pervez Musharraf, and Prime Minister Shaukat Aziz. They promptly named him as one of their most wanted terrorists and offered a reward of 20 million rupees for information leading to his arrest.[4] In May 2005 he

---

Ahmad, after the forces of the Northern Alliance entered Kabul in November 2001.

1 Tawfiq bin 'Attash, also known as Khallad, was captured in a raid in Karachi on 29 April 2003.

2 The real name of Abu Faraj al-Libi is thought to be Mustafa al-'Uzayti; he has also been known as Dr Tawfiq and Mustafa al-Libi.

3 According to the edition of the international Arabic newspaper *Asharq al-Awsat* published on 20 August 2004, Abu Faraj married the daughter of Bin Laden's personal bodyguard, 'Abdallah Tabarak (also known as Abu 'Umar al-Maghribi). The latter was captured in December 2001 attempting to cross the Afghan-Pakistani border, detained at Guantanamo Bay and subsequently handed over to his country of origin, Morocco.

4 Abu Faraj al-Libi is believed to have been behind two assassination attempts against President Pervez Musharraf of Pakistan in December 2003. In the first, on 14 December, a bridge in Rawalpindi was blown up moments after Musharraf's motorcade had crossed it; sophisticated jamming devices fitted to his car are

at last fell into their hands, captured in an ambush laid by the Pakistani
intelligence services north of Peshawar.

Al-Qa'ida's Brothers in Arms

It was natural that al-Qa'ida should bear the brunt of America's War on
Terror: it had, after all, been responsible for the very attacks which had
unleashed the conflict. But unlike bin Laden's organisation, other jihadist
groups caught up in the maelstrom had not known beforehand what was
coming, and so had no opportunity to prepare themselves or flee before
the arrival of the American juggernaut. 'The attacks of September 2001
cast the second generation of jihadists into the fiery furnace,' writes Abu
Mus'ab al-Suri. 'The dawn of the new millennium was for them a time of
carnage, a hellfire which consumed most of their leaders, fighters and bases,
leaving only a very few to escape either capture or death.'[1]

While acknowledging the difficulties bin Laden caused other jihadists,
Abu Mus'ab nevertheless describes him as 'the symbol of our jihad' and 'the
sun in the Muslim firmament'. His extravagant praise points to the way in
which the attacks on the US forced many independent jihadists like him to
side with bin Laden. Abu Mus'ab himself was well aware of this galvanising
effect. 'Whatever the different views in Islamist and jihadist circles towards
the events of September 2001,' he writes, 'it goes without saying that they
created a new reality. They provoked an American onslaught which in turn
demanded our attention and our resistance. Better this than squander our
efforts on mutual recriminations over what had happened. We were now
engaged in a battle for our own destiny.'[2] It was a conflict by which Abu
Mus'ab himself would not long remain unscathed. In November 2005,
months after publishing these very words, he was tracked down to his
hiding place in Quetta by the Pakistani security services. His fate since

---

thought to have delayed the explosion. Two weeks later, on Christmas Day, two
suicide bombers tried to drive vehicles packed with explosives into Musharraf's
convoy. The assassination attempt against Shaukat Aziz took place in Attock,
northern Punjab, in July 2004.

1 Abu Mus'ab al-Suri, *Da'wat al-Muqawama*, p. 41. In 2001 Abu Mus'ab was
running his own training camp in Afghanistan called al-Ghuraba'.

2 *Da'wat al-Muqawama*, p. 64.

then has been shrouded in mystery, with widespread speculation that he was taken, like other so-called 'high value detainees', to one of the secret prisons run by the CIA around the world.[1]

The Libyan Exodus

Abu Mus'ab al-Suri had been instrumental in persuading the LIFG to relocate to Afghanistan in the late 1990s, after the group's wilderness years in Sudan and the United Kingdom. It was a fateful decision that would lead to the LIFG suffering greater losses than almost any other group in Afghanistan.

In 1999 the LIFG's emir, Abu Abdullah al-Sadiq, moved to Afghanistan. He was soon joined by the group's head of Islamic law, Abu al-Mundhir al-Sa'idi, and Abu Anas al-Libi, who was fleeing prosecution for alleged involvement in the US embassy bombings.[2] The LIFG rapidly set about training Libyan would-be jihadists, many of whom had left homes in the West for what they saw as an Islamic state closer to their ideals. They soon came under pressure to sign up to bin Laden's agenda, initially by joining the World Islamic Front for Jihad against Jews and Crusaders, which he had co-founded with al-Zawahiri in 1998. Yet bin Laden's early efforts to bring the LIFG on board were in vain. 'People didn't take the idea of al-Qa'ida all that seriously to begin with,' explains the former LIFG member, Noman Benotman:

> Bin Laden was known as a millionaire, but it was the established groups such as al-Gama'a al-Islamiyya and EIJ which really caught their attention. Factions like the LIFG went almost unnoticed, partly because they were operating covertly at the time. However, al-Qa'ida tried to persuade us to form an alliance with them or even join their ranks. Yet merging with another group would have meant

---

1   Recent reports suggest that Abu Mus'ab al-Suri may be in prison in his native Syria.

2   Nazih al-Ruqay'i, also known as Abu Anas al-Libi, is accused of carrying out surveillance of the US embassy in Nairobi in 1993, in preparation for the bomb attack five years later.

the LIFG losing its freedom to operate independently in Libya: it was an idea that we rejected from the outset.[1]

The start of the War on Terror changed everything. The heads of the LIFG were now faced with three options: to join al-Qa'ida and help it take on the Americans, to stay in Afghanistan and fight US forces on their own, or to withdraw from the country altogether. With one notable exception, they settled on the last strategy.[2] Like hundreds of other jihadists uprooted by the conflict, the LIFG leaders made their way to Iran as soon as the Taliban regime collapsed in late 2001. 'The journey over the mountains was one of death and hardship,' relates 'Abd Rabbihi Nasir al-Jarrari, brother-in-law of the senior LIFG member, Abu al-Mundhir al-Sa'idi.[3] 'In some villages they passed along the way people would offer help, but others refused to do anything for them.' Moreover, when they eventually reached Iran, the LIFG leaders were soon swept up in mass arrests of Arabs fleeing Afghanistan.

Like many of his comrades, Abu al-Mundhir al-Sa'idi was interrogated. The Iranians told him that he and his family would be sent to Malaysia: he was not given any choice in the matter. The Malaysians appear to have conducted their own investigations, asking British intelligence, among others, about the nature of his activities when he had lived in the UK. According to al-Jarrari, the answer came back that he was a Libyan opposition member and an Islamist ideologue. Like the Iranians before them, the Malaysians decided to let al-Sa'idi go, on condition that he leave their country. At this point he headed to China, where he got involved in some kind of trade for eighteen months, taking care to do nothing that might arouse suspicion. Yet somehow he learned that he

1   Noman Benotman in interviews with the author in the summer of 2005 and spring of 2006.
2   The most senior LIFG figure to stay behind in Afghanistan following the attacks of 11 September 2001 was Abu Layth al-Libi. The role he went on to play in relations between the LIFG and al-Qa'ida is discussed in Chapter Twelve.
3   'Abd Rabbihi Nasir al-Jarrari, in an interview with the author in London in December 2004. The account of what happened to the LIFG following its withdrawal from Afghanistan is largely dependent on his version of events, as he was in contact with his brother-in-law, Abu al-Mundhir al-Sa'idi, at the time.

and his associates were being monitored by the Americans. Alarmed by this discovery, he decided to pack his things and head to an Arab country, where he assumed it would be safer. At Hong Kong Airport, as he prepared to leave the country, al-Sa'idi was arrested, separated from his family and then, according to al-Jarrari, blindfolded and taken to an unknown destination. CIA agents interrogated him about his links to al-Qa'ida, but during weeks of questioning they could find nothing to connect him to bin Laden's organisation. They then notified the Libyan authorities that he was in their custody, prompting them to send a plane to come and take him back to Tripoli in late March or early April 2004.[1] At the same time as Abu al-Mundhir al-Sa'idi's arrest, the LIFG's emir, Abu Abdullah al-Sadiq, was also detained in Thailand and subsequently handed over to Libya by the Americans. It was yet another devastating blow from which the LIFG would struggle to recover.

Algerians Under Pressure

Unlike other jihadist groups from Algeria, the Salafist Group for Preaching and Combat (GSPC) did not relocate to Afghanistan following the setbacks of the late 1990s. Instead, it stayed behind and tried to pursue what it saw as a legitimate jihad against the Algerian regime, distancing itself from the travesty which the GIA had become. Yet far removed though it was from the training camps of Afghanistan and al-Qa'ida's agenda, this would not be enough to protect the GSPC from the repercussions of 11 September 2001.

In persisting with the conflict in Algeria at that time, the GSPC was swimming against the tide. In 1997 the Islamic Salvation Army (AIS) had declared a truce and begun talks with the Algerian authorities.[2] These would eventually lead to President Abdelaziz Bouteflika offering an amnesty to

---

1 The Libyan authorities told al-Sa'idi's family that he was in their custody, at the same time informing them that two of his brothers had been killed in a prison mutiny in Tripoli back in 1996.

2 The AIS was the military wing of the FIS, which had been poised to win the elections of 1992. It was the regime's cancellation of the polls which ignited the Algerian civil war.

Islamist militants who renounced violence and turned themselves in.[1] Nor was the AIS the only faction to benefit from the pardon: others, including groups which had belonged to the GIA in central Algeria, signed up and handed themselves in to the authorities, in return for immunity from prosecution.

The widespread support for the reconciliation process in Algeria was a mark of the public's weariness of the conflict. The increasingly horrific and indiscriminate acts of murder committed by, or attributed to, the GIA during the late 1990s had alienated most Algerians and bolstered support for the state.[2] Little wonder, then, that the GSPC tried in vain to impose its vision of a jihad against the 'apostate' regime.[3]

Given the prevailing mood in the country, the GSPC had to ask itself whether there was anything to be gained from keeping up the fight. 'I could see that the situation was radically different from that of the 1990s,' says Hassan Hattab, the GSPC's emir at the time:[4]

> It was clear that the regime's policies had also changed. I had the definite impression that the president meant what he said about reconciliation. He had been out of the country when the events began [with the cancellation of the elections in 1992], so he was untainted by what had happened during the 1990s. But it wasn't

---

1   Abdelaziz Bouteflika came to power in April 1999; five months later his 'Charter for Peace and National Reconciliation' was overwhelmingly endorsed in a national referendum. The amnesty covered Islamists who had not been directly involved in murder or other serious crimes, including rape.

2   The high turnout in Algeria's elections from the mid-1990s onwards is also seen as a sign of public support for the reconciliation effort. However, opposition allegations of vote-rigging make it difficult to gauge the true extent of participation in the polls.

3   Remnants of the GIA would remain active under Antar Zouabri's leadership, until his assassination in 2002. Following his death, the group was almost completely dismantled.

4   In March 2009, the Algerian authorities permitted the author to meet Hassan Hattab, who had surrendered in 2007. The meeting took place at a secret location outside Algiers, where Hattab was being held by the Algerian security services. Three other senior GSPC members also attended, who like Hattab had laid down their arms and joined the peace process. They were Abu 'Umar 'Abd al-Birr, the former head of the Media Committee, 'Abd al-Qadir Bin Mas'ud (also known as Mus'ab Abu Dawud), the former head of the GSPC's 'Ninth Zone' (in the Sahara), and Abu Zakariya, the head of the group's Medical Committee.

just the regime: there had been a shift in society's attitude too. We could hardly claim to represent society's aspirations and go on fighting when the public was clamouring almost to a man for reconciliation.

There was a third reason for Hattab's change of heart:

Various Muslim clerics had started to oppose our continuation of the armed struggle. This was absolutely fundamental to our decision [to stop carrying out attacks]. There wasn't one cleric anywhere willing to support our campaign. We contacted some very learned scholars: members of the *Katibat al-Ghuraba'* got in touch with Sheikh [Muhammad bin Salih] al-'Uthaymin, for example.[1] But whereas before they had tended not to comment on the conflict in Algeria, now they began actively speaking out against it and issuing fatwas saying that it had to stop. That changed everything.

Following the attacks of 11 September 2001, Hattab issued a statement criticising the United States for rushing to blame Islamists for what had happened.[2] At the time, bin Laden had yet to claim responsibility for the attacks, and Hattab's statement seemed like an implicit denial that al-Qa'ida had been involved. 'I did not welcome the attacks,' Hattab says now, 'and I was sure that al-Qa'ida was behind them.[3] But I criticised America for accusing the Islamists because of what I thought the consequences would be. I was afraid of the harm that might come to the Taliban and Muslims more widely.'

In the aftermath of 11 September, no one in Washington was in any mood to make subtle distinctions between jihadists who did and did not support al-Qa'ida, much less to listen to the likes of Hattab. Just as the Americans tirelessly hunted down members of the LIFG, so they also turned their attention to the GSPC. In March 2002 the State Department designated the group a 'Foreign Terrorist Organisation', and

---

1 The *Katibat al-Ghuraba'* was a battalion of the GSPC which operated in Boumerdès Province, east of Algiers. Muhammad bin Salih al-'Uthaymin was a prominent Saudi scholar of Islamic jurisprudence; he died in 2001.
2 The author received a copy of Hattab's statement from the GSPC representative in Europe. Author's collection.
3 Author's interview with Hassan Hattab in Algeria, March 2009.

in September the following year the US Treasury Department branded it a 'Specially Designated Global Terrorist' entity. US support for the Algerian government's efforts to break up the group would prove highly significant. Since the early 1990s, the Algerian intelligence services had complained that Western countries tolerated the activities of 'terrorists' on their soil. In the past, these protests had never received a very sympathetic hearing. Now the United States added its weight, pressuring countries around the world to clamp down on the GSPC's logistical support networks.

At the same time al-Qa'ida was itself taking a greater interest in the GSPC. In 2002 its envoy, a Yemeni called 'Imad 'Abd al-Wahid Ahmad 'Alwan, arrived in Algeria and tried to make contact with the GSPC's leaders to propose a merger with al-Qa'ida. However, the Algerian security services were soon on to him: they knew he had spent time at various GSPC hideouts in Batna, in northeastern Algeria, and that he was trying to make his way to Hattab. After an intensive manhunt they got to him first, killing him in an ambush in Batna on 12 September 2002. The official Algerian news agency described him as 'al-Qa'ida's envoy to North Africa and the Sahel' and claimed that he had arrived in the region in June 2001. If true, this was evidence of the closer attention that al-Qa'ida was paying not only to Algeria, but to North Africa as a whole.

12

Al-Qaʻida & Co:
The Jihad Franchise

The United States began 2002 having achieved far more, far sooner than it could have ever dared hope. With the attacks of 11 September 2001, al-Qaʻida, its number one enemy, had bitten off much more than it could chew. The collapse of the Taliban regime and its replacement by President Hamid Karzai's administration had deprived bin Laden of the relative comfort of Afghanistan. When Pakistan and its powerful intelligence services sided with America in its War on Terror, al-Qaʻida lost a vital logistical support base there as well. Many of its men were killed or detained while attempting to flee the American advance; of those who made their way to Iran, hundreds were swept up by the authorities, to become mere bargaining chips in Iran's dealings with the jihadists' countries of origin.[1]

But the United States' jubilation would not last. In early 2003 it willingly embarked on a new war in Iraq, where its forces would become bogged down in a debilitating conflict not dissimilar to the Russians' misadventure in Afghanistan. And it was in the quagmire of Iraq that al-Qaʻida, which only months before had seemed on the brink of death, would start to revive. As the United States struggled with the combined effects of an Iraqi nationalist insurgency and Sunni extremist violence, it inadvertently provided al-Qaʻida with the breathing space it needed to regroup and

---

1 Initially the United States hoped Iran would extradite its jihadist prisoners to their countries of origin, which would in turn hand them over to the US for questioning and possible prosecution. These expectations would not be fulfilled.

rebuild. But this time the organisation would take a very different form, consisting of franchises which operated in al-Qaʻidaʼs name but not under its direct command, and sometimes in ways of which not even bin Laden would approve. It was a looser structure, one that was both more disparate and more resilient. From Iraq to the Maghreb, from the Levant to Sudan, from the Arabian Peninsula to Somalia, and perhaps even in Europe, the web of al-Qaʻidaʼs affiliates spread inexorably as the core of the organisation, still presided over by bin Laden and Ayman al-Zawahiri, clung on defiantly in the wilds of the Afghan-Pakistani border region.

The Arabian Peninsula

Bin Ladenʼs organisation had relied all along on a bedrock of Gulf support, money and manpower. It was, therefore, no surprise that al-Qaʻidaʼs first franchise to emerge after the fall of the Taliban appeared in its leaderʼs home country, Saudi Arabia. Al-Qaʻidaʼs conflict with the security services encompassed the entire Gulf region, but it was in the Saudi kingdom that the organisation carried out most of its attacks and suffered the worst of its setbacks.[1]

The sequence of events began on 18 March 2003, when a young Saudi called Fahd Samran al-Saʼidi accidentally blew himself up while mixing explosives in a flat in Riyadh. Weeks later, on 6 May 2003, the Saudi security forces raided a house in another area of the city, which they suspected was being used as a base by a group of extremists. Sure enough, inside they discovered weapons, forged documents and hundreds of kilograms of explosives. The next day the Saudi Interior Ministry published a list of its nineteen most wanted individuals, including photographs of the suspects.[2] Events were now gathering pace. On 12 May 2003 a group of nine suicide

---

1   Saudi Arabia had been taking action against al-Qaʻida long before 11 September 2001. However, from then on its security services would arrest hundreds of people suspected of involvement in what the Saudi media always referred to euphemistically as the ʻdeviant groupʼ, al-Qaʼida.

2   The nineteen individuals were alleged to belong to various terrorist cells; all but two of them were from Saudi Arabia itself. In December 2003 the Saudi authorities published another list of their twenty-six most wanted terrorists, most of whom were Saudis.

bombers, including several of those on the ministry's list, stormed three foreigners' residential compounds in Riyadh, killing at least thirty-five people and wounding hundreds of others. It was al-Qa'ida's declaration of war on the kingdom.

The security services were quick to hit back. At the end of May 2003 they killed Yusuf al-'Ayiri, the leader of 'al-Qa'ida in the Arabian Peninsula' (AQAP) and a close associate of bin Laden, during a shoot-out in Turba in the northern Saudi province of Ha'il. Each time a new chief was appointed, he would in turn be picked off, along with other senior members of the group.[1] AQAP managed to carry out numerous operations in Saudi Arabia over the next three years, with each one, its capabilities inside the kingdom being gradually diminished. By the beginning of 2006 the group's activities had dwindled to such an extent that it no longer even had a website to publish its statements, let alone a charismatic emir.

However, the diligence of the Saudi security services was not the only cause of AQAP's decline. Crucially, the organisation had failed to split Saudi Arabia's powerful religious establishment, which had backed the royal family since the birth of the kingdom in the eighteenth century. Nor could bin Laden come up with a convincing theological argument to persuade the Saudi public of their duty to rally to his cause. Ever since the Gulf War of 1991, bin Laden had used the presence of American troops on Saudi soil as justification for his campaign against the regime. However, once the Americans had evacuated most of their bases, it became much harder to defend continuing acts of violence in Saudi Arabia on the basis of an imaginary 'infidel occupation'.[2] Any attempt to do so would also have appeared ridiculous, given the very real American occupation of neighbouring Iraq. And it was there that al-Qa'ida's sympathisers now

---

1 The most senior AQAP members to die in clashes with the Saudi security forces were Khalid 'Ali Hajj, who was killed on 15 March 2004; Rakan al-Saykhan, fatally wounded in a gunfight on 12 April 2004; 'Abd al-'Aziz al-Muqrin and Faysal al-Dakhil, both killed on 19 June 2004; and Salih al-'Awfi, who died on 18 August 2005.

2 In April 2003 the United States announced plans to withdraw almost all of its forces from Saudi Arabia and relocate them to Qatar. The evacuation was completed by the following September.

shifted their focus, as the escalating conflict in Iraq attracted a steady stream of aspiring suicide bombers, above all from the Gulf.[1]

Al-Qaʻida did not formally announce a change of policy. However, its leaders may have hoped that a jihadist victory in Iraq would provide them with a base from which to take on the Saudi regime more effectively. Alternatively, they may have been persuaded by the religious arguments of clerics from the Gulf, who called on al-Qaʻida both directly and indirectly to cease its operations in Saudi Arabia and concentrate on Iraq. Either way, it would be years before al-Qaʻida carried out any more attacks inside the kingdom.[2]

As well as looking to Iraq, al-Qaʻida also began to take an increasing interest in Yemen. In November 2002 the Americans had killed its local leader, Abu ʻAli al-Harithi, by firing a missile at his car from an unmanned drone. A year later, al-Harithi's successor, Muhammad Hamdi al-Ahdal, was arrested. Earlier in 2003 the Iranians had deported one Nasir al-Wuhayshi to Yemen, and this man, perhaps more than any other, would prove crucial to the reversal of al-Qaʻida's fortunes in the Arabian Peninsula. Prior to his arrest in Iran, al-Wuhayshi had spent time in Afghanistan, where he had been one of bin Laden's lieutenants. Back in Yemen in February 2006, he and more than twenty other suspected al-Qaʻida members staged an audacious breakout from the prison in Sanaʻa where they were being held. No sooner had he escaped than he set about rebuilding the Yemeni branch of al-Qaʻida and launching a series of attacks against Western targets in the next few years.[3] Indeed, such was al-Wuhayshi's success that in January 2009 he was able to bring the remnants of al-Qaʻida's Saudi

---

1   See the report on the so-called 'Sinjar Records' by the Combating Terrorism Centre at the United States Military Academy at West Point. These documents include data compiled by al-Qaʻida in Iraq on foreign fighters operating in that country, and show that by far the largest number of fighters came from Saudi Arabia (see: http://www.ctc.usma.edu/harmony/pdf/CTCForeignFighter.19. Dec07.pdf).

2   In April 2007 the Saudi authorities announced that they had dismantled a network of al-Qaʻida cells comprising 172 individuals who had been plotting attacks in the kingdom. Some of the suspects were alleged to have trained as aircraft pilots, although the ultimate purpose of this training was not stated.

3   One of the most attention-grabbing operations mounted by al-Qaʻida in Yemen was its attack on the US embassy in Sanaʻa in March 2008.

franchise under his wing. In an interview published in an online jihadist newsletter, al-Wuhayshi claimed that the Saudi militants had pledged allegiance to him, pointing both to his own strength and their continuing weakness. However, within days Muhammad al-'Awfi, a Saudi national identified as al-Wuhayshi's field commander, handed himself in to the Saudi authorities.[1] It was yet another mark of their success in smashing al-Qa'ida in its leader's birthplace.

Iraq

Unlike its branch in the Arabian Peninsula, al-Qa'ida's franchise in Iraq was not established by members of the organisation. Its founder, Abu Mus'ab al-Zarqawi, had not only never belonged to al-Qa'ida, he had firmly resisted bin Laden's attempts to recruit him during his time in Afghanistan between 1999 and 2001. Instead Al-Zarqawi had preferred to operate independently, as head of his own group made up mainly of Palestinians, Syrians and his fellow Jordanians.

The US invasion of Afghanistan in 2001 forced al-Zarqawi to leave his base in Herat, in the west of the country, and make his way to the Taliban stronghold of Kandahar. When that too fell to the Americans, he fled to Pakistan and then went on, via Iran, to a new arena of jihad: the Kurdish region of northern Iraq. There in 2002 he joined the Kurdish Islamist group, Ansar al-Islam, helping to fight the Kurdish nationalist parties which had controlled the area since the Gulf War of 1991. Whether al-Zarqawi had the foresight to predict that the Americans would come to Iraq and was preparing for their arrival can never be known. But what is certain is that he was not a member of al-Qa'ida at this time.

How long al-Zarqawi remained with Ansar al-Islam is uncertain, but when US forces invaded Iraq he was running his own faction called Jama'at al-Tawhid wa al-Jihad, the 'Monotheism and Jihad Group'. It was only

---

1   Muhammad al-'Awfi is believed to have been an inmate at Guantanamo Bay who was later returned to Saudi Arabia. The Saudi authorities are said to have released him on parole; his appearance alongside al-Wuhayshi in the January 2009 video, together with another Saudi formerly held at Guantanamo, was thus a source of acute embarrassment to the kingdom.

in October 2004 that al-Zarqawi pledged allegiance to bin Laden, who duly appointed him emir of his franchise in Iraq.[1] The part al-Zarqawi had played earlier that year in fighting US forces in Falluja had already enhanced his prestige in jihadist circles.[2] Bin Laden's endorsement helped turn al-Zarqawi's organisation into a magnet for the stream of foreign jihadists heading to Iraq to join the insurgency, many of them keen to carry out suicide missions. This sheer weight of numbers soon helped turn al-Qa'ida in Iraq (AQI) into Iraq's pre-eminent jihadist group. However, what rival factions found harder to stomach was AQI's increasingly overbearing attitude, as al-Zarqawi tried to bully them into supporting his policies or merging with his organisation. It was the same domineering approach that the Algerian GIA had adopted in mid-1994 towards its rivals, and the effect in Iraq was much the same: to unleash vicious in-fighting among the jihadists. Other Sunni groups, repelled both by al-Zarqawi's imperiousness and his increasingly savage acts of indiscriminate murder, did what would have been anathema to bin Laden: they made contact with the US. The talks would lead the Americans to assist the Iraqi 'resistance' directly, on condition that they turned their guns on their new enemy: al-Qa'ida.

Al-Zarqawi did not realise until too late how deeply his conduct had alienated the Iraqi population at large, driving them into an uneasy alliance with their American foes for the sake of getting rid of him. His Sunni Iraqi opponents called themselves the 'honourable resistance', in an attempt to distinguish their nationalist agenda from the rabid religious extremism of al-Zarqawi and his ilk. Yet rather than trying to appease his critics, al-Zarqawi simply ignored them, apparently believing that they would have to side with him once he had driven the Americans out of Iraq.

---

1   After pledging allegiance to Bin Laden, al-Zarqawi's group assumed the name Tanzim Qa'idat al-Jihad fi Bilad al-Rafidayn, meaning the 'Organisation of the Jihad Base in Mesopotamia'. For the sake of simplicity it will be referred to here as al-Qa'ida in Iraq (AQI).

2   In late March 2004 four American security contractors were killed in Falluja, west of Baghdad, and their bodies mutilated. The incident led US forces to make an unsuccessful attempt to regain control of the city from Iraqi insurgents, who dubbed it the 'Battle of Falluja'. In November 2004 US forces again tried to recapture the city; the operation, known to jihadists as the 'Second Battle of Falluja', achieved its goals, although the cost in terms of bloodshed and damage to property is questioned in some quarters.

Indeed, so confident was al-Zarqawi of imminent victory that he began sending volunteers back to their home countries to establish al-Qa'ida cells and prepare to attack Western targets. The fact was that the aspiring jihadists who used to travel to Syria and then infiltrate Iraq were now surplus to requirements. Some of them went home and set up facilitation networks to help support the jihad in Iraq by other means. They included the Libyan, Khalid al-Zayidi, who was discovered and killed in Benghazi in October 2005, soon after his return from Iraq, where he had been wounded; only years later would it emerge that before his death he had succeeded in establishing cells with links to AQI. Much the same thing happened in Syria and Lebanon, but on a larger scale. The most significant example was the radical Sunni group, Fatah al-Islam, which operated out of the Palestinian refugee camp of Nahr al-Barid in northern Lebanon. Such was the threat posed by this AQI-linked faction that in mid-2007 the Lebanese armed forces surrounded and then shelled the camp to destroy the group. Hundreds died in what was the worst fighting Lebanon had seen since the end of its civil war in 1990.

Overseas affiliates were not enough to satisfy al-Zarqawi's ambition: he also wanted to expand his own area of operations outside Iraq. And he saw no reason to consult the core al-Qa'ida leadership before doing so. When in November 2005 three Iraqi suicide bombers carried out coordinated attacks on hotels in the Jordanian capital, Amman, the al-Qa'ida leadership was taken by surprise. More importantly, the bombings, in which dozens of Muslims died and hundreds of others were injured, provoked outrage in the Islamic world. For the already strained relationship between al-Qa'ida and al-Zarqawi, the Amman atrocity was the last straw. Even before the attacks bin Laden's inner circle had begun to express reservations about al-Zarqawi's conduct. In mid-2005 Abu Mus'ab received a message from Ayman al-Zawahiri containing advice mingled with mild criticism. Addressing one of the most controversial aspects of al-Zarqawi's campaign in Iraq, al-Zawahiri told him that 'many of your Muslim admirers ... are wondering about your attacks on the Shia ... Is this [conflict with the Shia] unavoidable?' He also alluded to the revulsion caused by al-Zarqawi's habit of beheading his captives. 'The Muslim populace who love and

support you', he wrote tactfully, 'will never find scenes of the slaughter
of hostages palatable.'[1]

By the end of 2005, core al-Qa'ida was no longer bothering to conceal
its exasperation with al-Zarqawi's waywardness. A letter written on behalf
of the leadership warned him against 'all acts that alienate': he was to
do nothing outside Iraq without consulting core al-Qa'ida, the 'greater
leadership that is more powerful and better able to lead the Muslim nation'.[2]
In a clear allusion to the danger of incurring the wrath of Iran, the letter
ordered al-Zarqawi not to 'declare war on the Shi'ite turncoats' or 'expand
the arena of the war to neighbouring countries'. Above all, the letter urged
him to adopt a more conciliatory approach to other insurgent factions,
and Sunni Iraqis at large. Tellingly, the letter pointed to the example of
Algeria and how, in 1994, just as the GIA 'was at the height of its power and
capabilities', its members 'destroyed themselves with their own hands, with
their lack of reason and their delusions, by ignoring others and alienating
them through oppression, deviance and ruthlessness ... Their enemy did
not defeat them: they defeated themselves.'

Al-Zarqawi responded to core al-Qa'ida's instructions by establishing
an umbrella group called the Mujahidin Shura Council (MSC), a notional
consultative body embracing AQI itself and several smaller jihadist groups.
The implication was that AQI was one among equals, now led by an Iraqi
called Abdullah Rashid al-Baghdadi.[3] The late 2005 letter from al-Qa'ida
had advised al-Zarqawi to 'beware of being zealous about the name "al-
Qa'ida"'; now he ceased using it altogether, claiming responsibility for
attacks only in the name of the MSC. Whether real or merely a front for

---

1   Ayman al-Zawahiri's message to al-Zarqawi was dated 9 July 2005; it was released
    by the United States' Office of the Director of National Intelligence in October
    2005. For a full translation of the text see: http://www.dni.gov/press_releases/
    letter_in_english.pdf.

2   The letter, which was dated 12 December 2005, was written on behalf of the
    al-Qa'ida senior leadership by bin Laden's Libyan envoy, 'Atiya 'Abd al-Rahman,
    whom he had sent to Algeria ten years earlier. The letter was discovered following
    al-Zarqawi's death in June 2006; for an English translation see: http://ctc.usma.
    edu/harmony/pdf/CTC-AtiyahLetter.pdf.

3   Abdullah Rashid al-Baghdadi, also known as Abu 'Umar al-Baghdadi, was never
    positively identified. There was widespread speculation at the time that he was
    a fictitious figure intended to give AQI a more Iraqi flavour.

AQI, the MSC did not last long: in October 2006 it was supplanted by the self-styled 'Islamic State of Iraq', in which al-Qaʿida's Iraqi franchise was again said to be only one of several players. Moreover, the very name of the organisation was a recognition of the need to limit the scope of the jihad to Iraq's borders. Though shortlived, the MSC outlasted al-Zarqawi himself, who was killed on 7 June 2006 when the Americans bombed his hiding place near Baʾquba, north of Baghdad. It was an appropriately violent end to a blood-stained career.

Yet even had he survived, al-Zarqawi's days at the head of al-Qaʿida's franchise in Iraq would have been numbered. Unbeknownst to him, the senior leadership had dispatched ʿAbd al-Hadi al-Iraqi, a prominent, longstanding member of core al-Qaʿida, with a remit to heal the rift between AQI and the other insurgent groups. Core al-Qaʿida may have hoped that, as an Iraqi himself, ʿAbd al-Hadi would have greater success than the Jordanian al-Zarqawi in winning other factions' support. If so, they were to be disappointed: in late 2006, as he made his way to Iraq from the Afghan-Pakistani border region, ʿAbd al-Hadi fell into the hands of the Americans. Instead of an Iraqi taking over AQI and repairing the damage both to its own reputation and that of its parent organisation, al-Zarqawi was replaced by an obscure foreigner known as Abu Hamza al-Muhajir.[1] It seemed a desperate choice for a group which only a year before had been al-Qaʿida's most powerful franchise in the world.

The Maghreb

In 1999 a war-weary Algerian public had overwhelmingly endorsed a plan to offer amnesty to the country's Islamist militants. It was never a compromise likely to attract the Armed Islamic Group, whose extremism had reached the point of condemning the country's entire population as infidels who deserved to die. But other militants were more receptive. They might have been expected to include the GSPC, the GIA offshoot

---

1   The United States identified Abu Hamza al-Muhajir as an Egyptian also known as Abu Ayyub al-Misri. He was killed in a joint operation by US and Iraqi forces on 18 April 2010, together with a man identified as Abdullah Rashid al-Baghdadi.

which had broken away partly in protest at the latter's excesses. The GSPC's first emir, Hassan Hattab, maintains today that he advocated just such a reconciliation between his faction and the state. But his failure to persuade his associates would see the GSPC gravitate ever further towards al-Qaʻida, until it eventually assumed the role of its North African franchise.

'I talked to senior GSPC figures behind the scenes,' says Hassan Hattab of his efforts to convince the group to talk to the Algerian government.[1] 'The problem was, there just wasn't the time they needed to change their outlook on things.' Abu al-Baraʼ, the group's expert in Islamic law, was one of these people; Hattab believed his support essential to winning around the others. But although Hattab claims he wavered, Abu al-Baraʼ was ultimately unable to overcome his own reservations. 'His extreme caution gave a boost to the other side [opposed to the national reconciliation process],' he says, 'even though they had no theological justification for continuing the conflict. The entire population was in favour of reconciliation; the only argument [the GSPC hardliners] had was that the regime wasn't really sincere in their intentions.' Unable to make headway, Hattab eventually withdrew from the group in August 2003, to be replaced by Nabil Sahraoui.

Within days Sahraoui released a statement pledging allegiance to bin Laden and his jihad against the US and its allies.[2] Less than a year later Sahraoui was dead, but, like him, his successor, Abdelmalek Droukdal, pursued ever closer relations with al-Qaʻida.[3] Having opened a direct channel of communication with the leadership on the Afghan-Pakistani border, Droukdal offered to merge the GSPC with bin Laden's organisation. This proposal followed a debate between Droukdal and other senior GSPC members over the advantages of unification. The group's ranks had been severely depleted as comrades laid down their weapons and accepted the

---

1   Author's interview with Hassan Hattab in Algeria, March 2009.

2   The statement was timed to coincide with the second anniversary of the attacks of 11 September 2001. In it, Sahraoui repudiated the statement Hassan Hattab had made at the time, implicitly exonerating al-Qaʻida of the atrocities. Chapter Eleven includes Hattab's account of that announcement.

3   Nabil Sahraoui was killed by the Algerian armed forces on 20 June 2004 in the coastal province of Béjaïa. Abdelmalek Droukdal, also known as Abou Moussab Abdelwadoud, was born in 1970 in the province of Blida, southwest of Algiers.

government's offer of amnesty. Those who were left behind had somehow to prove they were still a force to be reckoned with, in the hope of attracting new blood.

Core al-Qaʿida did not think twice before accepting the Algerians' offer. It may have had an eye on the GSPC's reputed cells in Europe, perhaps hoping to use them to carry out operations similar to the Madrid train bombings of March 2004. In September 2006 Ayman al-Zawahiri announced the GSPC's merger with al-Qaʿida; the following January the GSPC sealed the union by changing its name to al-Qaʿida in the Lands of the Islamic Maghreb (AQIM). 'We saw the merger with al-Qaʿida as giving us the breathing space we badly needed,' says Abu ʿUmar ʿAbd al-Birr, former head of the GSPC's media wing.[1] 'Faced with the national reconciliation process in Algeria, we'd had no choice but to stop fighting. But with the merger, we gained new authority in people's eyes: it allowed us to project an image of ourselves as a new group.'

But the alliance was not just about effective propaganda. AQIM soon began using suicide bombers to carry out mass-casualty attacks against local and Western targets: a tactic the GSPC had always eschewed, but which bore the hallmark of al-Qaʿida. The group also sought to extend its recruitment drive beyond Algeria's borders, drawing in new members from other parts of North Africa, some of whom went on to assume senior positions in the group. It even broadened its area of operations to include countries outside the Maghreb, such as Mali and Niger. Yet, however deadly some of its operations may have been, unlike the GIA in the 1990s, AQIM proved incapable of posing a serious threat to any North African regime. For all its ambition, its regional remit and its status as an al-Qaʿida franchise, nothing could disguise the fact that AQIM was a shadow of its Algerian forebears.

---

1   Author's interview with Abu ʿUmar ʿAbd al-Birr in Algeria, March 2009. Abu ʿUmar claims that the merger between the GSPC and al-Qaʿida was first proposed by the al-Qaʿida in Iraq leader, Abu Musʿab al-Zarqawi. In contrast, Hassan Hattab claims that Ayman al-Zawahiri sent a delegation to Algeria to discuss a merger with the GIA in 1995, but maintains that the group's then leader, Djamel Zitouni, rejected the proposal.

Libya

By 2004 the LIFG was paralysed. The arrest of its leader, Abu Abdullah al-Sadiq, and its legal expert, Abu al-Mundhir al-Sa'idi, had created a power vacuum which the members who remained at large had failed to fill. Part of this inertia may have been down to the group's internal regulations, which forbade the appointment of new leaders without a quorum of the existing ones. But it was also a reflection of how many of the group's members were in prison, under house arrest or in hiding.

It was against this background of defeat and demoralisation that two figures emerged who would play a key role in bringing the LIFG into al-Qa'ida's orbit. One was Abu Layth al-Libi, a longstanding member of the group who made a name for himself after breaking out of a Saudi prison in 1996.[1] By 1999 he had settled in Afghanistan, along with the LIFG leadership. However, while they fled to Iran following the US invasion of Afghanistan in 2001, Abu Layth decided to stay behind and fight. He was later joined by another LIFG member and scholar of Islamic law called Abu Yahya al-Libi, who had managed to escape from American detention at Bagram Airbase in Afghanistan.[2]

Video footage that had emerged showing Abu Layth with senior al-Qa'ida leaders fed speculation that he had joined their organisation. This was confirmed in the autumn of 2007, when Abu Layth announced the merger of the LIFG with al-Qa'ida. However, neither Abu Layth nor Abu Yahya represented the views of all LIFG members, whether imprisoned in Libya or living abroad. What the two men in Afghanistan did not know, or refused to believe, was that most of the leaders behind bars in Tripoli were engaged in secret talks with the Libyan regime.[3]

---

1   In 1996 Abu Layth al-Libi escaped with two other LIFG members from the al-Ruways Prison in Jeddah. They had been arrested in connection with a 1995 car bomb attack against a US-run training centre for the Saudi National Guard in Riyadh.

2   Muhammad Hasan Qayid, also known as Yunus al-Sahrawi and more commonly as Abu Yahya al-Libi, was detained following the US invasion of Afghanistan. In July 2005 he escaped from Bagram Air Base, north of Kabul, with three other high-profile detainees. He subsequently appeared in video recordings threatening the United States with humiliation by the mujahidin.

3   The most senior LIFG figures involved in the discussions were the group's emir,

Noman Benotman was the first LIFG member based overseas to be allowed to meet the leadership in prison. In January 2007 he flew to Tripoli for the first in a series of face-to-face meetings with his old associates. At one point they asked him if he would deliver a message about the talks to the LIFG leaders abroad: they were afraid of being seen as having sold out to the regime. The request naturally put Benotman in a difficult position, one which was resolved later in the year when, with the cooperation of the present author, the gist of the message was published in the international Arabic newspaper, *al-Hayat*. The LIFG leaders in Tripoli never received a direct response. But the joint statement by Abu Layth al-Libi and Ayman al-Zawahiri in October 2007 said it all: far from seeking reconciliation with the Libyan government, the LIFG was henceforth to form part of al-Qaʻida itself.

Within four months Abu Layth was dead, killed by an American air strike in January 2008. In his absence, his comrade, Abu Yahya, soon took on a prominent role in al-Qaʻida's propaganda activity, rivalling that of al-Zawahiri himself. But even this could not disguise the fact that both he and Abu Layth had diverged completely from the majority of their former associates. Back in Libya, the LIFG leadership had concluded that indiscriminate violence did far more harm than good. It had failed to bring down a single Arab regime or achieve the application of Islamic law, and instead had merely imperilled the lives of ordinary Muslims. In August 2009 this change of heart would lead to the publication of a document in which, in many hundreds of pages, the LIFG leaders refuted the very concept of violent jihad. CIA drones could eliminate al-Qaʻida's Libyan allies, but this was a major blow to the very ideas it embodied.[1]

ʻAbd al-Hakim Belhadj, also known as Abu Abdullah al-Sadiq; his deputy, Khalid al-Sharif, also known as Abu Hazim; the legal expert, Abu al-Mundhir al-Saʻidi; the military commander, Mustafa Qunayfidh, also known as al-Zubayr; the LIFG's first emir, ʻAbd al-Ghaffar al-Duwadi; and Abu Yahya al-Libi's brother, ʻAbd al-Wahhab Qayid. The Gaddafi International Foundation for Charity Associations, headed by the Libyan leader's son, Sayf al-Islam Gaddafi, mediated in the talks.

1   In March 2010, the Libyan authorities freed more than 200 Islamist prisoners from the Abu Salim prison in Tripoli. They included the LIFG's emir Abu Abdullah al-Sadiq, his deputy Khalid al-Sharif and Abu al-Mundhir al-Saʻidi.

Conclusion

The Arab jihadist groups emerged from the Afghan conflict of the 1980s. Lacking a unifying cause after the end of the jihad, the factions turned their attention to fighting the governments of their home countries. Yet in every case this proved too ambitious: the jihadists were no match for the repressive regimes of the Arab world. Some, such as the Algerian GIA, responded with increasing violence against and alienation from the societies they had been unable to dominate. Others, like the Egyptian al-Gama'a al-Islamiyya, and later the LIFG, took a pragmatic approach, renouncing the armed struggle and seeking an accommodation with the established powers.

A third category withdrew to Afghanistan, with the aim of regrouping and relaunching their respective jihads at a later date. Yet despite their common circumstances, most of these groups remained focused on their own limited, nationalist agendas. The exception was al-Qa'ida, which looked beyond the regimes of the Middle East to the United States, which it regarded as the origin of the Islamic world's decline.

Al-Qa'ida had limited success in persuading other jihadists of its priorities. However, the response to 11 September 2001 affected all jihadist groups alike, forcing them to define their stance towards bin Laden's manifesto. The years since have been a time of fragmentation, as al-Qa'ida and its sympathisers have come under unremitting pressure from armies, security and intelligence services and law enforcement agencies around the world. Yet this period has also seen a form of symbiosis between local and often increasingly violent Islamist movements and a 'core' al-Qa'ida. The latter confers prestige and legitimacy on its scattered franchises; at the same time, it is the actions of al-Qa'ida's affiliates around the world which ensure that the 'core' remains credible as a symbol, if no longer effective as a command-and-control centre. It is often said that a war cannot be waged against an idea. And yet the recantations of al-Gama'a al-Islamiyya and the LIFG suggest that in the realm of ideas a new front line has been opened. Whether these voices of moderation will prevail over the bloodthirsty battle cries, or whether they have already been fatally compromised by the discredited political regimes that have presided over them, remains to be seen.

INDEX